THE FOR DUMMIES®
COMPUTER BOOK SERIES FROM IDG

Creating Web Pages For Kids & Parents™

Cheat Sheet

Web Page "Do's"

✔ **Be creative.** Write and present information that is uniquely your own. Don't be a copy cat. Whatever is on your Web page should say, "Here I am. Take a look."

✔ **Be a designer.** Organize well so that your site is easy to access and view. Put out the welcome mat in a way that people can easily find their way to your front door (home page), even if they enter through a "side door."

✔ **Be a communicator.** Tell it like it is with spunky titles, headings, and subheadings. Give your reader a head start with a table of contents and a topic sentence that sums up what's on your page. Plus, don't forget to edit and proof.

✔ **Be a teacher.** Do some research, have some experiences, and then share what you've learned or done. Who knows, someone might even give you a shiny red apple.

✔ **Be an entertainer.** Use humor and details to tell stories in a way that will connect emotionally with each visitor. Make 'em laugh, or make 'em cry . . . just so they come back for more.

✔ **Be personal.** Show who you are and tell what you think without worrying whether it looks homemade.

✔ **Be visual.** A picture is worth a thousand words. Please the eye as well as the mind with graphic elements that effectively communicate the most important aspects of your Web site.

✔ **Be an explorer.** Visit lots of other sites on the Web to learn new things; then tell your visitors about other Web sites you admire and provide a link to those sites. That's what community is all about.

✔ **Be up-to-date.** Get rid of the cobwebs. Add new things, remove dated materials regularly, and keep reworking and improving your page.

✔ **Be a friend.** The Web is a friendly place. Send out and answer e-mail, be ready to listen and talk, and maybe even start up your own cyberclub.

List Your Personal Info Here

Your Internet Service Provider (ISP):

_____

Your E-Mail Address:

_____

Your Personal Home Page Address:

_____

Information about My Friends

Name	Web Page URL	E-Mail Address
_____	_____	_____
_____	_____	_____
_____	_____	_____
_____	_____	_____
_____	_____	_____
_____	_____	_____

The Dummies Guide to Family Computing™

COMPUTER BOOK SERIES FROM IDG

Creating Web Pages For Kids & Parents™

Cheat Sheet

Keys to Great Web Pages

___ Design your Web pages to be no more than one or two screens in length.

___ Make your titles clear, specific, and concise.

___ Use headings and subheadings to organize your topics and direct your readers' eyes.

___ Include a topic sentence that summarizes a page's contents.

___ Use hyperlinks to connect one page to others on your family "web" or to the wider Web.

___ Provide a link to your home page on every page on your site.

Web Page "Don'ts"

✔ **Don't overdo it.** Divide your text and images into several pages, and don't clutter a page with more than, say, two or three visuals.

✔ **Don't use big images.** Keep GIF or JPEG files small and crop closely.

✔ **Don't use copyrighted material.** Use art that is advertised as being freely available, or get permission in writing from the author(s) of material you want to use.

✔ **Keep backgrounds readable.** Avoid bright or busy backgrounds that are hard on the eyes.

✔ **Don't make "surprise" links.** If you provide links on your pages to large files, be sure to warn people about their size and how long it might take to download them.

✔ **No "caterpillars!"** Don't insert too many horizontal rules or bars across your page.

✔ **Keep URLs simple.** Use short filenames, without numbers or unusual characters.

✔ **No "Under Construction."** Web pages are always under construction, so don't add this label or graphic to your page.

✔ **Don't get obscure.** Avoid slang or obscure terms that readers from other countries might not understand.

✔ **No broken links.** Don't put a link on your page without checking to see whether it is accurate and that the URL is complete and spelled correctly.

My Favorite Web Sites

Name	URL
_____	_____
_____	_____
_____	_____
_____	_____
_____	_____
_____	_____
_____	_____
_____	_____
_____	_____

IDG BOOKS WORLDWIDE

The Dummies Guide to Family Computing™

CREATING WEB PAGES
FOR KIDS
& PARENTS™

CREATING WEB PAGES
FOR KIDS & PARENTS™

by Greg Holden
with Stylus Media

IDG Books Worldwide, Inc.
An International Data Group Company

Foster City, CA ◆ Chicago, IL ◆ Indianapolis, IN ◆ Southlake, TX

Creating Web Pages For Kids & Parents™

Published by
IDG Books Worldwide, Inc.
An International Data Group Company
919 E. Hillsdale Blvd.
Suite 400
Foster City, CA 94404
http://www.idgbooks.com (IDG Books Worldwide Web site)
http://www.dummies.com (Dummies Press Web site)

Library of Congress Catalog Card No.: 79-71806

ISBN: 0-7645-0156-9

Printed in the United States of America

10 9 8 7 6 5 4 3 2 1

1E/QY/QV/ZX

Distributed in the United States by IDG Books Worldwide, Inc.

Distributed by Macmillan Canada for Canada; by Transworld Publishers Limited in the United Kingdom and Europe; by WoodsLane Pty. Ltd. for Australia; by WoodsLane Enterprises Ltd. for New Zealand; by Longman Singapore Publishers Ltd. for Singapore, Malaysia, Thailand, and Indonesia; by Simron Pty. Ltd. for South Africa; by Toppan Company Ltd. for Japan; by Distribuidora Cuspide for Argentina; by Livraria Cultura for Brazil; by Ediciencia S.A. for Ecuador; by Addison-Wesley Publishing Company for Korea; by Ediciones ZETA S.C.R. Ltda. for Peru; by WS Computer Publishing Company, Inc., for the Philippines; by Unalis Corporation for Taiwan; by Contemporanea de Ediciones for Venezuela. Authorized Sales Agent: Anthony Rudkin Associates for the Middle East and North Africa.

For general information on IDG Books Worldwide's books in the U.S., please call our Consumer Customer Service department at 800-762-2974. For reseller information, including discounts and premium sales, please call our Reseller Customer Service department at 800-434-3422.

For information on where to purchase IDG Books Worldwide's books outside the U.S., please contact our International Sales department at 415-655-3023 or fax 415-655-3299.

For information on foreign language translations, please contact our Foreign & Subsidiary Rights department at 415-655-3021 or fax 415-655-3281.

For sales inquiries and special prices for bulk quantities, please contact our Sales department at 415-655-3200 or write to the address above.

For information on using IDG Books Worldwide's books in the classroom or for ordering examination copies, please contact our Educational Sales department at 800-434-2086 or fax 817-251-8174.

For press review copies, author interviews, or other publicity information, please contact our Public Relations department at 415-655-3000 or fax 415-655-3299.

For authorization to photocopy items for corporate, personal, or educational use, please contact Copyright Clearance Center, 222 Rosewood Drive, Danvers, MA 01923, or fax 508-750-4470.

is a trademark under exclusive license to IDG Books Worldwide, Inc., from International Data Group, Inc.

About the Author

Greg Holden is founder and president of Stylus Media, a group of editorial, design, and computer professionals who produce print and electronic publications and who create and publish Web pages. The company gets its name from a recording stylus that reads the traces left by voices or instruments on a disk and translates those signals into electronic data that can be amplified and enjoyed by many.

One of the ways Greg enjoys communicating is by writing books like this one so that nontechnical people can use the Web to share their own information and stories. He is currently working on his fifth book. Greg also writes poetry and short stories.

Greg received an M.A. degree in English from the University of Illinois at Chicago. After graduating, he worked as a newspaper reporter in his hometown and then in the publications office at the University of Chicago. In this latter position, computers came into Greg's life in a big way, first through desktop publishing and later via activities on the World Wide Web.

While at the University of Chicago, Greg met John Casler, who was a computer and technical specialist in the university's publications office and supervisor of the instructional laboratory in the Department of Computer Science. The two discovered many common interests. Now they are partners of Stylus Media and continue to be good friends. John's artwork is displayed in the clip art that accompanies the exercises on the CD-ROM that comes with this book.

Greg has created a number of Web sites for himself, for the books he has written, and for other companies and organizations. Seeing the excitement of the Web through the eyes of kids is something Greg does every day, in the company of his two daughters and his many nieces and nephews. They are full of questions, and he, from many years of working in communications and writing a number of other computer books, is happy to give them answers that they understand and enjoy.

Greg lives in Chicago with his wife and two daughters in an old house that he has been rehabbing for — well, for many years. Greg loves to travel, but with two daughters and his many other responsibilities, he admits to doing much of his traveling via the Web. He collects pens, cameras, radios, hats, and other things because he likes to take them apart, see how they work, and then fix them up — many of the same skills he uses in creating Web pages. Greg is an active member of Jewel Heart, a Tibetan Buddhist meditation and study group based in Ann Arbor, Michigan. Not surprisingly, he also produces a newsletter and a Web site for Jewel Heart.

ABOUT IDG BOOKS WORLDWIDE

Welcome to the world of IDG Books Worldwide.

IDG Books Worldwide, Inc., is a subsidiary of International Data Group, the world's largest publisher of computer-related information and the leading global provider of information services on information technology. IDG was founded more than 25 years ago and now employs more than 8,500 people worldwide. IDG publishes more than 275 computer publications in over 75 countries (see listing below). More than 60 million people read one or more IDG publications each month.

Launched in 1990, IDG Books Worldwide is today the #1 publisher of best-selling computer books in the United States. We are proud to have received eight awards from the Computer Press Association in recognition of editorial excellence and three from *Computer Currents'* First Annual Readers' Choice Awards. Our best-selling *...For Dummies*® series has more than 30 million copies in print with translations in 30 languages. IDG Books Worldwide, through a joint venture with IDG's Hi-Tech Beijing, became the first U.S. publisher to publish a computer book in the People's Republic of China. In record time, IDG Books Worldwide has become the first choice for millions of readers around the world who want to learn how to better manage their businesses.

Our mission is simple: Every one of our books is designed to bring extra value and skill-building instructions to the reader. Our books are written by experts who understand and care about our readers. The knowledge base of our editorial staff comes from years of experience in publishing, education, and journalism — experience we use to produce books for the '90s. In short, we care about books, so we attract the best people. We devote special attention to details such as audience, interior design, use of icons, and illustrations. And because we use an efficient process of authoring, editing, and desktop publishing our books electronically, we can spend more time ensuring superior content and spend less time on the technicalities of making books.

You can count on our commitment to deliver high-quality books at competitive prices on topics you want to read about. At IDG Books Worldwide, we continue in the IDG tradition of delivering quality for more than 25 years. You'll find no better book on a subject than one from IDG Books Worldwide.

John Kilcullen
John Kilcullen
CEO
IDG Books Worldwide, Inc.

Steven Berkowitz
Steven Berkowitz
President and Publisher
IDG Books Worldwide, Inc.

WINNER

Eighth Annual Computer Press Awards ➤1992

WINNER

Ninth Annual Computer Press Awards ➤1993

1995 COMPUTER CURRENTS READERS CHOICE

WINNER

Tenth Annual Computer Press Awards ➤1994

WINNER

Eleventh Annual Computer Press Awards ➤1995

IDG Books Worldwide, Inc., is a subsidiary of International Data Group, the world's largest publisher of computer-related information and the leading global provider of information services on information technology. International Data Group publishes over 275 computer publications in over 75 countries. Sixty million people read one or more International Data Group publications each month. International Data Group's publications include: **ARGENTINA:** Buyer's Guide Computerworld Argentina, PC World Argentina; **AUSTRALIA:** Australian Macworld, Australian PC World, Australian Reseller News, Computerworld, IT Casebook, Network World, Publish, Webmaster; **AUSTRIA:** Computerwelt Osterreich, Networks Austria, PC Tip Austria; **BANGLADESH:** PC World Bangladesh; **BELARUS:** PC World Belarus; **BELGIUM:** Data News; **BRAZIL:** Annuario de Informatica, Computerworld, Connections, Macworld, PC Player, PC World, Publish, Reseller News, Supergamepower; **BULGARIA:** Computerworld Bulgaria, Network World Bulgaria, PC & MacWorld Bulgaria; **CANADA:** CIO Canada, Client/Server World, ComputerWorld Canada, InfoWorld Canada, NetworkWorld Canada, WebWorld; **CHILE:** Computerworld Chile, PC World Chile; **COLOMBIA:** Computerworld Colombia, PC World Colombia; **COSTA RICA:** PC World Centro America; **THE CZECH AND SLOVAK REPUBLICS:** Computerworld Czechoslovakia, Macworld Czech Republic, PC World Czechoslovakia; **DENMARK:** Communications World Danmark, Computerworld Danmark, Macworld Danmark, PC World Danmark, Techworld Denmark; **DOMINICAN REPUBLIC:** PC World Republica Dominicana; **ECUADOR:** PC World Ecuador; **EGYPT:** Computerworld Middle East, PC World Middle East; **EL SALVADOR:** PC World Centro America; **FINLAND:** MikroPC, Tietoverkko, Tietoviikko; **FRANCE:** Distributique, Hebdo, Info PC, Le Monde Informatique, Macworld, Reseaux & Telecoms, WebMaster France; **GERMANY:** Computer Partner, Computerwoche, Computerwoche Extra, Computerwoche FOCUS, Global Online, Macwelt, PC Welt; **GREECE:** Amiga Computing, GamePro Greece, Multimedia World; **GUATEMALA:** PC World Centro America; **HONDURAS:** PC World Centro America; **HONG KONG:** Computerworld Hong Kong, PC World Hong Kong, Publish in Asia; **HUNGARY:** ABCD CD-ROM, Computerworld Szamitastechnika, Internetto online Magazine, PC World Hungary, PC-X Magazin Hungary; **ICELAND:** Tolvuheimur PC World Island; **INDIA:** Information Communications World, Information Systems Computerworld, PC World India, Publish in Asia; **INDONESIA:** InfoKomputer PC World, Komputek Computerworld, Publish in Asia; **IRELAND:** ComputerScope, PC Live!; **ISRAEL:** Macworld Israel, People & Computers/Computerworld; **ITALY:** Computerworld Italia, Macworld Italia, Networking Italia, PC World Italia; **JAPAN:** DTP World, Macworld Japan, Nikkei Personal Computing, OS/2 World Japan, SunWorld Japan, Windows NT World, Windows World Japan; **KENYA:** PC World East African; **KOREA:** Hi-Tech Information, Macworld Korea, PC World Korea; **MACEDONIA:** PC World Macedonia; **MALAYSIA:** Computerworld Malaysia, PC World Malaysia, Publish in Asia; **MALTA:** PC World Malta; **MEXICO:** Computerworld Mexico, PC World Mexico; **MYANMAR:** PC World Myanmar; **NETHERLANDS:** Computer! Totaal, LAN Internetworking Magazine, LAN World Buyers Guide, Macworld Netherlands, Net, WebWereld; **NEW ZEALAND:** Absolute Beginners Guide and Plain & Simple Series, Computer Buyer, Computer Industry Directory, Computerworld New Zealand, MTB, Network World, PC World New Zealand; **NICARAGUA:** PC World Centro America; **NORWAY:** Computerworld Norge, CW Rapport, Datamagasinet, Financial Rapport, Kursguide Norge, Macworld Norge, Multimediaworld Norge, PC World Ekspress Norge, PC World Nettverk, PC World Norge, PC World ProduktGuide Norge; **PAKISTAN:** Computerworld Pakistan; **PANAMA:** PC World Panama; **PEOPLE'S REPUBLIC OF CHINA:** China Computer Users, China Computerworld, China InfoWorld, China Telecom World Weekly, Computer & Communication, Electronic Design China, Electronics Today, Electronics Weekly, Game Software, PC World China, Popular Computer Week, Software Weekly, Software World; **PERU:** Computerworld Peru, PC World Profesional Peru, PC World SoHo Peru; **PHILIPPINES:** Click!, Computerworld Philippines, PC World Philippines, Publish in Asia; **POLAND:** Computerworld Poland, Computerworld Special Report Poland, Cyber, Macworld Poland, Networld Poland, PC World Komputer; **PORTUGAL:** Cerebro/PC World, Computerworld/Correio Informático, Dealer World Portugal, Mac*In/PC*In Portugal, Multimedia World; **PUERTO RICO:** PC World Puerto Rico; **ROMANIA:** Computerworld Romania, PC World Romania, Telecom Romania; **RUSSIA:** Computerworld Russia, Mir PK, Publish, Seti; **SINGAPORE:** Computerworld Singapore, PC World Singapore, Publish in Asia; **SLOVENIA:** Monitor; **SOUTH AFRICA:** Computing SA, Network World SA, Software World SA; **SPAIN:** Communicaciones World España, Computerworld España, Dealer World España, Macworld España, PC World España; **SRI LANKA:** Infolink PC World; **SWEDEN:** CAP&Design, Computer Sweden, Corporate Computing Sweden, Internetworld Sweden, it.branschen, Macworld Sweden, MaxiData Sweden, MikroDatorn, Nätverk & Kommunikation, PC World Sweden, PCaktiv, Windows World Sweden; **SWITZERLAND:** Computerworld Schweiz, Macworld Schweiz, PCtip; **TAIWAN:** Computerworld Taiwan, Macworld Taiwan, NEW ViSiON/Publish, PC World Taiwan, Windows World Taiwan; **THAILAND:** Publish in Asia, Thai Computerworld; **TURKEY:** Computerworld Turkiye, Macworld Turkiye, Network World Turkiye, PC World Turkiye; **UKRAINE:** Computerworld Kiev, Multimedia World Ukraine, PC World Ukraine; **UNITED KINGDOM:** Acorn User UK, Amiga Action UK, Amiga Computing UK, Apple Talk UK, Computing, Macworld, Parents and Computers UK, PC Advisor, PC Home, PSX Pro, The WEB; **UNITED STATES:** Cable in the Classroom, CIO Magazine, Computerworld, DOS World, Federal Computer Week, GamePro Magazine, InfoWorld, I-Way, Macworld, Network World, PC Games, PC World, Publish, Video Event, THE WEB Magazine, and WebMaster; online webzines: JavaWorld, NetscapeWorld, and SunWorld Online; **URUGUAY:** InfoWorld Uruguay; **VENEZUELA:** Computerworld Venezuela, PC World Venezuela; and **VIETNAM:** PC World Vietnam. 3/24/97

Dedication

To Stylus Media, my new company, and to all the young people who are and will be accomplishing wonderful things on the World Wide Web.

Author's Acknowledgments

This book was written for kids and their parents, and some of the good parts were written by kids. I especially want to thank my niece Clare Moseley (`dmoseley@mailserv.interhop.net`) and my nephew Brian Wolf for being stars of the show. You will meet them as you turn the pages of the book and look up their home pages on the Web, and I know you'll like them as much as I do. Dozens of other kids and their parents also allowed me to use their Web sites. Their imagination and intelligence were what attracted me to their pages in the first place, and I appreciate their generosity in being willing to share with all of us in this important way.

Quite a few "kids at heart" made writing this book fun for me. I'm sure you will love the drawings of John Casler (`jcasler@paranet.com`), whose zest for living always brightens up my day. The technical skill of Madonna Gauding (`madonna@interaccess.com`) is visible on nearly every page, and I'm thankful for her reassuring way of responding to my many requests. Mary Wisniewski Holden, in addition to being my loving and lovely wife, is a talented writer in her own right and helped with the organization and focus of the book when I really needed it. Ann Lindner used to be a school teacher, and her knack for doing "projects" and knowledge of communication added a lot to this book. Some of the parts that are especially fun to read came from Virginia Smiley, who likes to write about and meet kids and animals, both in person and on the Web.

The folks at IDG gave me plenty of challenges and also gave me the wherewithal to meet them. Special thanks first and foremost to my editor Melba Hopper, who braved a computer virus attack in the middle of this project and who helped me to be organized, focused, and clear so I could tell *you* how to be all of those things, too. Technical editor Linda Brigman kept me on my toes and made a lot of great suggestions. Thanks to Joyce Pepple and Heather Dismore for help with the book's CD-ROM and permissions issues and to Shelley Lea for help with graphics questions. Thanks also to my agent, Brian Gill, and his cohorts at Studio B.

My own two kids, Zosia and Lucy, are the reasons I'm writing this book in the first place. I'm truly a lucky man to be their father and am so glad that writing books like this one makes it possible for me to work at home and be with them.

Publisher's Acknowledgments

We're proud of this book; please send us your comments about it by using the IDG Books Worldwide Registration Card at the back of the book or by e-mailing us at feedback/dummies@idgbooks.com. Some of the people who helped bring this book to market include the following:

Acquisitions, Development, and Editorial

Project Editor: Melba Hopper

Senior Acquisitions Editor: Jill Pisoni

Product Development Director:
Mary Bednarek

Media Development Manager: Joyce Pepple

Associate Permissions Editor:
Heather H. Dismore

Technical Editor: Linda Brigman

Associate Technical Editor: Kevin Spencer

Editorial Manager: Mary C. Corder

Editorial Assistants: Chris H. Collins,
Michael D. Sullivan

Production

Project Coordinator: Cindy L. Phipps

Layout and Graphics: J. Tyler Connor,
Elizabeth Cárdenas-Nelson,
Angela F. Hunckler, Jane E. Martin,
Anna Rohrer, Brent Savage,
Gary Storey

Proofreaders: Christine D. Berman,
Joel K. Draper, Nancy Price,
Rob Springer, Karen York

Indexer: Sharon Hilgenberg

Special Help

Publication Services, Inc.

General and Administrative

IDG Books Worldwide, Inc.: John Kilcullen, CEO; Steven Berkowitz, President and Publisher

IDG Books Technology Publishing: Brenda McLaughlin, Senior Vice President and Group Publisher

Dummies Technology Press and Dummies Editorial: Diane Graves Steele, Vice President and Associate Publisher; Judith A. Taylor, Brand Manager; Kristin A. Cocks, Editorial Director

Dummies Trade Press: Kathleen A. Welton, Vice President and Publisher; Stacy S. Collins, Brand Manager

IDG Books Production for Dummies Press: Beth Jenkins, Production Director; Cindy L. Phipps, Supervisor of Project Coordination, Production Proofreading, and Indexing; Kathie S. Schutte, Supervisor of Page Layout; Shelley Lea, Supervisor of Graphics and Design; Debbie J. Gates, Production Systems Specialist; Tony Augsburger, Supervisor of Reprints and Bluelines; Leslie Popplewell, Media Archive Coordinator

Dummies Packaging and Book Design: Patti Sandez, Packaging Specialist; Lance Kayser, Packaging Assistant; Kavish + Kavish, Cover Design

♦

The publisher would like to give special thanks to Patrick J. McGovern,
without whom this book would not have been possible.

♦

Contents at a Glance

Cartoons at a Glance

By Rich Tennant • Fax: 508-546-7747 • E-mail: the5wave@tiac.net

"I SAID I WANTED A NEW MONITOR FOR MY BIRTHDAY! MONITOR! MONITOR!"

page 293

"No Stuart, I won't look up 'rampaging elephants' on the Internet. We're studying plant life and right now photosynthesis is a more pertinent topic."

page 271

"I NEED TO CONNECT TO OUR T1 LINE AND FTP A FILE FROM OUR CLIENT'S WEB SITE. CAN YOU GET MY KID ON THE PHONE?"

page 81

"YOU KNOW KIDS — YOU CAN'T BUY THEM JUST ANY WEB AUTHORING SOFTWARE."

page 129

"OH SURE, $1.8 MILLION DOLLARS SEEMS LIKE A LOT RIGHT NOW, BUT WHAT ABOUT RANDY? WHAT ABOUT HIS FUTURE? THINK WHAT A COMPUTER LIKE THIS WILL DO FOR HIS SAT SCORE SOMEDAY."

page 237

"LOOK AT THIS - THERE'S ROLLER COASTER ACTION, SUSPENSE AND DRAMA, WHERE SKILL AND STRATEGY ARE MATCHED AGAINST WINNING AND LOSING. AND I THOUGHT SETTING YOUR WEB BROWSER'S PREFERENCES WOULD BE DULL."

page 9

"Oh, Scarecrow! Without the database in your laptop, how will we ever find anything in Oz?"

page 179

Table of Contents

Introduction

● ●

My daughter Zosia and I were randomly browsing the Web, when suddenly I heard her exclaim, "Wow!" We had come across a page that a 5-year-old had created with the help of her mom. Zosia, who had just turned four, was enchanted by the colorful graphics. "Look, Daddy. Now look at this," she kept repeating as the little girl's smiling face appeared. Then Zosia's jaw dropped, and she stared wide-eyed as she heard her new friend's voice through the computer's speakers. The moment of awed silence was followed by a flurry of questions: "Daddy, how did she do that? Can I do it too? Will you help me? Please?"

That's when I knew I had to write this book. Both young and old are fascinated and informed by the Web, but kids are naturals for the Internet. At the moment I just described, my daughter and the little girl who had created the home page were in the same place. Even at age four, Zosia knew that she wanted to exchange messages, express what was important to her, and simply have fun. Kids have a splendid sense of wonder and excitement that melts away boundaries. So does the Web.

Kids respond immediately to what other kids put on the Web, and they want to do it, too. What's more, they have every confidence in the world that with just a little support and encouragement, they can create their own Web pages.

Where This Book Is Coming From

The goal of this book is to be there for parents and kids during those precious teachable moments. Instructions are provided in easy-to-follow steps written in language you can understand. My daughters and I have found the cyber community to be chock-full of knowledge, humor, and beauty. This book is written to inspire and encourage young Web authors (and their parents) to join the growing community of individuals who are sharing important parts of their lives by creating their own Web pages.

Everyone has something special to say about themselves. With the help of this book, kids and adults will soon be ready to create Web pages that reflect who they really are. Lots of people, both young and a little bit older, have helped with this book. Each of us have contributed our own talents and perspectives, but we all hope that you will:

> ✔ See how easy it is to create a Web page.
>
> ✔ Learn how to design and organize like the Web pros do.
>
> ✔ Plan an entire Web site of pages for you, your friends, or your family.
>
> ✔ Produce the cool effects you've admired in the Web pages of other kids.

How to Use This Book

Want to get on the Web with no muss or fuss? You can go straight for the basics and do what you wanna do easily and quickly. Want to know more detailed tricks of the trade and what goes on behind the scenes? That's here, too. Feel free to skip back and forth to what interests you. This book is organized as an easy-to-use reference tool to suit your level of experience with computers and the Web. You don't have to scour each chapter methodically from cover to cover to find what you want. The Web doesn't work that way, and this book doesn't, either!

If you want to make one simple Web page right away, you can find all you need to know in Chapter 1. If you want to plan out a Web site, go on to read the rest of Part I. The middle of the book explains in more detail how to make Web pages and publish them online. Those of you with more experience or those who want to know more techie stuff about making really fancy pages can find plenty of interesting advanced topics in the later chapters. The fun thing about the Web is that it's easy to keep revising. So start where you're comfortable, and come back later for more.

What This Book Assumes

This book is for you if you have or are ready to get the following:

> ✔ A computer and a modem
>
> ✔ Some technical know-how (maybe you have a friend to help you along)

I also assume that you're ready to share some interesting things about yourself. You don't have to know, right at this moment, exactly what those things are. You'll find plenty of ideas in this book to get you started.

If you're interested enough to buy this book, my bet is these are pretty safe assumptions.

What's Where in This Book

This book is divided into seven parts, and each part contains chapters that discuss a stage in the process of Web publishing. In each chapter, you find step-by-step instructions and icons that present short bits of useful information. Here are the parts of the book and what they contain.

Part I: A Web Page Primer

If you're an absolute computer novice or have been using computers and the Web for only a short time, this is the place to start.

Chapter 1 takes the "jump into the water with both feet" approach to Web publishing. After explaining the hardware and software you need to create a Web page, the chapter lets you follow along as my nephew Brian creates his own free Web page at the GeoCities Web site. People from all over the world are going to this site to create their Web pages and become part of GeoCities' virtual communities.

In **Chapter 2**, you take a step back and begin to plan your Web page and any other pages that you want to link together to form your own Web site. You even learn how you can get your family involved, too.

Chapter 3 contains lots of brainstorming exercises to help you come up with great contents for your Web pages. This chapter explains the exercises and free clip art included on the CD-ROM that comes with this book.

Chapter 4 shows you how to organize a Web site so that all the pages work well together.

Part II: Creating and Publishing Your Web Pages

This part focuses on putting together Web pages and shows how to actually publish your pages on the Web by moving your files from your computer to a Web server, a computer that makes documents available to visitors in cyberspace.

In **Chapter 5,** you find out how to make well-organized Web pages that include all the essentials. You also get some tips for creating pages that everyone can understand and that entice people to return, again and again.

In **Chapter 6**, you check out some cool tools for making Web pages. You also find out how to publish your pages with three different kinds of Web space providers: a free Web page service on the Web (GeoCities), a commercial online service (America Online), and an Internet Service Provider.

Part III: Cool Things You Can Do with Your Web Pages

This part opens up the Web publisher's bag of tricks to reveal how the coolest Web pages do their magic. With the help of this chapter, you can wave your magic wand and create your own awesome effects.

Chapter 7 describes some of the cool animations, sound, and other add-ons seen on many kids' Web pages.

Chapter 8 shows you how you can design your page the way the professionals do. It also describes some ready-made page layouts that you can copy from this book's CD-ROM and then complete by using your own words and images.

Chapter 9 provides pointers on locating and copying free art and other "eye candy" to make your Web pages truly sweet.

Part IV: Advanced Web Page Techniques

This part goes a step beyond explaining and showing you how to copy cool Web page contents by describing how you can create your own special effects.

Chapter 10 instructs you on the best ways to prepare photos or other images for your Web pages by scanning the images and then editing them in a graphics program.

Chapter 11 demonstrates how you, too, can be a Web page "movie director" by creating your own animated series of images.

In **Chapter 12,** you discover how to record voice and music clips and include them on your Web pages to involve your visitors' ears, as well as their eyes.

In Chapter 13, you learn how to draw images and convert them to formats that can be viewed by Web browsers.

Part V: Behind the Curtain: How Web Pages Work

The information in Part V is for those of you who aren't afraid of working with HTML and who want to really understand how the Web works.

Chapter 14 goes into the specifics of how to create Web pages, format text, add images, and do lots of other things by entering the HTML instructions yourself.

In **Chapter 15,** you learn all about making links within your site and to other Web sites so that your pages are connected to other locations on the Web.

Part VI: The Part of Tens

Filled with tips, cautions, suggestions, and examples, Part VI presents many kinds of information to help you plan and create your Web pages.

Chapter 16 presents lists of procedures and describes strategies that a smart Web publisher like yourself will want to follow (or, in the case of the "don'ts," avoid).

Chapter 17 describes cool features commonly seen on kids' Web pages that you might want to add to your own site.

Chapter 18 honors ten (actually 11) kids' pages that the author found worthy of recognition and that contain plenty of features you can add to your own soon-to-be-award-winning pages.

Part VII: Appendixes

You can find a grab bag of information in the appendixes that are part of this book.

If you want to know more about the hardware you need to connect to the Web, read about how to set up your Web page toolbox in **Appendix A.**

Appendix B describes some essential software for Web page developers. A variety of Web page authoring tools are compared.

In **Appendix C,** you find lots of great resources on the Web that can help you find other kids online or help you create Web pages.

Appendix D tells you all about using this book's CD-ROM, which contains Web browsers, Web page tools, clip art, a graphics program, and more.

Conventions Used in This Book

I have tried to address both the Windows 95 and Macintosh users in this book. But while I love the Mac, the reality is that in terms of computer users, PCs are more widespread, so most of the examples and instructions address Windows 95 users.

By the way, whenever you see "I" in this book note that it refers to Greg Holden, the author and head honcho of Stylus Media. "We" refers to Greg and his colleagues, Ann, John, and Madonna.

Important bits of information are formatted in special ways in this book to make sure you notice them right away. Here they are:

"In This Chapter" lists: These are the lists at the very beginning of each chapter. They represent a kind of table of contents in miniature. They tell you the Web page contents covered and suggest why you might want to learn how to add those features yourself.

Numbered lists: These lists are for steps or instructions that you need to follow in a specific order.

Bulleted lists: These lists are for special descriptive information or things that you can do in any order.

Web addresses: These addresses, known as Uniform Resource Locators (URLs), are shown in a special typeface, for example: `http://www.dummies.com/`.

Don't be surprised if your browser cannot find a Web address you type or if a Web page shown in this book is no longer at the given address. It's not your fault, and it's probably not our fault either! Blame it on the ever-changing World Wide Web: Web addresses (and sites themselves) can be pretty fickle. Try looking for a "missing" site by using an Internet search engine. And try shortening the address by deleting everything after the `.com` (or `.org` or `.edu`).

Note: By the way, most of the kids' Web pages we mention in this book, as well as copyright-free image archives and other resources, are listed in a set of bookmarks that you can open in your Web browser. (See Appendix D for more information.)

Icons Used in This Book

Creating Web Pages For Kids & Parents also uses special graphical elements, called icons, to get your readers' attention. Here's what they look like and what they mean:

Indicates really important lists or ideas for you to remember.

Introduces a tip or other comment by a real kid just like you named Clare Moseley, who lives in Canada, surfs the Web, and makes her own Web pages. You find these icons beside sidebars at the end of most chapters in this book.

Emphasizes ideas for using the techniques you employ to create Web pages to complement your classroom learning.

Alerts you to together-time activities that will help kids, siblings, and parents get more mileage out of creating Web pages.

Points out some technical details you may want to know but don't necessarily need to know.

Indicates that the CD-ROM at the back of this book contains a version of the software mentioned.

The TakeCharge icon alerts *kids* to activities, tips, or strategies that empower you and propel you on the way to becoming a dynamite Web publisher.

Points out things that can cause problems.

Marks your gateway to online fun and learning. It's always followed by suggestions for useful Web sites, software, or other kid or family-oriented resources.

Flags practical advice about equipment, privacy questions, or other issues of importance to kids and parents.

Feedback!

The whole point of this book is to help you express yourself and communicate in the exciting new medium of the World Wide Web. If you have something to say about this book, you can reach us online or by *snail mail* at:

IDG Books Worldwide Inc.
7260 Shadeland Station, Suite 100
Indianapolis, IN 46256

You can e-mail us at feedback/dummies@idgbooks.com. And remember to check out the *...For Dummies* Web site at http://www.dummies.com/.

If you want to reach the author, you're welcome to do that, too. Send e-mail to Greg Holden at gholden@interaccess.com.

Part I
A Web Page Primer

The 5th Wave   By Rich Tennant

©RICHTENNANT

"LOOK AT THIS - THERE'S ROLLER COASTER ACTION, SUSPENSE AND DRAMA, WHERE SKILL AND STRATEGY ARE MATCHED AGAINST WINNING AND LOSING. AND I THOUGHT SETTING YOUR WEB BROWSER'S PREFERENCES WOULD BE DULL."

In this part . . .

Some of you probably try out new projects right away: You simply jump in with both feet. Some of you probably like to read and plan before starting: You don't want to miss any important steps. Whether you're a jumper or a planner, Part I gives you a way to create your own Web page.

For those of you who want to get on the Web *now,* this book isn't going to make you wait for the good stuff. In the very first chapter, you find out what sort of hardware and software you need. You also make your own Web page with GeoCities, a place on the Web that provides free Web pages and e-mail for kids. Just follow the simple directions, and you'll be a proud citizen in *cyberland* before you know it. For the planners among you, Chapters 2 through 4 help you brainstorm and gather ideas for lots of different Web pages.

After you decide what you want to do and have a notion about what you want to say, how do you put it all together? In the rest of Part I, you find suggestions for organizing and connecting your individual Web pages to weave your own *Web site.* You discover how to create a welcome page, the page that introduces your Web site. Then you divide your site into levels of information so that your visitors can quickly and easily find engaging text and graphics.

Chapter 1

Weaving Your World on the Web

• •

In This Chapter

▶ Finding out what Web pages are and how they are displayed by Web browsers

▶ Understanding the parts of a Web address

▶ Discovering what Web browsers do and locating the latest versions

▶ Creating a free Web page on GeoCities

• •

*Y*ou probably browsed the World Wide Web a little and thought about how great it would be to have your own pages on the Web. Now you probably want to know a little more about it, and are wondering whether you can put your own pages on it — right?

Well, you *can*! And this book is going to help you do it. Actually, you're probably already doing what all Web page authors do before creating their own masterpieces — asking good questions, thinking about what they want the world to see, or better still, considering *why* the world will want to see it.

Maybe you want to share stories or poems you've written. Maybe you're totally crazy about a hobby, a TV show, or a movie star, and you want to find people who like what you like. Perhaps your friends have Web pages of their own, and you just want to join the crowd and make pages with bright colors and interesting graphics or with photos that appear to move on-screen. My point is that if you know why you want a Web page, you're well on your way to having one.

Now that you've determined that you — yes, I'm talking to you — can be a Web page author, take a brief look at some of the reasons some people might be *afraid* to make a Web page, and after you read them, just banish them from your brain, because they are wrong!

▶ You have to be a computer programmer to do be a Web page author. (Negative!)

▶ You need special permission from America Online (AOL) or some Internet company. (Nope!)

▶ You need a special computer program or a really fast modem. (No way!)

▶ Having a Web page costs extra. (No — no more than you already pay to get on the Web.)

The truth is that if you have a computer and a modem, you have the basic hardware you need to make a home page. ***Note:*** If you need basic information about using PCs and Macs, you may want to check out *PCs For Kids & Parents* and *Macs For Kids & Parents,* both published by IDG Books Worldwide. If you already have a connection to the Internet and have surfed the Web, I have only one thing to say: C'mon! What are you waiting for?

A *guide* of course. Everyone needs a guide to help them learn something new, and that's what *Creating Web Pages For Kids & Parents* is: a friendly, *cyberspace* guide to show you how to make your own Web pages about yourself, your family, and even your pets, if you want. Later in this chapter, you'll follow along as a 5th-grader named Brian becomes a member of a site that lets anyone create and publish free Web pages. You'll learn how he made his own page, and if Brian can do it, you can, too.

Note: When you're delving into the basics of the Web and Web pages, you have a great chance to check out the rest of the Internet, too. These days, people use the term *Web* almost exclusively, as though the rest of the Internet doesn't exist. But the Web is just one of a number of Internet services. People just talk about the Web all the time because it's fun, colorful, and exciting. To find out more, check out some of IDG's books, such as *The Internet For Dummies Quick Reference,* 3rd Edition, by John Levine, Margaret Levine Young, and Arnold Reinhold. You may also want to check out *The World Wide Web For Kids & Parents,* by Viraf D. Mohta, also published by IDG Books.

Before you start connecting to the Web and creating a Web page, take a moment to review the equipment you have on hand. Make sure you have everything you need. In general, you need these items (see Appendix A for more about online requirements):

    ___ Computer with enough memory and processing power to operate a Web browser

    ___ Modem, either built into your computer or an external one

    ___ Web browser that supports frames

    Some pages use frames. Netscape Navigator 2.0 or later and Microsoft Internet Explorer 3.0 or later support frames. ***Note:*** If you don't have a Web browser, you'll find what you need to get connected on the CD-ROM that accompanies this book (see Appendix D).

If you use Netscape Navigator 3.0 and have a PC running Windows 95, you need these:

    ___ 386SX or later processor

    ___ Minimum of 6MB RAM (random access memory); 8MB preferred

    ___ At least 9MB space available on your hard drive

Mac users using Netscape Navigator 3.0 need these:

___ 68020 processor or Power Macintosh computer

___ Minimum 16MB RAM; 32MB preferred

___ At least 15MB space available on your hard drive

To run Microsoft Internet Explorer on a PC that uses Windows 95, you need:

___ 386DX or later processor

___ Minimum 8MB RAM

___ 5–10MB of space on your hard drive

To run Microsoft Internet Explorer on a Mac running System 7.1 or later, you need these:

___ 68030 or Power Mac processor

___ Minimum 8MB RAM

___ 2–8MB of space on your hard drive

Square One: Getting to Know a Web Page

Chances are that you've peeked over the shoulders of your friends or parents as they explored cool Web sites. What you probably don't know is how they're made, where they come from, and how people get them on the Internet so that you and everyone else can see them. The following sections provide some quick, _pseudotechnical_ answers to these and other burning questions.

Defining a Web page

A Web page is a group of words and images that someone has assembled and saved in a document in ways that let cyberspace _visitors_ like you see those words and images on the Web. Actually, there's no such thing as a real Web page because the Web isn't a book. Calling what you see a _page_ is just a way of saying that this set of information is grouped into a single document (or file).

These documents are formatted with instructions contained in a language called _HTML (HyperText Markup Language)_. HTML is the set of commands (called tags) that _marks up_ text or images so they can be displayed on the Web. For example, using HTML commands, some text is identified as headings, other text can be formatted to appear bold, and image files can be identified so that they appear on a page, too.

How do you create all these nifty HTML commands? One of two ways: The easy way is to use a software program that lets you select the function that a part of your Web page is supposed to perform. These user-friendly Web authoring tools let you click on buttons or select menu items to insert images, mark up selected text as italic, or even create links that your visitors can click on to go to other places on your site or to other Web sites. See Chapters 14 and 15 for more information on HTML and links. Also check out Appendix B, which lists some authoring tools.

Web pages don't have a standard length. Sometimes you have to scroll down quite a bit to get to the bottom of one. Other times, the page's entire contents fit on a computer screen.

Puzzling out Web addresses

Web pages *are* similar to pages in the books you find on shelves, however. Every document that is formatted with the mysterious HTML language has its own electronic *page number,* you might say. This page number is an electronic address on the Web. The techie name for this address is Uniform Resource Locator, more commonly called a *URL.* A URL is a series of letters, colons, slashes, dots, and other strange things you type in order to get to a particular Web page or site out in cyberspace. Web pages always have to be marked up with HTML, and they must always have `.html` or `.htm` at the end of the filename in order to be displayed by a Web browser.

Exploring the Web — with a browser

A Web browser is a special computer program that makes it possible for you to view the words and images on Web pages. Microsoft Internet Explorer, and Netscape Communicator, previously called Netscape Navigator, are two popular browsers. Web surfers use quite a few other browsers as their surfboards, but chances are that you use (or will use) one of these two browsers to do your Web surfing.

A Web browser's job is to display documents that have been created with HTML. Browsers are programmed so that they recognize HTML markup commands like `<BLOCKQUOTE>` for a block of text, such as a quotation, that needs to be indented or `<OL>` for the beginning of an ordered list of items. A browser recognizes the HTML and displays the text and images on the page the way the author of the page intended for them to be formatted; the actual HTML instructions don't appear on-screen.

A browser's main purpose is to enable you to really *experience* a Web page: see words, colors, or photos, hear music and other sounds, watch movie clips and other cool things included on the page. (And, guess what? You're going to find out how to put all those things on your Web page, too!)

Here are some other nifty things browsers do:

- ✔ Give you a place to type URLs so that you can go somewhere online (which you'll do shortly, when you start making your own page)
- ✔ Save addresses of pages you want to visit frequently (by using things called Bookmarks or Favorites)
- ✔ Let you fill out forms (you'll get to do that, too — big time)
- ✔ Help you download (get a file from another computer on the Internet, which is the opposite of *upload*) software, send e-mail, copy images, and lots of other things

You don't have to worry about all the details mentioned in this section when you're zooming from site to site. A lot of the details are handled in the background, but when you want to create your own Web page, believe me, knowing about browsers, URLs, and HTML eventually comes in handy.

Nevertheless, some sites on the Web give you tools that make creating a Web page a piece of cake. And you're ready to head to one of those sites right now. All you do is type a URL and, using your browser, go right to the site. You can follow along with my nephew, Brian, as you make your first Web page.

OPEN

Some Web Page Questions

In the course of creating his first Web page, Brian asked some questions that have probably occurred to you, too. So before getting started, you may want to look these over.

Q. How do I get graphics on a Web page?

A. In order to be included on a Web page, graphics must be created as documents on a computer and saved in a format that makes them easy to see and send. Drawings on paper won't work unless they are scanned by a machine called (guess what?) a *scanner.* Often, the stuff you see on Web pages starts out as graphics that someone drew on a computer by using a drawing program like MacPaint or CorelDraw. Then a computerized version of the drawing is saved as a GIF or JPEG file (the most common formats). As the file is saved, these formats *compress* it automatically to a smaller size so that the drawing will appear faster on your computer screen. (See Chapters 7 and 13 for more about graphic file formats.)

▶▶

Q. How do I get drawings or photos to move on a Web page?

A. Usually, these elements are animations made up of several separate images. The images are drawn or arranged in such a way that they give the effect of motion. A format called an *animated GIF* lets you save a series of images as one image. See Chapter 11 for information about creating animated GIF images.

Q. Why do I have to type Web page addresses (URLs) exactly right?

A. URL (pronounced *Earl* and short for Uniform Resource Locator) is the *address* that lets you find a particular file or Web page on the Internet. Web browsers don't know how to read English, or any other human language, for that matter. They recognize only a particular sequence of characters that someone enters into a text box on a computer screen. You have to type the address with all the dots and backslashes in just the right places so a browser can connect to the right computer, burrow through the right directories, and finally locate exactly what you're looking for.

When you type a Web address, you always enter `http://` at the very beginning of the address. This prefix tells the Internet that the site you want to go to is a Web site. (See Chapter 15 for more about the specific parts of a URL.)

Square Two: Finding Your Home on the Web

On a snowy day in February, I drove to the suburbs of Chicago to visit my 10-year-old nephew, Brian Wolf. Brian is in the 5th grade at Forest Elementary School. Brian started surfing the Web about a year ago. Now he's a frequent visitor to the Disney Adventures chat room on AOL and the Beanie Babies Web site (`http://www.ty.com/`). A *chat room* is a site on the Internet that allows you to communicate in real time with other computer users who are connected to the same site and who are using special chat software. You communicate by typing messages back and forth in a sort of *cyberconversation* about virtually anything you want to discuss.

Like most kids, when Brian sees a Web page that looks especially colorful or interesting, he often wonders how all those great pictures get out there.

Step 1: Dive into the Web

Where do you start? Well, that part's easy: Turn on your computer.

Next you need to get your computer connected to the Web. Almost everyone who connects from home uses a *modem,* a handy little device that lets a computer make a telephone call. In this case, you want your computer to be capable of calling another computer that is connected to the Internet all the time. When you connect to this computer you, too, are connected to the Internet — at least for as long as the phone call lasts.

The computer you connect to is operated by an Internet Service Provider (ISP), a company that enables people to get online in order to send e-mail, visit Web sites, gab on chat sites, or any number of online activities. An ISP connects a house or business to the Internet either by running a cable connected to the Internet to a house or business or by letting people use their existing telephone line (you connect your phone to the modem on your computer) to dial in to the Internet.

Brian's father, Kurt, works in a computer store, so he gets to try out lots of software and hardware for his business. For a while, the family was on AOL. Now they're on the Microsoft Network. Brian double-clicked on the icon labeled "msn" on his computer desktop. He entered his password and typed **Connect**. The modem did its dialing, and in a few seconds, he was connected.

Brian uses Microsoft Internet Explorer as his Web *surfboard* (browser). To get started, he got on his surfboard, paddled out into the deep water, and pointed his surfboard in a certain direction (to the Web address for GeoCities, as mentioned later).

Don't be bashful. If you have a computer and a modem, you, too, can get connected to your own online service. Just open Microsoft Internet Explorer, Netscape Communicator (Netscape Navigator), or whatever browser you use, and follow along. It's important to remember, however, that whether you decide to use AT&T, America Online, or another ISP, you'll be charged a monthly bill for the service. Usually, this charge is deducted from one of your parents' credit cards. So don't sign up without telling them what's happening.

Remember: If you don't have a Web browser or an ISP, you'll find everything you need to get connected on the CD-ROM that accompanies this book. Kids can ask Mom or Dad to do this: They can install the sign-on software to AT&T WorldNet Service from the CD and get connected in minutes. (See Appendix D for more information.)

Step 2: Connect to GeoCities

1. **PC and Mac users: From the menu bar at the top of the Netscape Navigator or Internet Explorer screen, select File⇨Open.**

   A dialog box labeled Open Location (or Open Page, if you're using Netscape Navigator rather than Microsoft Internet Explorer) appears on your screen. (It's called a dialog box because you "talk back" to a program by typing characters and pressing buttons like OK or Browse within the box.) A text cursor is blinking in the box, waiting for you to type one of those URLs I mentioned earlier.

2. **In the Open text box, type the following characters exactly as they appear here:** `http://www.geocities.com/`.

3. **Click on OK.**

   The Open Location dialog box closes, and you're back at your browser's main window. In just a few seconds, the GeoCities Home Page (`http://www.geocities.com/`) appears. See Figure 1-1, which shows the page as seen in Netscape Navigator's browser window.

GeoCities' home page, like many other nice home pages, gives you a lot of options to click on and a lot of things to view. You can spend as much time as you want looking around and finding out about GeoCities — but if you're like Brian, you'll be in a hurry to get your home page going, and you'll click on the link <u>Free Home Pages & Free E-mail.</u> This action takes you to the GeoCities Personal Home Page Program page (`http://www.geocities.com/BHI/freehp.html`), shown in Figure 1-2.

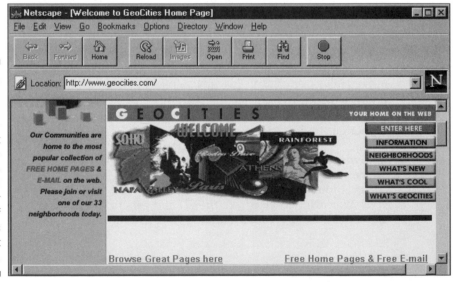

Figure 1-1: Welcome to GeoCities, a Web site that provides free Web pages and e-mail for lots of customers just like you.

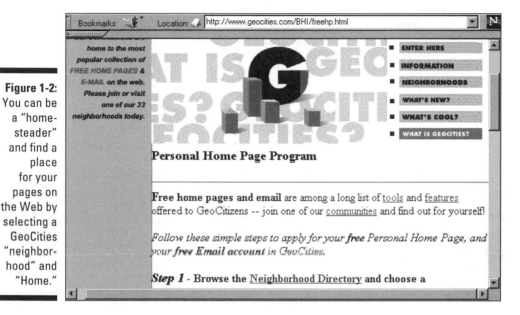

Figure 1-2:
You can be a "home-steader" and find a place for your pages on the Web by selecting a GeoCities "neighbor-hood" and "Home."

The GeoCities Web pages, like lots of other pages, contain images that can take a long time to appear on your computer screen. They are actually being downloaded from the Web site to your computer, one by one, which is why they seem to creep along. You don't have to sit there, tapping your Nikes, waiting for all the images to appear before moving on to the next step. While they are still downloading, scroll down a page, and if you see a place you want to go to, click on a link (remember, links are underlined). That'll save you a lot of time.

You may be wondering why GeoCities lets people do all this for free. The answer is pretty simple: Just look at all the ads on the GeoCities site. One of the few ways a company can make money on a Web site is to attract a lot of visitors. The more visitors it has, the more money it gets from advertisers. However, just because GeoCities is now providing free Web pages doesn't mean it will always provide them for free.

Step 3: Become a homesteader

The Personal Home Page Program Page also contains lots of useful information that you may want to read, but Brian is on a mission. His mission? To get on the Web. He scrolls down to the first step on the screen, which tells you that, like anyone who wants to build a home (or a home page), you first must find a place to live. So click on the link Neighborhood Directory. This link takes you from the Home Page Information page to the Neighborhood Directory page.

Choosing a neighborhood

Like any prospective homesteader, when looking around for a place to stake your claim, you look for a part of the country you like. In its Neighborhood Directory, GeoCities gives you about 30 different *virtual neighborhoods.* You can choose to live in any one of them.

Brian chose an area called <u>EnchantedForest</u>, which is especially for kids and is set up as a sort of electronic bulletin board where kids can post their own home pages. I suggest that you, too, click on the words <u>EnchantedForest</u> so that you can find a spot for your page. Now Netscape Navigator takes you to the Enchanted Forest page at `http://www.geocities.com/ EnchantedForest/`.

At some point, you may want to check out the special content guidelines for the Enchanted Forest site or any other "neighborhoods" your kids join in GeoCities. Basically, GeoCities advises participants to keep it clean: no profanity or naughty pictures on their Web pages. You may also want to look into the GeoRewards program, which makes you eligible for prizes if you agree to include advertising banners on your Web page.

Next, click on the words <u>Join this Neighborhood</u>. This link takes you to the Enchanted Forest Description page. You can decide to move into the Enchanted Forest neighborhood itself or one of its newer "suburbs." Click on one of the links for <u>EnchantedForest</u>, or <u>EnchantedForest/Dell</u>, or one of the other suburbs available. Brian clicked on the <u>EnchantedForest</u> link, which took him to the GeoCities Vacancy Locator page for EnchantedForest.

Don't just skip through this page. Read the description, and jot down a few items you might want to put on your page. Of course, like Brian, you may wind up saying, "I wish I didn't have topics like that." Although you may not want to talk about cartoons or fairy tales, you probably have some hobbies to talk about. And you have a family, too, remember? You'll need these descriptive topics in a minute, when you fill out the Homesteader Program application form. Click on Yes to confirm that this is the area on GeoCities where you want your Web pages to reside.

Picking a vacant address

Netscape Navigator now takes you to the Vacancy Locator, where you can search for a vacant address for your page. You have to find a place to put your Web page, which is a little like finding an address on a street. GeoCities will look for a spot for you, but you have to tell GeoCities where to look. Scroll down to the bottom of the Vacancy Locator page to the Choose Address Range text boxes (see Figure 1-3). You have to choose two numbers between 1000 and 8799. The numbers you choose must have a difference of 200. The first time Brian did this, he didn't find any vacancies; I suggest you enter some very high numbers. Brian entered 8400 and 8600 and clicked on the Submit button at the bottom of the page.

Figure 1-3:
Search for
a "block"
in the
Enchanted
Forest
neighbor-
hood that
has a
vacancy
where you
can set up
your Web
page.

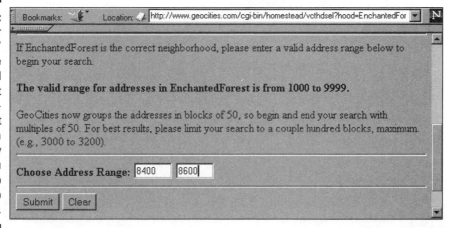

If this section of Enchanted Forest has any *vacant* spots, you receive a list of *blocks* in the forest where there are vacancies. Click on one of these blocks. Brian found plenty of vacancies, and clicked on the link for the EnchantedForest 8580 block.

The next page that appears is great visually. It's the block where your Web page will reside. Scroll down, and you see the rest of the people who already live on this block. Some of the *houses* on the block are labeled *vacant.* Click on one of the underlined links labeled vacant, and you can move into this space. Brian picked 8582 (see Figure 1-4).

Figure 1-4:
Brian's
block
doesn't
have
vacancies
right now,
but keep
searching,
and you'll
find just the
right spot.

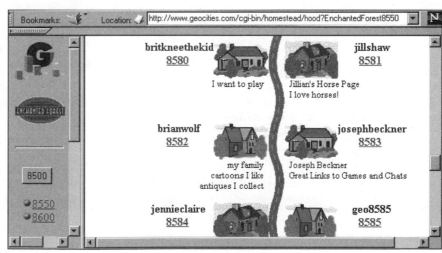

At this point, Brian sighed: The process of getting a free home page takes a while, doesn't it — so many choices to make and forms to fill out. Take heart. You're almost there.

Filling in the blanks to get your Web page

Now you have to fill out the GeoCities Membership Application Form (see Figure 1-5). Naturally, GeoCities wants to keep a record of people who have a free home page, where they can be reached by e-mail, and so on. You don't have to fill out all the boxes in the form. Scroll down and fill in only the boxes that are marked with an asterisk (*) as being required. You can press the Tab key to move from field to field on this form.

What you're filling out is a Web page form. You fill out text boxes and check off options and submit data about yourself to a Web site. The data you send to the site is read by a computer program, which doesn't know how to read English, but only processes numbers and letters that appear in the right spots. That's why everything has to be filled out in exactly the way the form requests. For example, when you're working on the Membership Application Form, be sure to fill out your birth date exactly in the month/day/year (mm/dd/yy) format the form requests (enter 02/08/87, for example, if your birth date is February 8, 1987). If you don't, you'll have to fill it out again the correct way. And when you're entering your e-mail address, be sure to use the standard @ symbol — rather than type the word "at."

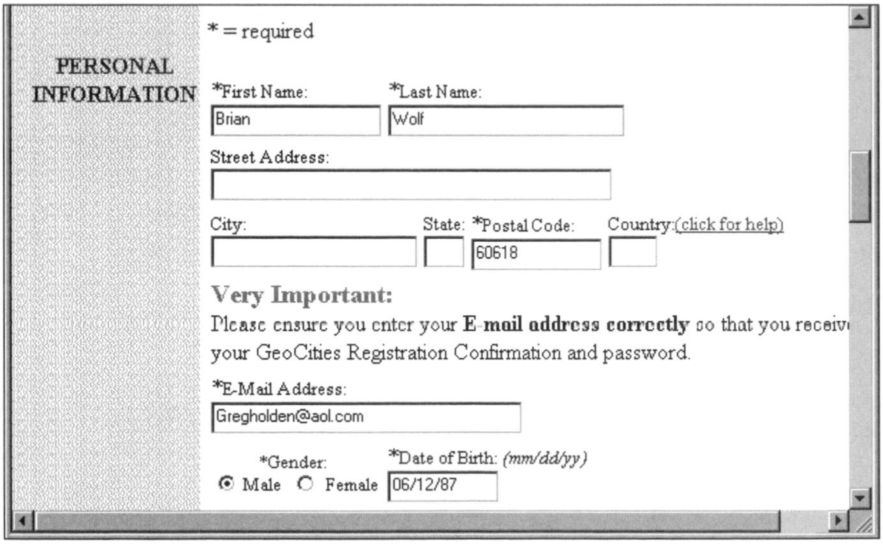

Figure 1-5:
In order to get your free Web page, you must fill out this interactive form and submit it to GeoCities.

```
* = required

PERSONAL
INFORMATION    *First Name:        *Last Name:
               [Brian        ]     [Wolf         ]

               Street Address:
               [                              ]

               City:              State:  *Postal Code:  Country:(click for help)
               [             ]    [   ]   [60618     ]   [        ]

               Very Important:
               Please ensure you enter your E-mail address correctly so that you receive
               your GeoCities Registration Confirmation and password.

               *E-Mail Address:
               [Gregholden@aol.com        ]

                    *Gender:      *Date of Birth: (mm/dd/yy)
               ⦿ Male  ○ Female  [06/12/87  ]
```

Enter your e-mail address

You'll need to enter an e-mail address on the Membership Application Form. If you or your parents have one, that's cool; just enter it. If not, enter the e-mail address of someone else you know, such as a friend or relative — but be sure to let that person know that he or she will be getting e-mail for you from GeoCities. If that person doesn't know what the e-mail is about, it might seem like "bogus" or junk e-mail and end up getting deleted. Another thing to remember: This has to be an *outside* e-mail address, that is, not a GeoCities e-mail address. Why? After you fill out this form, GeoCities will send you an e-mail message that provides your password, which you need to start making your Web page.

Say Yes or No to discount notices

One of the lines on the form asks: "Would you like to receive special offers from advertisers based on your interests?"

Notice that the Yes box is already preselected. You may want to click on No instead. If you leave Yes selected, you'll receive junk e-mail of the sort that already floods your postal mailbox, only you'll get electronic advertisements about software programs.

Get your own e-mail address

The application form also gives you the chance to get your very own e-mail address with GeoCities. If you don't already have an e-mail address, this is a good chance to get one. The member name for your Web site with GeoCities serves as the first part of your e-mail address, as well. Be sure to enter a really simple member name — so that you can remember it. E-mail addresses are not supposed to be creative or clever; you'll have plenty of time for that later on.

Brian had to try a few member names because his first choices were already taken by other GeoCities members. He finally settled on this one:

```
brianwolf@GeoCities.com
```

Discuss beforehand with your kids whether you want them to use your e-mail address or have their own free e-mail address with GeoCities. Having their own e-mail address with GeoCities doesn't cost anything and may provide them with a certain sense of autonomy. Also discuss exactly how much personal information they should provide when filling out registration forms, such as the one required by GeoCities. Security measures on the Web are still pretty uncertain; you have no way of knowing who's going to see this information and what they're going to do with it.

Describe your site

The application form makes you to look into the future: You have to pick three keywords or phrases that describe your Web page, even though you haven't made that page yet. If you jotted down some descriptions, as I suggested earlier in the section "Choosing a neighborhood," enter your descriptive topics now. Otherwise, make up some words or phrases that describe the theme of your page — enter cartoons, stories, or whatever you want your page to be about.

You include these keywords, phrases, or complete sentences so that people with similar interests who are scrolling through the list of GeoCities users — just like you did a few minutes ago — will become curious about your site. If you're interested in collecting model race cars, you can put down "Matchbox cars," or "model racers," for example, and someone else who is a race car collector might find you. Brian typed: **This page is about me, collectibles, and Boy Scouts.**

Internet phone book listings

The Membership Application Form asks whether you want to be listed in "Who Where," which is a huge Internet phone book. It's not actually a book, but an extensive directory that lists individuals and gives their e-mail addresses. There's no harm in being listed here, if you want.

If you don't have a primary e-mail address, just click on the button next to "Yes, please list my name and my GeoCities e-mail address."

Finally, you're done! Click on Submit. Don't be surprised if the next screen informs you that you have filled out something incorrectly or that you have chosen a member name already claimed by someone else. Brian found out just how many people use this free home page service. The first two names he tried, "briman" and "briguy," were taken. "brianwolf" went through okay, however, so his GeoCities member name is "brianwolf." Go back to the Membership Application Form page by clicking on the left-pointing arrow in your browser's toolbar. If you're using Microsoft Internet Explorer, you can also select Go⇨Back from the menu bar.

If all the information seems correct to GeoCities, you will receive a page that lets you review your information and make any changes you want. Review the information, and then click on Accept.

You might record your GeoCities member name and address on paper at this point — in case you have a problem getting the e-mail message that provides your password and confirms that you're an official member of GeoCities.

Get your password

At this point, you can pat yourself on the back for a job well done. Take a break, call a friend, get some refreshments, stretch your legs. Now that you have finished filling out the Membership Application Form and submitted the information, it's up to GeoCities to make the next move. It will process your application and assign you a password. It will then e-mail that password and some other important information to the address you entered back in the section entitled "Enter your e-mail address."

If you entered a friend's address, now is a good time to see whether your friend has received the GeoCities e-mail. If you specified your mom or dad's e-mail address, all you have to do is return to your computer, and check your e-mail for the message from GeoCities. The e-mail message you are looking for tells you your password. It also tells you the Web address that has been assigned to your Web page (the page you're about to create, that is).

In Brian's case, he told GeoCities to send his information to me. I received a message from a sender listed only as Webmaster. The message read in part, as follows:

```
Your member name is: brianwolf.
Your Neighborhood is: EnchantedForest.
Your Address is: 8582.
Your Current Password is: cxzfdj

The URL for your Personal Home Page is:
http://www.geocities.com/EnchantedForest/8582
```

(That's not Brian's real password, by the way.) The URL you receive is your actual address on the Internet where anyone can find you — after you create your home page, that is.

Write down all the information in this e-mail message (better yet, save the message, and print it). If you go to the URL specified in the message right now, you won't see anything because you haven't made a Web page yet. You'll see only a blank screen and a message like, "brianwolf has not moved in yet. Please check back later."

Square Three: Making Your Own Home Page

Congratulations! Way to go, dude! You're now a member of GeoCities, and you can begin to make your home page. Now the fun begins. In the following sections, you go through the process with Brian.

Creating a Web page with the Basic HTML Editor

By this time, you're probably in a hurry to see your name on the Web. Well, you're in luck, my friend. You can use a free utility put out by GeoCities that lets you create a simple page right away. The following steps describe how to do that:

1. **From your browser's menu bar, select File⇨Open Page, enter the address** `http://www.geocities.com/BHI/freehp.html`**, and click on OK.**

   This step takes you back to the GeoCities Personal Home Page Program page.

2. **Click on the link** tools **near the top of the page (refer to Figure 1-2). This link takes you to the GeoCities Homesteader Utilities page.**

   GeoCities offers a lot of software and other resources on the GeoCities Homesteader Utilities page. You can make use of some of these programs in later chapters.

3. **Scroll down, and click on the link The File Manager.**

   The GeoCities File Manager page (`http://www.geocities.com/homestead/file_manager.html`) appears.

4. **Scroll down this page, fill in the text boxes that ask for your member name and password, and click on Submit.**

   A new page appears entitled GeoCities File Manager. Below this title, you see your neighborhood name, your GeoCities "street address," and your member name.

5. **Scroll down the page, and click on the arrow next to the Choose Your Editor text box (see Figure 1-6).**

   GeoCities gives you the choice of three different programs for creating Web pages. For beginners, the best choice is the first one: Basic HTML Editor.

6. **Pressing your mouse, select Basic Home Page Editor from the drop-down menu list.**

7. **Click on the button Create New HTML File.**

   The GeoCities Basic HTML Editor page appears.

8. **Scroll down to the second part of the page.**

   You see a group of text boxes labeled "Background Color," "Text Color," "Visited Link Color," and "Unvisited Link Color" (see Figure 1-7).

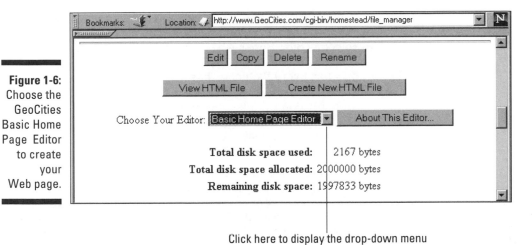

Figure 1-6:
Choose the
GeoCities
Basic Home
Page Editor
to create
your
Web page.

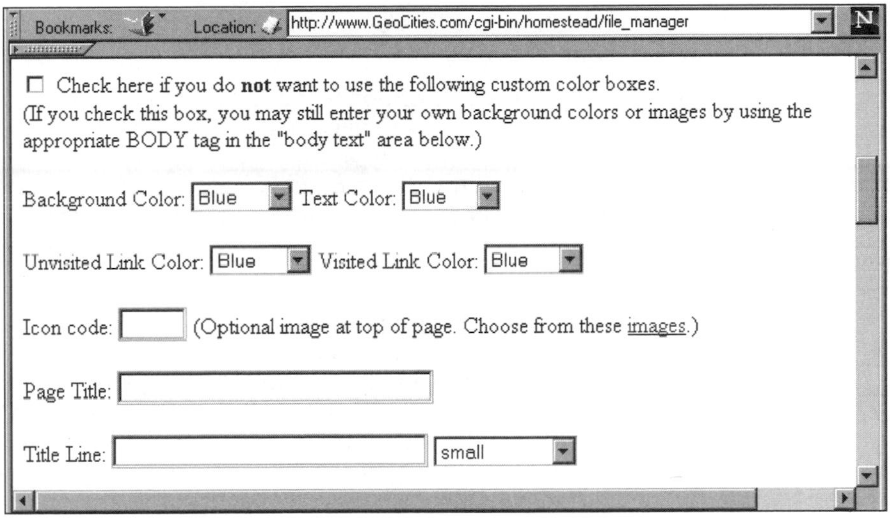

Click here to display the drop-down menu

Figure 1-7:
You can
use these
Personal
Home
Editor
buttons and
menus to
create your
own Web
page.

Show your colors!

If you know something about HTML already, feel free to choose any options you want on this page. If you're still in the dark, just follow my suggestions for now. You'll be able to go back later and customize your page.

The first checkbox at the top of the screen shown in Figure 1-7 asks you to decide whether you want to use the colors for backgrounds and links that GeoCities provides or whether you're adventurous enough to enter your own. For now, leave the box unchecked.

The four boxes, which each have an arrow next to them, let you select the colors you want on your page. Click on an arrow, and a menu drops down enabling you to select a color. Here's what you can *colorize:*

- **Background Color:** Every Web page has a background. This area appears behind the type and images. Backgrounds are one of those things you probably don't think about until you see one that's really outlandish or striking. It's best to pick a very light color for your background so the type appears easy to read on a computer screen. There's nothing wrong with white, so select that color.

- **Text Color:** You can also assign a color to the text that will appear on your page — the headings (the large type that appears at the top of a page or that starts major sections of the page), and the body text — the words you want people to read. The rule of thumb here is to pick a color that looks good against the background. If you have chosen a white background, don't pick white type, or you won't be able to read anything! Be a little adventurous, and choose blue.

- **Unvisited Link Color:** This option is for links that you haven't clicked on yet. For now, leave it blue.

- **Visited Link Color:** This option is for links that you clicked on when you previously visited a Web page. These links change color and stay that color for a while (usually, about 30 days). That way, if you're looking for a page you visited previously, you can follow the trail of "visited links." For now, set the Visited Link Color on red.

Choose a graphic

Ever wondered how folks get graphics on a Web page? You can take a graphic, for example, a photograph, and scan it. A scanner is a device that takes a photo or other image and turns it into little squares called pixels that computers can display (see Chapters 11 and 13, respectively, for information about scanning and graphics). If you don't have a scanner, find a friend who has one, or scrape a few bucks together and go to your local Kinko's branch (many branches will scan images for you). You can draw an image on the computer; and from sites on the Web, you can copy images that helpful people offer for free to budding Web page creators like yourself (see Chapter 9).

GeoCities offers you its own set of free images *(clip art)* that you can put anywhere in your Web page. Here's how to shop through and then select a graphic:

1. **Click on the word** Images **to go to** http://www.geocities.com/ homestead/homef12.html, **which contains icons you can use.**

   Most of this page (the Images page) contains links to other pages that contain pictures of flags from many nations. At the bottom of the page, you see the link Other icons. Click on this link, and you go to a page that contains all sorts of different icons (see Figure 1-8).

Figure 1-8:
Scroll
through the
screen full
of free
icons to
find one
you'd like to
add to your
Web page.

2. **Notice that each icon has a code next to it. Write down the code for the icon you want (for example, enter** bm **if you want to use the bomb icon, as shown in Figure 1-9).**

   Brian decided to put a rainbow on his page, so he wrote down the code rb.

3. **Click on your browser's Back toolbar button twice to go back to Home Page Editor.**

4. **In the box next to Icon Code, enter the code for the image you want, for example** rb.

Title your page

Now that you have selected colors and added a graphic to your Web page, you get to create some headings so people will know what your Web page is all about. GeoCities lets you create two headings: a *Title Line* and a *Second Title*. The Title Line is the main heading for the page. The Second Title is a sort of subheading, which appears in smaller type than does the main Title Line.

1. **For your Title Line, just enter two or three words in the Title Line text box, for example: Brian's Home Page.**

2. **Click on the arrow next to the Title Line text box, and choose the font (or type) size and style for your Title Line.**

   To get people's attention, your main title should be pretty large and "with-it." Brian chose large italic for his font size and type.

3. **For your Second Title, enter a few words that tell people something about the contents of your home page in the Second Title text box.**

   Brian entered All about my family, my collections, and my Boy Scout troop.

4. **Click on the arrow next to Second Title, and choose how you want your Second Title to appear.**

   Brian chose small italic.

Pick a separator

After you enter the headings for your page, you're ready to pick a line that will separate the headings from the text you are about to enter. Here's what you can do.

1. **Click on the arrow next to the Separator box.**

   A menu drops down containing the names of lots of different kinds of horizontal lines. These lines run across your Web page from left to right; they separate one section of a page from the next section. You can preview the lines by clicking on the underlined word in the phrase "Choose from these Separators" next to the Separator text box. Otherwise, you have to guess how the lines look. You can change the lines later on if you want.

   Brian chose blue_mrble_thick. This adds a blue, thick horizontal rule with a marbled design to the Web page. When you preview the page (soon, very soon), you'll be able to see how this line actually looks on the page.

Type your text

Now scroll down to the large box at the bottom of the Personal Home Editor page, the box under the heading "Body Text: HTML." This is where you enter the text for your Web page. Right now, the text says something like "[username] has not moved in yet — please check back later."

1. **Position your text cursor at the end of the line of text that reads "[username] has not moved in yet — please check back later," and press the Backspace key until you erase all these words.**

   If you're like Brian, you may respond to this by saying, "But what do I say instead?" If you don't have any ideas, don't worry. You can find plenty of suggestions in this book for things to put on your home page. The paragraph in Step 2 is a suggestion for something you can type now, just as a way of getting started. (***Note:*** Press the Return or Enter key once after every paragraph.) Figure 1-9 indicates where you should type your own comments in the large text box labeled "Body Text."

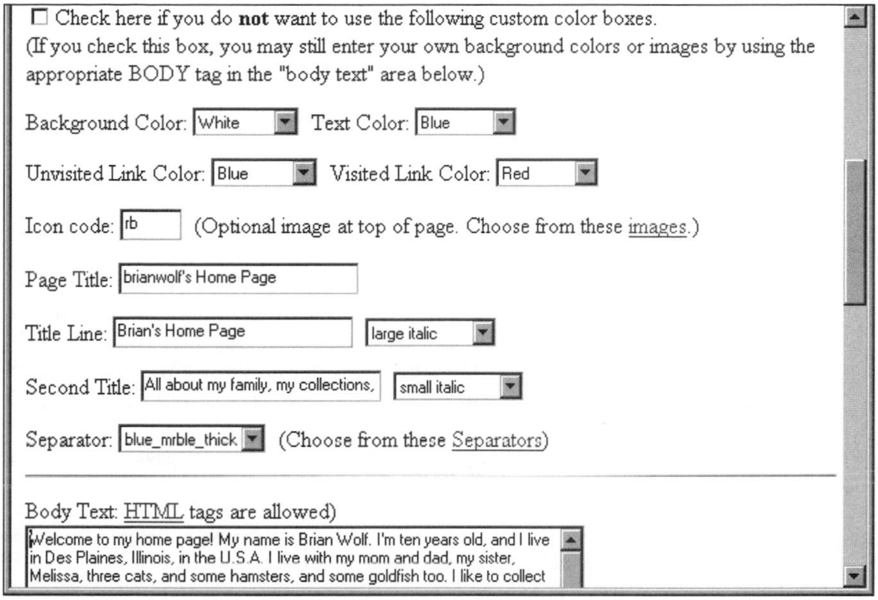

☐ Check here if you do **not** want to use the following custom color boxes.
(If you check this box, you may still enter your own background colors or images by using the appropriate BODY tag in the "body text" area below.)

Background Color: White ▾   Text Color: Blue ▾

Unvisited Link Color: Blue ▾   Visited Link Color: Red ▾

Icon code: rb   (Optional image at top of page. Choose from these images.)

Page Title: brianwolf's Home Page

Title Line: Brian's Home Page   large italic ▾

Second Title: All about my family, my collections,   small italic ▾

Separator: blue_mrble_thick ▾   (Choose from these Separators)

Body Text: HTML tags are allowed)

Welcome to my home page! My name is Brian Wolf. I'm ten years old, and I live in Des Plaines, Illinois, in the U.S.A. I live with my mom and dad, my sister, Melissa, three cats, and some hamsters, and some goldfish too. I like to collect

Figure 1-9: After you enter a title and a separator, you can create the main contents for your Web page in the Body Text text box.

2. Enter some text similar to the following:

> Welcome to my home page! My name is Brian Wolf. I'm ten years old, and I live in Des Plaines, Illinois, in the U.S.A. I live with my mom and dad, my sister Melissa, three cats, and some hamsters, and some goldfish too. I like to collect antique food boxes — I've got old Lipton Tea tins from the turn of the century, lots of old Wheaties cereal boxes, some cool bottles that are in different colors, and some Coca Cola plates. My grandma is a real antique hunter and she helps me find a lot of this stuff. I'm a member of Cub Scout Troop 128. But I'm going to be a Boy Scout soon.
>
> I plan to be improving this page a lot in the weeks to come — so come back soon!
>
> Here are some of my favorite places on the Web:

That last line is in anticipation of links you're going to make in a moment.

3. **After you type your text, scroll down, and click on the arrow next to the text box labeled Separator.**

   Brian chose blck_beaded_line. This adds a black, beaded line to the Web page. You can't see it just yet, but soon (very soon!) you will.

Make some links

I've talked a lot about links. Now you get to create some on your Web page so that people visiting your page can actually click on the links (those underlined words or graphics) to go from your page to other Web pages. Links have a number of advantages. They make your page an integral part of the Web; they also give you a way to let people know the kinds of things you like on the Web and to suggest sites they may want to visit. So before moving on, jot down a couple of sites you might like to tell people about.

For each link you want to add, you use the two text boxes shown in Figure 1-10.

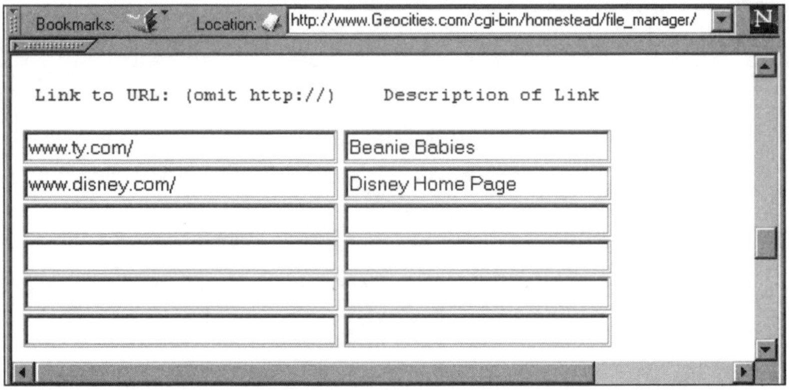

Figure 1-10:
Make like a spider; link your page to the rest of the Web by entering Web addresses in these text boxes.

```
Bookmarks:        Location:   http://www.Geocities.com/cgi-bin/homestead/file_manager/    N

Link to URL: (omit http://)        Description of Link

www.ty.com/                        Beanie Babies
www.disney.com/                    Disney Home Page
```

1. **Scroll down to the section of the Basic HTML Editor labeled "Link to URL." In the box on the left, enter the URL for a Web page.**

   For example, if you enter the URL www.ty.com/, you'll be creating a link to the Beanie Babies page. Your visitors will be able to click on this link and go to the official Beanie Babies Web site.

2. **In the box to the right (next to the box where you just typed the URL), enter two or three words that describe the page.**

   These are the words that will appear as the underlined link, so it's best to keep this short. If you use the URL www.ty.com/ entry, you can enter the words Beanie Babies as the link.

   Brian entered the URL for the Beanie Babies site (www.ty.com/). Because he likes Disney movies and characters, he entered the URL for the Disney Home Page (www.disney.com/).

The Web is becoming so popular that chances are pretty good you can find a Web page relating to something you're interested in. How do you find the addresses of one of these great Web pages so that you can make a link to it from your own page? By using an Internet search service. A *search service* is an organization that indexes Web pages and their contents and holds the information in huge computer databases so you can find them — for example, Excite (http://www.excite.com/), AltaVista (http://altavista.digital.com/), or Yahoo! (http://www.yahoo.com/). Using one of these services, you can find the URL for a page you're interested in. Then you can add it to the Link to URL text box while you are creating your page in the Basic HTML Editor.

Using Microsoft Internet Explorer, follow along with Brian:

1. **Select Search the Web from the Go menu, or press the Search toolbar button. (If you're using Netscape Navigator, select Internet Search from the Directory menu.)**

   It's best to do this after you begin to create your home page. That way, you have the Basic HTML Editor filled out with some of your Web page contents. You might even have the Basic HTML Editor still open and not yet completed when you decide to search for some pages you can link to. You can have your browser go to a search service like Yahoo! while you are still working on your page. After you find a page you want to link to, you can go back to the Basic HTML Editor by pressing your browser's Back toolbar button a few times. After you return to the Basic HTML Editor, you can then add the new Web addresses to the Link to URL text boxes.

   Mac users: Choose Search the Internet from the Go menu if you're using Internet Explorer. If you're using Netscape the steps are the same.

   The Find it Fast page appears.

2. **In the text box near the upper-left corner of this page, type** Boy Scouts of America home page.

3. **Click on the button next to the name of the search service you want to use.**

4. **Click on Search.**

   A page appears with links that respond to the search term you typed.

Brian found tons of local Boy Scout Councils. He clicked on one of the links to a page for Troop 112 in Illinois. The home page of the Troop 112 Web site contained a link to the <u>Official Boy Scouts of America Web page</u> (http://www.bsa.scouting.org). That's the way you find things on the Web: by searching, burrowing around Web sites, and following links. Often, you discover things you never even knew existed. To try one of the Internet search services, follow these steps:

1. **Right-click on the link for the page you want to copy.**

   A menu pops up in your browser window with a list of options.

   A PC that uses Windows 95 as its operating system has two *clickers* on its mouse: one clicker on the left and one on the right. In this example, use the clicker on the right, and click on the underlined words <u>Official Boy Scouts of America Web page</u>.

2. **If you're using Internet Explorer, select Copy Shortcut from the pop-up menu. Netscape Navigator's pop-up menu contains the option Copy Link Location.**

   Both of these menu options do the same thing: They copy the address of the Web page that is associated with the clickable hypertext link, so you can paste the address somewhere else.

3. **Click on the Back button in your browser's toolbar until you return to the Basic Home Page Editor.**

One more separator

After you add some links to your Web page-in-progress, it's a good idea to add another horizontal line to separate the "links" section of that page from the next section. You just click on the arrow next to the Separator box. A menu drops down containing lots of different names of separators. For his next separator, Brian chose the inimitable red_thick_line_1.

Footer text

The *footer* of a document is the stuff that goes at the bottom (as opposed to the "header" stuff, which goes at the top). In the case of a Web page, the footer includes information such as who you are, when the page was created, and your e-mail address. To add this information in the Basic HTML Editor, you just scroll down to the text box labeled Footer Text (HTML tags are allowed). Then click inside the text box so you can begin typing. This is what Brian typed for his footer:

```
Created by Brian L. Wolf
Last updated February 12, 1997
```

Brian also checked the box next to Include E-Mail Address On Page (see Figure 1-11).

This time he did not select a separator; a few lines on a page is more than enough.

See your results!

You're through — and it hasn't been so long since you started, has it? Now, you get to reap the rewards of your work and see what your page looks like. Here's what you do:

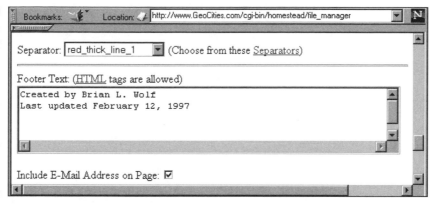

Figure 1-11:
Sign your
page to
include a
return
address
(your e-mail
address,
that is) by
adding
footer text.

1. **Scroll down to the bottom of the Basic HTML Editor window.**

   You see a bunch of gray buttons labeled Preview, Save, Save and Continue Editing, Return to File Manager, and Reset.

2. **Click on the Preview button.**

   Your new page appears on-screen. Figure 1-12 shows a preview of what Brian's home page (`http://www.geocities.com/EnchantedForest/8582`) looks like.

If something doesn't look quite right, select Back from the Go menu, and change the item. For example, you may want to change one of those snazzy colors you picked, if the words are too hard to read.

Figure 1-12:
Hello,
World!
Here's 10-
year-old
Brian
Wolf's own
Web page.

Chapter 2

Deciding What You Want to Do

· ·

In This Chapter

▶ Gathering ideas for your Web site

▶ Recruiting Mom and Dad and the rest of the gang

▶ Surfing other family Web sites

▶ Becoming the family news reporter

▶ Making a Web site table of contents

▶ Who will be the Webmaster?

· ·

*I*n Chapters 1 and 6, you find out how to create Web pages. When you put all your pages together, you have what is called a Web site. A *Web site* is a group of pages that are linked together and share a common theme. In this chapter, you explore ideas for themes and topics that you can use to develop your Web site.

In case you are worried that you just can't think of anything to put on a bunch of pages and transform into a Web site, don't worry. You are virtually unlimited as to themes for your Web pages. For example, in your travels around the Web, you've probably visited sites that talk about hobbies, TV shows, movie stars, art, science, history, sports, you name it. And, if you haven't browsed the Web yet, I'll point you to a few of my favorite sites where you can go to get ideas.

Near the end of this chapter, you find out how to become Webmaster. "Who, *Me, a Webmaster?*," you ask! Yes, I'm talking about you — or a member of your family. A *Webmaster* is someone who takes care of a Web site. Actually, there are two sorts of Webmasters. One kind actually creates the pages, links them together, sends them to an Internet Service Provider (ISP), and later updates them. The other kind is an employee of an ISP; this person is responsible for posting pages, writing scripts, answering e-mail, keeping computers running, and making sure the network works right.

Gathering Ideas for Your Web Site

A good way to begin organizing your site is to identify the main topics you want to cover and draw up a list of those subjects so that you can turn them into a table of contents. A good place to start is with your family. Another brainstorming resource is the GeoCities Web pages, which contains free pages created by and for kids. These pages contain lots of ideas that may apply to your Web site. In this section, you learn how to search GeoCities and then the rest of the Web.

Creating a Web page table of contents

Before you start shopping around for ideas for your Web site, you need to make a list of the people and the activities that are most important to you — a sort of Web page *table of contents*.

Write or draw your list on paper, and keep it handy as you gather ideas. Jot down activities, hobbies, jobs, or other things that each member of your family is interested in. The important thing is to get a lot of ideas now; later when you actually start mapping out your Web site, you can select the ones you want to work on. (See Chapter 4 for information about mapping out your site.) Figure 2-1 shows one way you might do this.

Figure 2-1: When fishing for ideas, pick up your old-fashioned pencil and paper and sketch activities and people you might present on your Web pages.

Things I Like To Do	My School	Mom
Boy/Girl Scouts Baseball/Softball Coin collecting My stories	My classroom My homework	Loves folk tales Is an artist Writes poetry
Dad	**Jill**	**My Favorite Web Sites**
Travels all over Just went to Germany Likes photography Likes golf	Likes *The Little Mermaid* Plays computer games	My friends' sites KidsWeb Boy Scouts of America/Girl Scouts of America home pages

Over the next few days, you'll probably come up with new ideas and cross out some that don't seem as good as they did when you wrote them down. Just be open to all possibilities at this point. You can use this table of contents later in this chapter.

If you just enjoyed a big family event such as a birthday, a wedding, or an anniversary party, you have a ready-made occasion for a Web page. Perhaps some relatives couldn't make it to the party: You can do these folks a good deed by creating a page about the event and putting some photos online. That way they don't have to wait until the next big family gathering to see who danced with whom, who's been putting on a little weight, and all the other family gossip.

Fishing the GeoCities waters

You might, for starters, skip back to Chapter 1, and go to the GeoCities Web sites for ideas. The Web pages that people have published on GeoCities can be accessed visually; GeoCities presents these pages as *homesteads* that are arranged in blocks, much like the neighborhood you live in. Look in a *block* in EnchantedForest, and check out the pages listed there. If you don't see pages that relate to kids or families, you can click on nearby blocks on the left side of the page. For example, if your address is 8582, you'll see links to the blocks 8000, 8100, 8200, 8300, and 8400.

You can also search the Web pages in GeoCities by filling out a simple search form. You need to connect to the Internet and start up your Web browser. Then select File➪Open Location if you arc using Netscape Navigator or File➪Open if you're using Microsoft Internet Explorer. The Open Location (or Open) dialog box appears.

Sudden appeals

After you're on the Web, don't be surprised if people come to you, asking you for advice, or suggesting things you can put on the Web. Suddenly, your dad is asking how you made your Web page because he has been assigned to make one for his company. Your friends want you to look things up on the Web to help with their homework. You start getting e-mail from people you never met who want to make links to your page.

Sound farfetched? It's not. Take my 14-year-old niece, Clare, who is contributing the "Clare Declares" sidebars throughout this book. After she made a couple of Web pages, her brother asked her to make a page about his rock band. Next, a friend asked her to start up a fan-club page about an actor they both

admire. Clare used one of the pages she attributes to her alter-ego, Mina Skywalker, to include an image that is linked to this fan-club page. The image is a montage of photos of Jerry O'Donnell. The image has a border around it; this border indicates that it is a link. When you click on the image, you go to another page (in this case, the JOD fan club page).

Then she was asked to set up a page for her school. And *then* I asked her to put some of her work in this book. That's how things can work: One page leads to another, then another, and before long, you've spun a Web of friendships and resources, all bounded only by your imagination and ambition.

1. **In the Open Location (or Open) dialog box, enter the URL for the GeoCities Search Page (**`http://www.geocities.com/search/`**).**

   The GeoCities Search Page appears in your browser window.

2. **Scroll down the page a bit, and click on the type of search you want to perform.**

   The search page lets you search through the GeoCities site for a subject covered in a Web page (represented by the button, Search by Subject), a region of the country (Search by Topic/Geography), a member's name (Search for a Member), an e-mail address (Search for an E-Mail Address), or a specific phone number (Search for a Phone Number).

   Assume that you want to find pages that refer to coin collecting. For this search, you search GeoCities for pages that contain the subject coin collecting.

3. **Click on the Search by Subject button.**

   A page entitled "Search the GeoCities neighborhoods by subject" appears (`http://www.geocities.com/search/search_subject.html`).

4. **Scroll down the page, and click on the arrow just to the right of the box labeled Neighborhood.**

   A drop-down list appears with a roster of GeoCities neighborhoods. Pick a neighborhood that you want to search, and your search is restricted to that neighborhood. Heartland is a good place to find family Web pages; EnchantedForest is good for finding kids' pages.

5. **In the Search String text box, enter** coin collecting or coin collection.

6. **Click on the Search button.**

   In a few seconds, a page entitled "WhoWhere? Home Pages Search Results" appears. This page contains a link or links, that is graphics or text you can click on to go GeoCities pages that contain the words you just searched for. In the case of the search for "coin collecting," GeoCities found only one link, as shown in Figure 2-2.

7. **Scroll down the list, and click on the link for the page you want to visit.**

   In this example, the link is to a page (`http://www.geocities.com/EnchantedForest/6154/`) created by a GeoCities member who calls himself "Legoguy" and who is interested in coin collecting, Legos, among other things.

8. **When you're ready to visit another page, just return to the list of links by selecting the Back button located on your toolbar, or select Go⇨Back.**

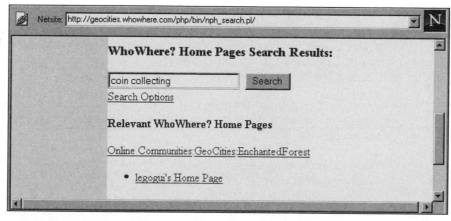

Figure 2-2:
This page
shows links
to all
GeoCities
pages that
include
the words
you are
looking for.

Starting at home base

The best place to find interesting, exciting, meaningful, wonderful things to put on your own Web pages is right under your mouse pad. What do I mean? Your desk or table? Actually — believe it or not, I mean your very own home!

Look to the people you live with as the best source of material for your Web pages. Those fun-loving people who use up the toothpaste, leave their socks in the hallway, and play video games on the TV when you'd rather watch *Star Trek:* your family.

Get with these folks, and create a *family Web site.* Parents often — and kids *sometimes* — complain that their families don't get to spend enough time together. Wouldn't it be great if you and your Web site became a project that your whole family could plan and work on together?

You don't have to be a computer genius to provide support with your kids' Web page projects. But in case they ask a lot of questions you can't answer, you might consult the following books to get up to speed: *The World Wide Web For Kids and Parents,* by Viraf D. Mohta, or *TakeCharge Computing For Kids and Parents,* by Pam Dixon, both published by IDG Books Worldwide.

When it comes to helping you make your Web pages cool and exciting, Mom and Dad may be your best sources for help and support. Even if they don't know a thing about computers, they can probably come up with stuff like photos that you can use (see Chapters 10 and 13 for more about scanning and graphics). Or maybe they can suggest family members to write about. You may even be one of the lucky few whose Mom or Dad is totally *techno-savvy* and can help you create a really sizzling Web site.

Be a family reporter

You might want to think of yourself as a family reporter. In her book, *Harriet the Spy,* Louise Fitzhugh wrote about a girl who liked to find out everything about the people in her neighborhood and who kept her observations in a little notebook.

You can be like Harriet. Start by finding out interesting things about the people you live with. Then you can gather addresses for different family sites around the Web.

Who are the members of your family? Introduce them, and tell what they do. Are they students, workers, volunteers? Also describe your extended relatives, neighbors, and friends.

What about hobbies and collections? Don't just list things; show examples of artwork or poetry. How about other living things in your house, such as pets or plants? Do you have an imaginary companion? On the Web, anything that is important to you can come to life.

Like a good reporter, you can record your family stories in a composition notebook. Online, you can keep a record of cool sites by making a set of bookmarks (or Favorites, as Microsoft Internet Explorer calls them). *Bookmarks* are a Web browser's way of recording the URLs of sites you visit. When you know that you will want to visit a particular site again, you save the page's address as a bookmark. Sometimes bookmarks contain a space where you can record some notes about a site.

As for gathering family stories: Who would love to talk to you, either on the phone or in person? Take a wild guess: Okay, they're your grandparents. Grandma and Grandpa can be a great source of stories. Not only can they tell you about when you were younger, they can also tell you about times before you were born, including what the world was like when they were your age.

Here are some of the things you might ask them:

- ✔ Where did our family come from originally?
- ✔ Where were you born, and where did you go to school?
- ✔ What kinds of things did you like to do when you were a kid?
- ✔ Do we have any family legends or funny stories to tell?
- ✔ Do any of our long-lost relatives have names or stories that other folks, especially kids, might recognize or relate to?

Checking out the Web

Another great place for ideas on family and kids' Web pages is the Web itself. In fact, the Web offers you one of the greatest sources of information in the world. Right at your fingertips, you'll find links to pages about every conceivable subject. After reading this book, I suspect that whenever you have a question about a particular topic, you'll say, "I wonder what I can find about this topic out on the Web?"

Using the Web browser of your choice, you might begin by searching for families that have the same last name as your family.

Say that your last name is Jones. If you're using Microsoft Internet Explorer, you follow these steps:

1. **From your menu bar, select <u>Go</u>⇨Search the <u>W</u>eb.**

   The Find it Fast page appears (`http://home.microsoft.com/access/allinone.asp`).

2. **Scroll down the page a bit, and select one of the Internet search services from the list provided by clicking on the little circle.**

   A little black dot appears within the circle. For more about search services, see Chapter 1.

3. **In the text box near the top of the Find it Fast page, enter the words** Jones Family.

4. **Click on the Search button and have fun scanning.**

Investigating Other Family Web Sites

A great way to develop content about your family members is to see how other kids describe their nearest and dearest on their Web pages. GeoCities is a great place to start looking because it contains lots of Web sites created by families and individual kids, too. You can always look through Yahoo! (`http://www.yahoo.com/`), which is a great index that helps you locate just about anything that's contained on the Web. Here are some suggestions for family-related topics you might want to cover in your Web

OPEN

publishing project, along with suggestions about where to find more information about them online.

Rachel's Page

You can find a terrific Web site created by a mother-daughter team at Rachel's Page at `http://www.mcs.net/~kathyw/rachel.html`.

Rachel Williams has won all kinds of awards for this Web page, and that's due in large part to the help she received from her very talented mom, Kathy.

Kathy Williams created much of the artwork, cool lettering, and detailed background for the pages. Rachel came up with most of the content, which includes her favorite movie, *Aladdin,* as well as links to her friends' Web pages. The team even added sound clips of the voices of Rachel's friends! See Chapter 12 for more about sound clips.

Mom added some valuable pages dealing with child safety on the Internet, self-esteem for girls, and many other issues. Together, their pages make a beautifully designed and very moving family Web site.

A family photo album

For some folks, a family's Web site isn't complete without photos of all the *very important people* in the family. Ten-year-old Kim Bonney of South Africa created a page showing thumbnail sketches (small drawings), which are a good way to present photos. You an find her page at `http://www.geocities.com/EnchantedForest/1616/`.

This site won the 1996 GeoCities award for Best South African Children's Web Site. Kim linked each thumbnail to a full-size version of the photo. See Chapter 13 for more information on using graphics.

FAMILY FUN

Sit down with your family after you clear away the dinner dishes — and before the TV is turned on! Look through some family photo albums. Photos are a great way to get ideas for graphics to put on your Web pages. You might decide to write about

▶▶

a vacation you've taken or places you've lived. Those old photos showing Mom and Dad when they were kids can look great on a Web page, especially next to their more up-to-date photos.

Family gatherings

Families that have several members connected to the Web can use a family Web page to announce and plan family gatherings. Norma Harwood's family-reunion page on GeoCities (http://www.geocities.com/Heartland/2144/) includes a recipe for a fruit salad "that everyone was raving about" at the family reunion.

The Baker Family home page (http://www.geocities.com/Heartland/1526/) announces some exciting family news — a wedding — and provides a schedule of events. Farther down this page is an interactive form that announces a family reunion and in which relatives can submit their suggestions for activities at the reunion (certainly a busy year for the Bakers).

A page for everyone

Every member of the family can have a personal home page with at least one photo and perhaps a description of the things that person likes to do and the places he or she likes to visit on the Web. A good example is the Buchanan Family Web site (http://www.buchanan.com/), on which Larry Buchanan created a home page for each of his five kids (see Figure 2-3).

Stories, poems, and artwork

Web pages also provide a wonderful way for the creative types in your family to be *published* or to stand in the spotlight. Not only do the visitors to your pages view and enjoy the fruits of your labors, but also they can give you instant feedback, either by commenting on your work in person, or by sending you e-mail about your pages.

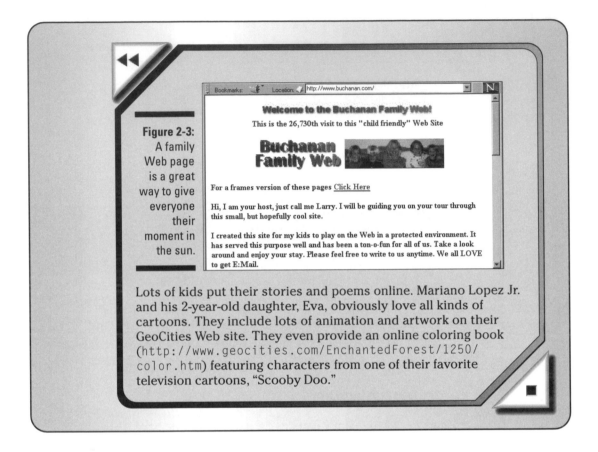

Figure 2-3:
A family
Web page
is a great
way to give
everyone
their
moment in
the sun.

Lots of kids put their stories and poems online. Mariano Lopez Jr. and his 2-year-old daughter, Eva, obviously love all kinds of cartoons. They include lots of animation and artwork on their GeoCities Web site. They even provide an online coloring book (`http://www.geocities.com/EnchantedForest/1250/color.htm`) featuring characters from one of their favorite television cartoons, "Scooby Doo."

Holding a family summit

Now might be a good time to ask for your *first* family summit (conference, forum, whatever you want to call it). Perhaps you can schedule the summit during one of those little *windows of opportunity* between dessert and TV.

Family summits can be great ways to gather and select information and even decide how to get on the Web. Bring out the table of contents that you created earlier in this chapter and say something like, "Okay, I've got some ideas for our family Web site. Would you all look at them and tell me what you think?" In the course of going over the list, everyone just might come up with some new and better ideas.

Here are some suggestions for running a family forum:

____ Schedule a time when everyone can be present.

____ Decide how long to meet, and start and stop on time. If you're still going strong when time is up, schedule another forum.

___ Take turns being the leader and note taker. Even the youngest family member can speak into a tape recorder, and someone else can transcribe.

___ Make decisions after *everyone* has a chance to share ideas.

___ Avoid making one person feel like a winner and another a loser.

___ If you can't agree on something, talk about it again at the next meeting.

___ End the family forum on a fun and positive note, maybe by munching on a delicious snack or going on a special outing.

Communicating on the Web with E-Mail

Besides creating Web sites to tell people about you and your interests, you can get your messages out to people in cyberspace via e-mail.

E-mail provides some big advantages:

✔ **It's popular.** Not everyone has a Web page, but most people who have a connection to the Internet send and receive e-mail.

✔ **It's easy to use:** You just type your messages in plain-text format without having to format a Web page using HTML. (See Chapter 14 for more about formatting with HTML.)

Here are three practical ways to use e-mail to publicize your Web page:

• **Link your e-mail to your Web page:** One of the most useful things you can include in your e-mail messages is a link to your Web site. These links are easy to create: Just type **Visit** and the name of your site, press Enter or Return to skip to the next line, and then type the URL for your site. Here's how Brian did it:

Visit Brian's Home Page

```
http://www.geocities.com/EnchantedForest/
8253/index.html
```

• **Include a signature file:** Some e-mail programs allow you to use a signature file. A *signature file* is a short text file added to the end of your e-mail messages. It can contain one or all of several possible components, including, for example, your name, a link to your Web site, and a bit of playful art made up of ASCII text characters.

To create a signature file, you use a word-processing program, such as SimpleText (Mac) or Notepad (PC) to type and save whatever you want in the file. The text file should contain your name and a few lines of information (remember to keep this short!) about you or your Web site. Next, you save your text file on your hard drive. Then using the software program you use to send and receive e-mail, find the file and select it as a signature file. It will be added automatically to your e-mail messages. When you use a signature file, you don't have to type your personal information at the end of your e-mail messages; the software does it for you. Go to your e-mail program's Help menu, and look up "signature file" to see whether you can use this feature. If you can, a signature file is a useful way to provide people with information about you as well as a link to your Web page.

• **Create ASCII art:** ASCII (pronounced "as-key") essentially stands for *standard plain-text characters.* Normally, ASCII characters are used to type text and other computer instructions. However, you can also use ASCII symbols as graphic elements. You actually make intricate little designs by typing common characters that aren't part of the alphabet on your keyboard, for example, things like the asterisk (*), the "at" symbol (@), the plus sign (+), or anything you like (see Figure 2-4 for an example). When added to your signature file, these little drawings attract attention to links in your e-mail messages to your Web page or other pages.

If you work really hard and enter the blank spaces just right, you can design these characters so that they fit into a pattern that looks like a drawing or a word. Try it yourself — if you have the time to experiment, this can be a lot of fun. It's also a simple way to get art on a Web page without drawing a picture or scanning a photo.

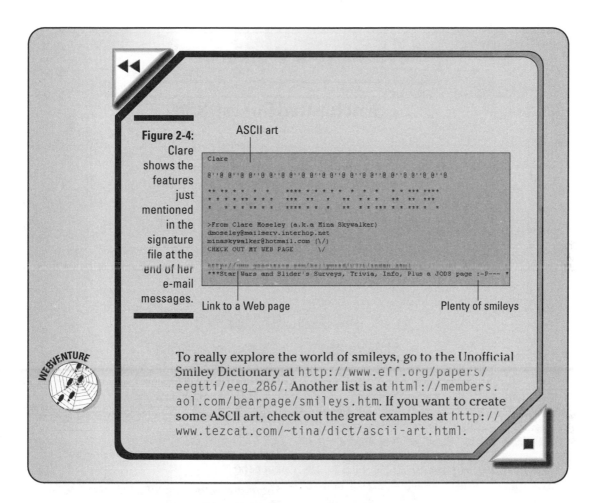

Figure 2-4: Clare shows the features just mentioned in the signature file at the end of her e-mail messages.

ASCII art

```
Clare
@'@ @'@ @'@ @'@ @'@ @'@ @'@ @'@ @'@ @'@ @'@ @'@ @'@ @'@
** ** * * *   *  *   **** * * * * *   *  *   * * *** ****
* * * * * * *   *** ** *  ** *  * ** * ***  ** *  ***
* * * * * * *   **** * *  *  ** * * *** ** * * * *

>From Clare Moseley (a.k.a Mina Skywalker)
dmoseley@mailserv.interhop.net
minaskywalker@hotmail.com  (\/)
CHECK OUT MY WEB PAGE       \/

http://www.geocities.com/hollywood/5512/index.html
***Star Wars and Slider's Surveys, Trivia, Info, Plus a JODS page :-P~~~ *
```

Link to a Web page   Plenty of smileys

To really explore the world of smileys, go to the Unofficial Smiley Dictionary at `http://www.eff.org/papers/eegtti/eeg_286/`. Another list is at `html://members.aol.com/bearpage/smileys.htm`. If you want to create some ASCII art, check out the great examples at `http://www.tezcat.com/~tina/dict/ascii-art.html`.

Who's the Webmaster?

Now you and your family have a list of Web site themes, you've held your first family summit, and you've selected some family photos to include on your pages. It's time to decide who's going to be in charge of putting everything together. In other words, who will be the family Webmaster?

The young people in your family exhibiting the most enthusiasm about the Web may end up having to do everything all alone, which can be quite a burden — maybe even impossible. Create a ballot so family members can divvy up responsibilities. This approach is a great way to get everyone involved.

Revising your Web page

When you want to revise your Web page, whether that page is on GeoCities or another organization's Web site, you can take advantage of a software program that you use to edit Web pages. Often, such a program is called an HTML editor. For this example, follow along with my nephew Brian as he edits a page he created on GeoCities. Like other GeoCities members, Brian has access to a group of HTML editor programs. This group of programs is collectively called the File Manager. You can find a link to the File Manager on the Homesteader Utilities Page (http://www.geocities.com/Utilities/utilities.html). You can also go to the page directly and use the File Manager by following these steps:

1. **From the Microsoft Internet Explorer menu bar, select File⇨Open.**

   In Netscape Navigator, select File⇨Open Location.

   The Open Location (or Open) dialog box appears.

2. **Enter the following URL for the File Manager page:** http://www.geocities.com/homestead/file_manager.html.

3. **Scroll down the page, and enter your GeoCities member name and password (if you have one).**

4. **Click on Submit.**

   The File Manager appears on your screen, as shown in the figure in this sidebar, with your member name and address at the top of the Web page. Click on the checkbox next to "index" to make sure you revise the Web page you created in Chapter 1 — if you created one. (Your page has the standard name index.html.)

5. **Scroll down the page, click on the arrow next to the Choose Your Editor text box, and select Basic HTML Editor.**

6. **To revise your** index.html **page, click on Edit.**

   The contents of the Web page you created earlier show in the Web page (entitled Basic HTML Editor) that now appears on-screen. If you want to create a new Web page at this point, you can click on Create New HTML File.

7. **To change text, links, and background colors on your page, click on the arrows to the right of the boxes labeled Background Color, Text Color, Unvisited Link Color, and Visited Link Color.**

   You can change the body text for your page by scrolling down the Basic HTML Editor page to the Body Text text box. When you delete or retype the text contained in this box, the textual content of your Web page changes.

8. **To reap the rewards of your work and see what your page looks like, scroll to the bottom of the Basic HTML Editor window.**

   You see a bunch of gray buttons labeled Preview, Save, Save and Continue Editing, Return to File Manager, and Reset.

9. **Click on the Preview button.**

   Your new page appears on-screen with all the new contents, new colors, and any other changes you made.

Before selecting your Webmaster, consider the following tasks that the Webmaster must "assign."

- ✔ **Typing the text on a computer:** A nimble-fingered family member might accept this task.

- ✔ **Checking for typos and other errors:** The pages are going to be visible to lots of people, and presentation is important. Does your family have a good proofreader?

- ✔ **Creating the Web pages:** The Webmaster will probably end up formatting the Web pages, but Mom or Dad can help select or scan photos.

- ✔ **Putting the pages online:** Someone with an eagle-eye should test the pages before and after they're published on the Web.

- ✔ **Making sure that links work:** If several Web pages are linked together, someone must make sure all the links work correctly. (Don't worry — you learn how to do this in Chapter 15.) The best course is to have someone who didn't work on the pages check them after they're put on the Web.

✔ **Scanning photos:** If you include photos on the Web pages, someone must use a scanner to (that's right) scan them. If you don't have one, you'll need to locate one (see Chapter 10 for more about scanners).

✔ **Updating the site:** Last but by no means least, the Webmaster (or an assigned person) must keep the pages current by updating the pages with new information as it becomes available. You can't simply plop your pages on the Web and leave them there forever, or they'll be *cobWeb* pages that simply grow old and stale.

As people grow up — go to camp, celebrate birthdays, take trips, graduate from kindergarten, high school, and college, get married — you'll have new things to talk about. The best Web pages are an ongoing project, not a one-time amusement.

You've covered a lot of ground in this chapter and read about some ways to develop ideas for your Web pages. Planning is hard work, so take a deep breath, step back for a moment, and review the steps involved in planning your Web site so you can get your ducks in order. Remember to identify the main topics, sketch them on paper, and discuss your Web site with the members of your family. Decide who will be in charge. And always remember that the main idea is to have fun! Making Web pages shouldn't be like doing chores around the house. Don't be afraid to be come up with creative, crazy ideas to share with your friends and family.

One kid's opinion

My family and I love the Internet. We started using it as soon as we could, and we keep on finding new ways to have fun with it. Our local service provider is Interhop, and the phone calls we make to get connected are local, which saves us money! The really important thing that happened when we started on the Web was that we got a better computer! Our modem is a 14.4 Kbps external modem, which cost quite a bit, but my Web pages basically don't cost anything to put together.

I have free Web space with GeoCities. My dad's office is really nice and lets us borrow a scanner when we want to scan photos. Plus, I use a shareware HTML program, World Wide Web Weaver, to make the pages.

Everyone in our house always wants to use the computer! That's probably just like your house, right? My older brother Ethan (he's 16) is making a page for his band. My younger brother Robert (he's 12) always wants to surf the Internet. So we finally got a second phone line so we could make phone calls, even while someone is on the computer. Of course, we all want to use the phone all the time, too. They're pretty good about sharing, but sometimes I ask them to use the computer on Tuesday and Thursday afternoons when I'm at band practice. Then I can get on the Web and work on my Star Wars pages when I get home.

Chapter 3

Awesome Ideas for Cyber-Phat Web Pages

● ●

In This Chapter

▶ Ideas for Web pages that are all about you

▶ Web pages about your school, friends, hobbies, interests, and more!

● ●

Some people love to talk about themselves. In fact, it often seems like they think of nothing else. Others are shy. Calling attention to themselves is the last thing in the world they call fun. No matter what kind of person you are, a Web page can be a discreet way to blow your own horn and tell the whole world how unique, fascinating, and talented you are. (By the way, if you've been working through this book, you really *are* all of those things. Stop and think for a moment: You made your own GeoCities Web page (in Chapter 1), you're getting ready to create more pages, and you're smart enough to use this book! You're not only on the cutting edge, my friend, you're obviously clever and a trendsetter, too!)

Now it's time to make some *new* Web pages devoted to you, yourself, and you! But getting your thoughts and words together so that you can communicate effectively on the Web can be a challenge. Maybe you need someone to suggest topics or even get you started with things you might say. Well, guess what? This chapter offers lots of suggestions that will start your brain pumping out ideas.

Throughout this chapter, you find references to Web pages that other kids have created and that are related to the subject at hand. You can visit those sites or find others by yourself to get more ideas. You can also copy a set of Web page addresses you might like to visit from the CD-ROM that accompanies this book, as explained in Appendix D.

The clip art in this chapter was drawn by John Casler, who's an artist as well as the designer for Stylus Media, the group of publications professionals who helped me put this book together. You'll find electronic versions of each of his drawings on the CD-ROM accompanying this book. Figure 3-1 presents small versions of each of these drawings. Feel free to copy the drawings and use them on your own pages. Notice that the graphics correspond with the topics suggested in this chapter.

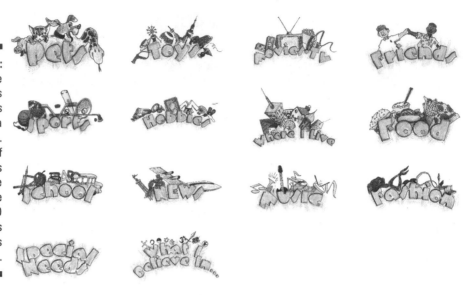

Figure 3-1:
An image always helps enliven a Web page. This set of images is available for your use on the CD that comes with this book.

At this age, kids are really getting social. They are making lots of new friends and becoming interested in team sports. The ideas in this section encourage young people to include a widening circle of people, places, and activities in their Web pages.

Note: The suggestions in this chapter are arranged by age ranges. However, just because a topic is targeted at 7- to 10-year-olds doesn't mean that the teenagers among you can't use them for inspiration. Flip through the whole chapter and see which subjects interest you the most — or which ones make you think of some other really cool stuff.

Each exercise contains a number of questions that can help you develop topics to discuss on your Web pages. Think about each question, and answer the ones that make you think of things you'd like to talk about. Feel free to come up with topics that aren't suggested. If you're confused about how to proceed, see "Developing Your Web Page: An Example," later in this chapter.

Web Page Ideas for Kids Ages 7–10

Nothing is more exciting to a child than learning. The Web provides a way to organize and reorganize all that they can comprehend about themselves and the world in which they live. The Web allows growth to be a truly creative process, too; by browsing through Web pages, each child chooses the aspects to which he or she will respond. By sharing parts of themselves on their own Web page, they affirm and consolidate what is important to them. Working with other family members on this project provides valuable teachable moments and important times of bonding. The ideas in this section examine topics that kids ages 7–10 will know well and feel comfortable discussing.

Pets and other animals

Millions of dogs and cats live with families all over the country. Are you lucky enough to have an animal companion? Maybe you have more exotic pets, such as birds, ferrets, and turtles. If you live in a rural area, you may be the envy of all of us because you have horses. (You may also be unlucky enough to have to get up at dawn to milk the cows or feed the chickens.) If you have a pet or love a particular kind of animal, tell people about it.

Even people who don't have their own pets love to read funny stories about other people's animals. A kitten, puppy, lamb, colt, or other small animal is sure to guarantee you a popular Web site. Start thinking of all the ways you can describe your furry or scaled friend as smart/stupid, cute/ugly, funny/boring, brave/cowardly, or whatever.

My friend Raymond breeds canaries every spring and always has cute little ones for sale or to give away to good homes. My friend Virginia has a Welsh terrier named Parker who always falls asleep on the pillow on her bed. When Virginia wakes him and tells him to move over, he growls at her and makes *her* sleep at the foot of the bed!

Other kids are interested in animals they don't live with. You might want to talk about how prairie dogs live in towns, how beavers build dams, or how porcupines defend themselves. Or maybe you have visited a different country or like animals in the zoo that come from a particular part of the world. Africa is known for its lions, elephants, giraffes, zebra, and antelopes. But you might want to describe the okapi or potto, or talk about the differences between gorillas, baboons, and mandrills.

If you're interested in making a Web page about your pet, go to the file, pets.htm, on the CD-ROM that comes with this book, and fill in the blanks. See Appendix D for information about the CD.

Toys and games

Everyone has a favorite toy (even parents and grandparents!). Maybe you collect a particular kind of stuffed animal, or perhaps you spend hours constructing elaborate towers and castles. You may also love playing an adventure or fantasy game.

Some toys are special because they are homemade or because they are a gift from someone you love — or maybe you saved your allowance just to buy one. Sometimes it's fun to share stories about toys you had when you were small. I actually know someone who is not ashamed to admit she still sleeps with the baby blanket she was wrapped in when she came home from the hospital — and she's in college now. You might also think about what you would buy to play with if you suddenly inherited a fortune.

A Web page is a great way to share your fascinations with others and meet kids who love to do the same things you do. You might even find kids with whom you can trade toys, games, or fantasy adventures. For some playful suggestions for ways to talk about your favorite toys and games, open the file, `toys.htm`, on the CD-ROM, and fill in the blanks.

Movies and TV shows

Unless you're living most of your life on a planet other than Earth, you probably have a couple of favorite TV shows and movies. Surf around some kids' Web sites for a little while, and you'll see images from *Aladdin, Star Wars,* "Sliders," and lots of other movies and TV shows. I bet you don't always agree with your sisters or brothers about those choices, but this is your Web page we're talking about here, and this is your chance to tell people about your favorite sources of video entertainment.

Try answering these questions in order to come up with some creative ideas: Did you ever try to dress like a famous character or a movie star? Have you ever celebrated a birthday party with a theme based on a movie? What objects do you treasure that have something to do with entertainment?

You might imagine yourself as a movie critic. Make lists of thumbs-up and thumbs-down movies, put them on your Web site, and have a great time arguing with those who disagree with you. Why should movie critics like Siskel and Ebert have all the fun?

The file, `movies.htm`, found on the CD has some spaces where you can create lists of your top five movies or TV shows.

Web sites for kids ages 7–10

You'll find plenty of sites for kids 7–10 on the Web, including some devoted to pets and animals. Purebred dog and cat owners have breed clubs that meet on the Web to discuss their Collies or Persian cats. You may be able to find the breed you're interested in by checking out this site: `http://www.<breedname>.com` (where *breedname* is the breed of your pet). You can also contact the American Kennel Club at `http://www.akc.org/`.

Petstation Kids! (http://petstation.com/kids.html) is devoted specifically to kids and their pets. This site allows you to send photos of your
pets, which it will then scan and post on its pages. Pet Ring (http://www.
albritons.com/petring/) also has a good collection of pet pages.

Younger kids will enjoy a page created by Ed Menuey, a 13-year-old from
Australia who is fascinated by sharks. He hopes to be an oceanographer one
day. Visit his Ed's Sharks and Stuff page at http://www.geocities.com/
EnchantedForest/3545.

The official Beanie Babies Web site is at http://www.ty.com/. The authors'
young friend David Price is fascinated with the game Magic: The Gathering.
You can find out about this and other wizard/fantasy games at http://www.
wizards.com/. You can find a British Web site devoted to the movie *Toy Story*
at http://www.bvi.co.uk/toystory/. Each toy in the film has its own
Web page. Visit Metrolegoland at http://www.geocities.com/SoHo/7750/.

Seven-year-old Heather Shade came up with the concept for Heather's
Happy Holidaze Page (http://www.shadeslanding.com/hms/). With some
help from Mom and Dad, who do the HTML Web page coding, Heather
celebrates a new holiday every month.

Web Page Ideas for Kids Ages 9–12

At this age, kids are really getting social. They are making lots of new friends
and becoming interested in team sports. The ideas in this section encourage
young people to include a widening circle of people, places, and activities in
their Web pages.

My friends

Almost everyone has a couple of buddies or chums to hang out with, but if
you're lucky, you've got a super best friend. That's the person you talk to
about everything, who likes a lot of the same things you do. Tell folks in
cyberspace about them. How did you two meet? Did you like each other
right away, or did it take some time for things to warm up between you?
What do you all like to do together?

The television show, "Friends," presents a bunch of people who hang out
together. Do you have a *crew* you spend time with? What happens when
disagreements arise? How do you keep in touch when people move away
(***Hint:*** Think "Web")?

Speaking of cyberspace friends, do you already have any? If so, how do you communicate? Will you ever meet in person? Visitors to your Web page (who probably have their own cyberspace friends) will love to hear about friends with whom you regularly exchange e-mail or chat messages. You can use the file, `friends.htm`, on the CD to create your own Web friends page.

Sports

Sports are a great way to bring kids together, whether on the playing field or in cyberspace. Tell your Web page visitors about your own athletic activities. Can the people in your household tell the season by the kind of ball or athletic shoes they trip over as they walk from room to room? Were you born to boogie with tap, ballet, or hip-hop? Lots of kids like to tool around town on their skateboards, their BMX bikes, or their inline skates. Who are your male and female sports heroes? Different sports are big in different countries, but I bet everyone would want to hear about the time you met Michael Jordan or had your baseball signed by your favorite major-league baseball player.

Does your family play softball, touch football, or some other game together? Does your dad or mom coach one or more athletes on their own teams? Are you all proud of some family member's athletic achievements? Make a Web page about these kinds of things.

Tell other kids what you like to play and where. Tell them what you've accomplished — especially if you've won awards, placed well in competitions, or if you're simply admired in your area of competition. Who knows, if you talk about your particular athletic pursuits on the Web, you might even get to meet a fellow *cybersports* nut at a particular competition or summer athletic camp.

Open the file, `sports.htm`, on the CD if you're interested in creating a sports-related Web page.

Hobbies

The good thing about having friends is that you have someone to share your hobbies and collections with. Whether you like to collect things, build things, or take things apart, you'll find friends on the Web who will be willing to compare notes and give and take advice.

Speaking of taking things apart, Alex and Steve, two 10-year-old friends in my neighborhood, have an old car engine in Steve's garage. They spend hours taking the thing apart and putting it back together. I'm just waiting for the day when I hear VAAAAAROOOOOOOM!!! When these guys aren't working on the car engine, Steve collects old Zippo lighters and Alex has matchbooks from restaurants that no one has even heard of. *Note:* These boys don't collect these items to use, which would be prohibited! — only to display.

So stop and think about your hobbies and the kinds of things you collect. In the old days, stamps and coins were big collectibles. Have you or anyone in your family been fortunate enough to inherit an old blue coin collection book, maybe baseball cards, or anything else from an older cousin, aunt, or uncle? If so, tell folks about it on your Web pages.

The file, `hobbies.htm`, on the CD includes a space where you can share the Web address of a wonderful Web site that has the latest and greatest info on your particular passion. Maybe somebody who loves what you do will return the favor.

Where I live

In Chapter 5, you hear about Daniel Warsaw, a young person who is really proud of his home country, New Zealand. If you've moved around a lot (or even a little), talk about that. If you'd rather share details about where you'd prefer to live, don't be shy. But the bottom line is that everybody lives somewhere, and (believe it or not) that *somewhere* can be interesting to others. You probably know a lot of entertaining tidbits about the people who are your neighbors — where they work, play, shop, worship, go to school, and so on. Tell about where you live. Tell what it looks like. Pretend you're a tour guide and are giving your Web page visitors instructions on what they don't want to miss.

You'll find some suggestions for ways to describe your own home base in the file, `myhome.htm`, on the CD.

Cooking and favorite foods

Lots of kids like to cook — even though some kids, just like some adults, are better at it than others. When my friend Noah was 3, he dictated the following recipe to his teacher at school. She thought it was so good (I mean, hysterically good) that she printed a whole cookbook of recipes by 3-year-olds.

Note: Although this recipe is fun to read, *do not* try it at home:

> **Chocolate Cake:**
>
> You need chocolate and I think sugar. I think baking powder. I think some eggs. In mixing — a big mixing bowl — I think you do it with a mixer or grinder — about ten hours. Put it in the oven — we have a stove that's pretty, pretty hot — and it has something that looks like a wheel. It gets very hot. Cook it for about ten hours. I think you take it out.

Anyway, your own favorite recipe (or maybe a younger sibling's recipe) can make a fun addition to your Web page.

When you get ready to write about food, you might ask yourself the following kinds of questions: Do you eat three square meals a day or graze your way through the day (though probably your folks don't allow that)?

Do you prefer your own cooking, your parents' cooking, or do you hang around waiting for a dinner invitation at someone else's house? What is on the table when it's someone's birthday, a holiday, or another kind of celebration? *Remember:* If you can't help nibbling while writing this up for your Web site, don't get crumbs on your keyboard.

You'll find some mouth-watering subjects you can sink your teeth into in the file, `food.htm`, on the CD.

Scott Beatty, an 11th-grade student in British Columbia, describes himself as a soccer fanatic. Visit his Scott's Soccer Corner Web page at `http://www.bcsupernet.com/users/jazz/soccer.htm`.

Cosanna, a 7th-grader from western Canada, collects erasers, shells, rocks, stamps, coins, and more. She lives in a geodesic dome. Check out her photos at `http://midxpress.com/midxpress/cos/collect.htm`.

Web Sites for Kids Ages 13–15

The social horizon begins to expand, making the Web a perfect place to explore new ideas without leaving home. Whereas a teen might not want to be seen talking to an adult in public, on the Web, all age groups can share concerns about common issues. The goal is to go from dependence on parents to independence in their own lives, and the Web can be a place to safely explore choices such as careers and colleges. As they create and re-create their own Web sites and explore the Web sites of others, kids foster emotional growth and provide a meaning for and direction to live their lives.

My school

Like it or not, you spend many of your waking hours at school. School can provide you with plenty of material for a Web page. You can write about your class, teachers you like, extracurricular activities, or special projects you've done. Describe what school would be like if you were principal for the day. Share sources for school-related clip art or your school's Web address. What? Your school doesn't yet have a Web page. *Ah,* there's your chance to get tons of extra credit.

My niece, Clare Moseley, includes a photo of her class on one of her pages (`http://www.geocities.com/Heartland/plains/7942/me.html`).

Go to the head of your class by creating a Web page about where you go to school; just open the file, `school.htm`, on the CD, and answer the questions.

News

One good reason for having a Web page is to keep your cyberspace friends informed of the latest goings-on in your busy life. You can post photos of a great vacation, where you work, an event you attended, you name it. You might even start a newsletter devoted just to you. Imagine that!

You can create Web pages that keep track of current events by opening the file, `news.htm`, on the CD.

Jobs and chores

The questions below are meant to stimulate your thinking and suggest ideas for things you can say on your Web pages about jobs and chores you do. A kid's life is not all games. Not that doing stuff to help out the family, whether out of a sense of *charity* or to earn some extra cash can't be fun. In fact, some kids say they learn as much at work as they do at school.

Grown-ups get a lot out of networking — having lunch with people who have jobs similar to theirs or joining groups or workers who have the same challenges and experiences. When you're on the Web, you can network about your work, too.

Jobs

Some of you older kids may have part-time jobs after school or on weekends that you can talk about on your Web page. Here are some questions you might think about: Are you slinging burgers for McDonald's? Do you work in a florist or craft shop? Do any of you work with your folks at their place of business? How many of you baby-sit to make extra money? Some of you probably work just to make money; others may have jobs that you really like and might like to do all your life.

Putting your thoughts on the Web can help you clarify what "doing what you do" means to you. You can share tips for getting along with your boss and your coworkers. You can also figure out your budget and find ways to make your dollars go further so you can put some in the bank or invest in some necessary computer equipment.

Chores

Once kids start walking, most parents find chores for them to do around the house. If both your parents work or if you're part of a single parent household, you may have some fairly adult responsibilities, too. Maybe you do some of the grocery shopping or cooking. If you live in the country and have farm animals to tend, you may be responsible for the cows getting their evening meal. List the chores you actually like to do — well, okay, the ones that you, at least, don't mind doing.

Here are some questions that might help you come up with subjects to discuss: Do you receive an allowance? Is the amount of money you receive determined by the quantity or the quality of the work you do? Is your floor clean? Have you *seen* your floor lately? You might share ways to do your chores more efficiently or get out of them altogether. (Maybe you and your Web friends could find ways to get your brothers and sisters to do them. That would make your Web site really popular!)

Vacations

Some of you get to go on really neat vacations. Whether you visit relatives, go fishing, or tour eight countries in seven days, you will come back with plenty of stories to tell about people and places. My friend Isaac and his family just got back from the Galapagos Islands! Isaac saw huge turtles and walked the same paths Darwin walked in the 1830s when he was forming his theory of evolution. Use the Web to get travel tips for faraway places with strange-sounding names. Or if you have a vacation home, check out things to do and people to see when you get there.

Awards

Some of you probably don't like to brag, but here's the place to list all the awards you've received. Are you on the honor roll at school? A national merit scholar? Did your sports team win an award? Are you the best speller in all of Montana? Keep us posted about the good news! Another positive way to use the Web is to get encouragement for current pursuits. Tell about your goals, and maybe someone will have a tip that will help you achieve them.

Music

Everyone likes music, and everyone marches to the beat of a different drummer. From country and western to heavy metal, from opera to rap, music takes people out of themselves, helps them transcend the boredom of their daily lives, and gives them something to listen to on their portable CD players.

Are your musical tastes *eclectic?* That means you like to listen to lots of different stuff. Or maybe you're the kind of kid who holds your fingers in your ears and whistles "Dixie" if anything but the Smashing Pumpkins is playing. Whether you're into making music or just listening to it, describe your tastes on the Web and find others who think you're way cool (and argue with those who think your favorite group stinks). Is there a song — or two — that expresses your feelings more clearly than you ever thought possible? Maybe it needs to be mentioned on your page.

Sing out about your favorite kinds of music by opening the file, `music.htm`, on the CD.

Fashion

Lots of fashion trends are happening every day. You might not be able to jump on a plane and see the latest fashions yourself, but on the Web, you can get there with just a click of the mouse. When you're thinking of things to say about fashion, ask yourself: What's cool at your school? Do you care about what you wear? Do you go baggy or slim-fitting? Do you try to stay in fashion, or have you created your own unique look? Many people feel they have to dress like the crowd to fit in. In my day, there were *Collegiates* (sometimes called preppies) and *Greasers* (or homeboys).

Share your fashion likes and dislikes by opening the file, `fashion.htm`, on the CD.

Political causes/personal issues

Tons of things happen daily in your community, state, and country that have a strong impact on your life. Are you active in political or social organizations? Are you, or members of your family, fighting or working with the local authorities over things like parking lots, new schools, better parks, or troublesome garbage dumps? Getting together with other like-minded people on the Web can sometimes be more effective than passing around a petition. Here are some sites created by kids ages 11 and up.

Lauren Bush, an 11-year-old from Pennsylvania, plays the flute and the piano and sings in her school chorus, too. Read all about it on her Web page (`http://milo.chem.usouthal.edu/%/Enix/`).

At the other end of the musical spectrum, 16-year-old Aurora from Toronto, Canada, plays bass guitar and likes industrial music. She also wants to form her own "chick band." She includes a Hair Gallery on her Web site. Check out her interests at `http://www.interlog.com/%7Eeidolon/home3.htm`.

Debbie Zapf, a 13-year-old from New York, has started a newsletter for girls, and she has lots of other material on her Web site (`http://www.li.net/ ~edhayes/debbie.html`). Debbie Hayes started a girls' newsletter on her page (`http://www.li.net/~elhayes/debbie.html`).

Try not to include hard-to-remember or unusual symbols in your Web addresses. The %7 in Aurora's address crops up when you leave a blank space in a filename and open the file on your computer. The blank space is interpreted as %7. Be sure to delete these symbols or any blank spaces from your filenames before you put your files on the Web.

By the way, if you're interested in environmental issues, you can check out the environmental page on GeoCities at `http://www.geocities.com/ RainForest/4560/`.

More Web Page Ideas for Kids Ages 13–15

The following ideas cover some thoughtful topics and might require you to put on an extra-large thinking cap. If you can write about one of these topics, though, the additional effort will be worth the effort. The pages will have a personal and sincere effect, and the subjects will be important to lots of readers. Read the following list of topics, and try to create a page about one or more of them.

- ✔ **Chosen people:** Thirteen-year-old Kelly is an adopted child; she has started an online adoption group. Check out her Web page at `http:// www.angelfire.com/pg0/Kel/adopt.html`.

- ✔ **Disabilities:** Many kids and families know people with special needs. Are you or someone in your family living with a disability? Some kids have found support and made new friends by sharing the challenges they face. *Note:* Some suggestions for pages about kids with special needs can be found in the file, `special.htm`, on the CD.

- ✔ **Illnesses and accidents:** Some kids live with illnesses everyday. My friend Noah has asthma. You'd hardly know it until his inhaler slips out of his pocket when he's playing tennis. But some kids have more serious problems. You may want to tell others about accidents or illnesses you've had to overcome or live with.

  As Elizabeth says on her Snow White Home Page: "I have Down's Syndrome, Cerebral Palsy, and very bad asthma. But that doesn't slow me down!" Visit her at `http://www.ecnet.net/users/gjmuzzo/ lizzie1.htm`.

- ✔ **Nearest and dearest:** In this big, crazy world, kids acquire families in all kinds of ways. Some just arrive to be with their moms and dads, some come with one parent and get another one when Mom or Dad remarries. Some kids are adopted by a man or woman or family, and together they create a new family for themselves. Every group needs to communicate with others. Tell about your own family on the Web.

✔ **Religion:** Being part of a religious community plays an important part in the lives of many people. Even those who don't belong to a particular group think about spiritual things and live their lives according to some kind of philosophy. The Web can be a good place to figure out some important ways to become a better person or to make the world a better place.

✔ **Show who you are:** Web pages are also the perfect place for you to communicate with the world about the thoughts that fill your mind. Are you a list maker? Do you daydream? What about a section that tells other browsers what you'd do with a million dollars. You could list your loves and hates. Or how about a section entitled, "If I Ruled the World"?

✔ **What I believe in:** Your Web page needs to make a statement. There's no reason why the statement has to be subtle. This is your page, and you're in charge, so feel free to state your opinions on issues about which you feel strongly. Your Web page can be a place where you write or show all your wishes and dreams for yourself, your friends, family, and the world.

You can make your own personal statement by filling in the blanks in the file, `beliefs.htm`, on the CD.

Now that you've discovered what you already knew — what a great and interesting kid you are — you can figure out exactly what you really want to put on your Web page. Even if you don't use all the material this chapter has generated, save your lists. When you update your Web page, you'll have new ideas on hand to make your page look great and be of interest to others.

Developing Your Web Page: An Example

Here is an example that shows how to develop the contents of a Web page following the suggestions in this chapter. In this example, the subject is one that might apply to a young person of virtually any age: Whether to celebrate a birthday, anniversary, a holiday, or other special occasion, it's fun to plan a party for your friends. Here are steps you can follow to develop a Web page:

▶▶

ON THE CD

1. Open your favorite Web page authoring tool.

If you haven't chosen one yet, Appendix B provides some suggestions, and Appendix D describes some programs you can install from the CD that comes with this book.

2. **Either start a new Web page document (if you're coming up with your own Web page idea) or open one of the exercises in the directory** `D:\POTPOURI\CH3IDEAS` **found on the CD with this book.**

3. **Create a main heading for your page, unless you're working on one of the exercises and you like the heading that's there already.**

Make it something fun. In this example, you might write something like "Party Time! Tips for Planning Your Gathering."

4. **Start with a topic sentence that tells why you are talking about this subject and what you plan to discuss.**

You might start out with this: "I love to get ready for parties, and people say I do such a good job that I ought to go into the party-planning business. So I decided to come up with a Web page on the subject."

5. **Develop main subjects that apply to your topic.**

Consider creating one page per subject. On your opening page, you can make a *clickable link* that leads to each of these pages. (See Chapter 15 for details on how to connect a set of pages with same-site links.) Here are some subjects related to parties, some questions you might consider, and some answers and approaches you might come up with:

- **Subject: Clothes**

- **Question:** Should you tell people what to wear? What should they wear? Why does it matter what they wear?

  Answer: Whether you are wearing a costume or other festive dress, your clothes start to set the mood. Sometimes hats or other accessories are part of the party itself. Click here for ways to dress or clothes to make for parties.

- **Subject: Decorations**
- **Question:** What kinds of decorations can you choose from? Where do you get them? Where do you put them?

   Answer: The first thing you notice when you walk into a party is the way the room is decorated. Zany or romantic, we all get excited when we see streamers, balloons, banners, and other room decorations. Click here for ideas on how to make a room come alive.

- **Subject: Activities**
- **Question:** How do you come up with things for people to do that don't end up being corny or hokey? Does everyone have to participate? What can people do?

   Answer: Activities are an important part of the fun. Where there are arts and crafts projects, a show or performance, a piñata, or games, you get to have fun with long-time friends and people you just met. Click here for lists of things to do.

- **Subject: Don't Forget the Food!**
- **Question:** Do you have to spend a fortune on a fancy caterer? Do you have to make all the food yourself? Should you ask someone to help? How do you make "party food"?

   Answer: Not if you know how to make simple things fancy. Take cake, for example. Cutting it into different shapes, adding candy arrangements, and making the frosting a particular color can transform it for any occasion. Click here for lots of ideas for party food.

CLARE DECLARES

One kid's opinion

Sometimes I get ideas for my own Web pages by reading something on someone else's Web page. If they write about something that I'm interested in, I'll think of things I'd like to say about the same subject. I also get lots of ideas from books that I read. Since I have a Web page about a TV show called "Sliders," sometimes while I'm watching an episode of the show, I'll write some notes about the show, and later on I'll put some comments on my Web page.

Chapter 4

Mapping Out Your Web Site

· ·

· ·

*1*n *The Hobbit,* the dwarves have a map that shows them how to reach Smaug the dragon; in *Treasure Island,* Long John Silver has his treasure map; in *Star Wars,* Luke Skywalker follows a diagram of the Death Star in order to destroy it. As you probably know, most adventure or fantasy games give you an overview of the terrain you have to follow to play the game. You may have to move through different rooms, journey from kingdom to kingdom, or descend through several levels. In every case, someone has organized the routes you can take and arranged the things you'll encounter along the way.

Whether you're searching for treasure or trying to achieve an important goal, you need a map so you can follow the right path and get where you need to go. This is especially true when you're designing your Web site or browsing other sites on the Web. When you're planning a Web site, you get to plan where your visitors can go when they visit your pages. You arrange paths that people can follow, and you publish the words and images that they are able to see.

I like to arrange my Web pages so that they form a triangle. The point at the top of the triangle is the "welcome page" (or home page) for the site, the place where you want your visitors to come first. The bottom of the triangle contains pages about specific subjects. This arrangement makes it easy for me to see how the pages move in a logical way from general (at the top of the triangle) to specific (at the bottom). You find out more about the triangular arrangement in this chapter.

Depending on what works for you, you might imagine your site as a *virtual* shopping mall. Your visitor can enter the mall through any number of doors, but each door leads them to a welcome sign or an information center that provides a list of the stores in the mall. This location is where the mall lists each store according to a numeric code so shoppers know how to find it, and gives a brief description of what each store sells. The stores in the mall are divided into levels: Some are on the first floor, some are on the second, and so on.

You can do the same thing with your Web site. Before the *building* process begins, you draw a map or a blueprint (much like an architect does), provide an arrangement that makes sense, and make your welcome page in which you tell your visitors what they can find on your site and the path they can follow to find it.

Being large and in charge is one of the best things about making your own Web pages. In this chapter, you discover ways to plan where the visitors to your Web site will go and consider paths you can draw to help them get there.

Here are some Web site map-making materials that will probably come in handy during your planning process:

— **Drawing software:** A good computer drawing program, such as MacDraw (for the Mac) or CorelDRAW (for the PC), is a great tool for coming up with a visual map of your site.

— **Pencil and paper:** You'll probably want these for making a handy list of sites you want to link to, as well as for making a visual map of your own site.

— **Web browser:** You need a browser to get around the Web and check out other pages and to find out which ones you want to link to your own Web pages.

Scoping Out Your Web Site Map

In this section, you find out how to make a well-organized, user-friendly site that just might win some awards, or, at the least, make your visitors happy they dropped in. But before you actually get started mapping out your site, here are some steps to go over:

1. **Refer to Chapter 2, where you make a list of possible Web page contents.**

In case you skipped over that part, you can draw up a list now: Make a column for each member of your family, one for yourself, one for your friends, one for school, and so on. List the main topics that might go on a Web page. Don't get too specific here: You're looking for general areas such as "me" and "The Web."

2. **Look over the topics on your list, and divide them into two or three main categories that include just about everything (if you come up with four, five, or six categories, that's fine).**

3. **Make subdivisions of each of the main categories so that your whole Web site is divided into *levels* of information.**

4. **Make a welcome page that shows the main categories in your Web site and includes graphics and links to pages in each of those categories.**

You may draw a map of the whole site so that it assumes the shape of a triangle, which is what I like to do. Figure 4-1 gives you an idea of what I'm talking about.

The following sections explain these steps in more detail so that you — like a traveler in a fantasy adventure world or a shopper in an immense mall — won't lose your way as you plan a really cool, informative, and irresistible site that keeps visitors coming back. You also find out how to you express yourself effectively and provide ways to get feedback from cyberspace visitors around the world.

Figure 4-1:
Start with a welcome page, divide your site into levels of information, and before you know it, you have a well-organized Web site.

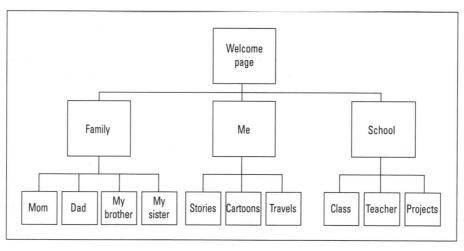

A "game plan" for your Web site

Planning your Web site is a good excuse for checking out some adventure games on the Web. The way the pages on the sites are arranged may spark some thoughts about how you can organize your site. An index of adventure games can be found at `http://www.yahoo.com/Recreation/Games/Computer_Games/Genres/Adventure/Titles/`. A list of interactive games you can play in real-time (that is, you can play them even while you're connected to the Web) is at `http://www.yahoo.com/Recreation/Games/Internet_Games/` `Interactive_Web_Games/Interactive_Fiction/Adventure/`. Check out the DCity "interactive landscape" site, which is set up to resemble a game but is actually a good map of Web pages (`http://dc.viper.net/map.cgi`). When you're visiting the Yahoo! site, keep in mind that you're making use of a very complex and well organized Web site; you might just go to the Yahoo! home page (`http://www.yahoo.com/`) to see how the authors categorize information and provide paths that visitors can follow easily to find virtually anything.

Getting organized: Divide your site into categories

Why, you ask, do you want to spend all this time getting organized? The Web is made up of millions of pages, not all of which are easy to locate, and now your pages are about to join them. Part of your challenge becomes how to attract, and keep, visitors' attention. You begin with organization. In fact, organization is the key to everything on the Web. As you begin, here are two basic problems to consider:

✔ Because most users connect to the Web with fairly slow modems, lengthy, complex Web pages (especially those with lots of detailed graphics) take too long to appear on-screen. For example, if your visitors use a 14.4 Kbps modem to connect to the Web, they'll spend about one second to load 1K of data. If your Web page takes up 40–50K of disk space, your visitors will have to count up to 40–50 before seeing everything. So you definitely want your pages to be well planned! (See Appendix A for information about modems.)

✔ Because the Web is constantly changing and growing and because no single guide is available for everything on the Web, most users have a hard time finding things.

To minimize these problems, all successful Web sites need to follow some basic rules (so you're going to follow them, right?):

- ✔ Don't try to do too much on any one Web page. Each page should cover only one subject, for example, "The Country I Live In."

- ✔ Don't load up any one page with too many complex images, such as scanned photos, that take lots of time for your visitors to see. Consider using only two or three images per page, at most.

- ✔ Spend most of your time and energy making your welcome page outstanding. An eye-catching and well-organized first page can make or break a Web site.

- ✔ Link all of your Web pages into an *interconnected Web* that has a coherent theme and organization. By interconnected Web, I mean a set of related Web pages that are connected by hypertext links. Each page contains links that will take visitors to other parts of the site (for example, a set of buttons or links at the bottom of each page). Clicking on a particular link might take them to <u>Home</u> (your site's welcome page), <u>Back</u> (to the previous page in a series of pages), or <u>Next</u> (to the next page in the series). For more on making links on your Web pages, see Chapter 15.

Spinning your Web pages into a triangle

You can map out your Web pages many ways, but as I mentioned earlier in the chapter, I find that arranging my Web pages into a triangle enables me to see easily how the pages move from the most general (at the top of the triangle) to the most specific pages and topics (at the bottom).

Here's an example that you may consider and a triangular structure you can follow for all your pages. Do you play or watch a team sport? If so, think about how the team is organized. At the top of the heap, you have the head coach, who is in charge of everything (at least, that's what *he or she* thinks). The team may have one or two assistant coaches working under the head coach. The starting lineup reports to those assistants. At the bottom of the team's organizational structure are the rest of the players. A large team's structure might look something like the triangular arrangement shown in Figure 4-2.

By the way, all the pages on your site should *wear* the same *uniforms* and *play* well together. You can find out more about all that in Chapter 5, where you learn about principles of making Web pages, such as how to use graphics and how to compose your headings so that everything is organized and consistent.

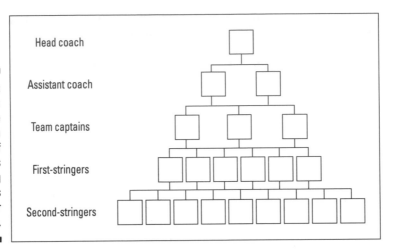

Figure 4-2:
You can
organize
your own
"team" of
Web pages
by using
this
triangular
organization.

Head coach

Assistant coach

Team captains

First-stringers

Second-stringers

If you do belong to an athletic team, you may actually want to create a Web page for it. You can provide an online roster of players, publish your schedule of games for the upcoming season, and urge your fans to attend and cheer you on. Chances are your fellow teammates and your coaches will welcome the attention. If your school puts out a printed program for fans, see if you can have the URL for your team's new Web page printed on it.

Thinking in terms of levels

As shown in the triangular illustration in Figure 4-2, the pages that make up a Web site fall into different levels. The top-level page welcomes people to your site, describes what the site is about, and lists the main contents. Second-level pages introduce major topics covered in the site. Pages at or near the bottom level are more narrow in scope. They do only one or two things. If you were to create a Web site about baseball, for example, the pages at the bottom would be about topics like how to pitch, how to play center field, how to pick off a base runner, and so on.

You divide your site into pages so that you can distribute information evenly. The following sections describe the various levels of Web site pages.

Level 1: Your welcome page

The top-level page (which is equivalent to the head coach in Figure 4-2) is your welcome page, or home page. I prefer welcome page because it describes the purpose of the page: to welcome people to your home on the Web. This page is the front door through which people enter to visit the various rooms (that is, pages) you have set up. This page tells visitors something about who made the site (you), and it provides links to the lower level pages on your site.

If you try to load up this first page with too many graphics and examples of information within your site, visitors may become impatient while your page *slowly* appears on their computer screen. They may even (and probably will) click their browser's Stop button and check out. Instead of sticking around to see everything you've put together, they may try someone else's Web site. So just include a photo or two, a couple of sentences introducing and describing your site, and some links to the main topic areas on other pages on your site. That's all you need.

Try to put all of your links to other areas on your site at or near the top of your welcome page so that they appear in the first or second *screen* of information the viewer sees. (Readers really don't like to scroll down to get to the links.) The Teel Family Web Site (`http://www.teelfamily.com/`) is pleasant to look at, full of good information, and well organized. The links to the main areas of the site are presented in the left column, as shown in Figure 4-3.

Level 2: Major categories

The second-level pages on a site are the ones that introduce your major categories. One page might be entitled "My School." Another might be "All About Me." You can provide more specific information on this page than you did on your welcome page. However, if you have a lot of topics to cover about your school or about you, this second-level page can be another welcome page, only this time it is welcoming you to an area *within* your Web site rather than to the site as a whole.

Figure 4-3: Try to keep your top-level page simple, and present all the main links quickly, as is done here in The Teel Family Site's welcome page.

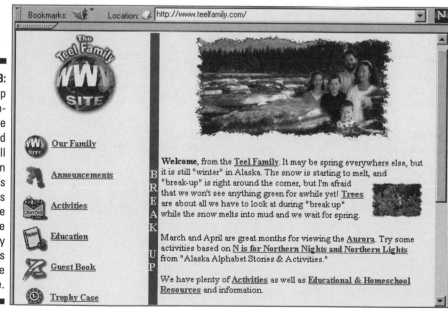

The KIDZ Online Games & Activities page in Figure 4-4 is not the welcome page for the whole WorldVillage KIDZ site (`http://www.worldvillage.com/kidz/`). It is a second-level page that introduces the main category (games kids can find online) and provides links to third-level pages, each of which describes a specific game.

When you map out your own site, it's a good idea to limit yourself to only two levels of Web pages. A site like KIDZ Online not only has lots of games and projects to present, but it also probably has lots of paid employees to help prepare and organize the Web pages. If you're lucky, your family members are helping you create your site; otherwise, you may be doing most of your Web page preparation yourself. Keeping it simple makes your job easier, and you don't make your visitors do a lot of clicking on lists to find what they want to know about you.

Level 3: Details . . . details!

Third-level pages get into specifics. These pages give detailed information about a topic. They don't have to be the bottom-level pages of your site. Depending on your penchant for organizing and putting things in the proper place, you can go on and on as long as you like.

Figure 4-4:
In a second-level page, you get into more detail about your Web site. You can also provide visitors with links to specific topics.

Here are some examples of the role third- or (if you simply *must* get into even more detail) fourth-level pages can play in the triangular hierarchy of a Web site:

Example 1
Level 1: Randy's Cool Web Site

Level 2: My School Activities

Level 3: My Trip to Washington

Level 4: A Speech I Gave to the National 4-H Club

Example 2
Level 1: Oliver Twist Elementary School Home Page

Level 2: Room 12-B Home Page

Level 3: Our Teacher, Mr. Fagin

Level 4: Math Problems that Mr. Fagin Likes

If you're into family history, all this organizing and *triangulating* of Web site contents might just remind you of how a family tree is drawn. If you or someone in your family has done research on your ancestors and traced your lineage back to the pilgrims, put the information online. Family history is a great project for a Web page. You can say something about what country you or your ancestors are from, how you are proud of your heritage; you can put out old photos, dates of birth and death, and all kinds of information that one of your second-cousins-thrice-removed just might find valuable. You can put everything on one page, or you can devote a single page to each of your forebears. The world is your oyster. Tell your family genealogist to type the information on a computer and save each file as a text-only document. You can then convert the documents to HTML (see Chapter 14 for more about HTML).

Genealogy is a *big deal* on the Internet. As more databases are put online and more amateur family researchers put out information about their families, the chances get better and better that you can actually find out something about your long-lost relatives by searching the Internet. If you want to dig around the roots of your own family tree on the Internet, a good starting point is Matt Helm's Genealogy Toolbox (`http://genealogy.tbox.com/genealogy.html`).

OPEN

Other Ways to Map Out Your Site

Paper and pen are easy and convenient, but, hey, this is almost the twenty-first century. If you really get into making maps and drawing up Web sites, here are a couple of programs you can use to help you create a visual representation of your entire site and map out links between documents within the site. You can use the following two programs to provide a visual representation of your site. You can see how the pages are linked together and rearrange them if you want.

Note: You don't have to use these two programs in order to get your site started; nothing is wrong with drawing your pages on paper. Use your written plan at the beginning. Then after you have your site up and running, if the links between the pages start to get complicated, you can investigate these cool (but expensive) tools.

Microsoft FrontPage (Windows 95 and Power Mac)

Microsoft FrontPage is one of the coolest programs around for creating a Web site. FrontPage is actually made up of several separate programs. One (*FrontPage Editor*) lets you edit Web pages without having to type HTML. Another (*FrontPage Web Server*) lets you explore your Web site and test your pages before you put them online. Another (*Image Composer*) lets you edit images.

Appendix B contains a more complete description of FrontPage and where you can get it. The big drawback is that it's not shareware: You have to purchase FrontPage in order to use all its features. I found the program for $99.95.

If you're planning a Web site, *FrontPage Explorer* lets you see how your pages are linked together (see the demo page from the Microsoft Web site in Figure 4-5; you can see how the

▶▶

whole site works and revise it without erasing and re-drawing.

To use Microsoft FrontPage, you need a 486 or higher processor, the Windows 95 operating system, 8MB of memory, 15MB of available hard-drive space, and a VGA or higher resolution video monitor (SVGA 256-color recommended).

Figure 4-5:
Each page shown in this diagram is one of the Web pages on your site; lines are drawn between pages that are linked.

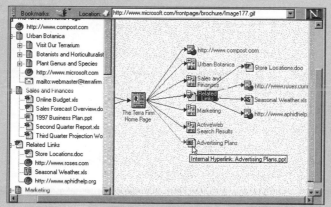

Adobe SiteMill (Mac only)

Adobe SiteMill is a variation of a similar Mac-only product, *Adobe PageMill.* PageMill's main purpose is to help you create individual Web pages. SiteMill does that, too, but it also enables you to link pages and check your links to see whether everything works. In addition, it lets you see the pages on your site and how they're linked. However, the pages don't appear in a nice visual *tree* (a diagram that shows the pages in your site and how they're linked) as they do in FrontPage.

SiteMill, like FrontPage, is also not shareware. It costs about $199. SiteMill requires a color monitor, a Macintosh System 7.5 or later, and a 68040 or Power Macintosh with 6MB RAM available for the program, which means you need 12–16MB total RAM in your computer. See Appendix B for more details.

Drawing it out

Whether you do your drawing on the computer or on paper, the final step is to get all the pages down so you know where everything fits. Depending on how many pages you have, you may need a big sheet of paper for this operation.

This doesn't have to be the last word on how things are arranged. On the contrary, one of the great things about making Web pages is that you can upgrade and improve your work as often as you please, without having to pay to get anything reprinted. Remember that you're in charge of your Web site *map;* you can enlarge it, simplify it, or tear it up and do it all over again whenever you want.

CLARE DECLARES

One kid's opinion

I never did a map of my site when I was coming up with all the Web pages for me and my family. I started out with a few pages containing my stories and my fan club information, and then I just added pages as I went along. I *do* write down the names of the pages I want to link to and the URLs for each page before I actually design a page. Then I write down the *titles* of the links by hand — that is, the text that's going to be underlined as links that people can click on. When I get ready to add the HTML for my page, I refer to this list of titles and URLs, so it's easier to make the links with my HTML editing program (World Wide Web Weaver, which comes on the CD with this book).

Part II
Creating and Publishing Your Web Pages

The 5th Wave   By Rich Tennant

"I NEED TO CONNECT TO OUR T1 LINE AND FTP A FILE FROM OUR CLIENT'S WEB SITE. CAN YOU GET MY KID ON THE PHONE?"

In this part . . .

Having a page on the World Wide Web means you can show the whole wide world who you are. But how can you make sure that you put your best foot forward? To be a good communicator, you need to figure out what you want to say, organize your thoughts clearly, and include all the essential elements. Creating a Web page is a lot like writing an essay. The difference is you're not in English class. And you have some tricks up your sleeve that your teachers never dreamed possible when they were going to school.

Part II gives you the tools you need to create outstanding and well-organized Web pages. First, how about a game of *tag?* You get a brief, painless introduction to HTML, the language made up of instructions called *tags,* which makes Web pages work. You discover "must-have" contents to include on every Web page, and you find tips for preparing pages that everyone can understand — and love reading, too.

After you have the rules of the Web page game, you're ready to be a player. You find out how to create the Web page of your dreams with some easy-to-use programs. Then you learn how to get those exciting pages on the Web. Part II also goes into the pros and cons of the various online service providers that are lining up to meet your needs. You are the customer they are all trying to please, so you want to be educated enough to choose the very best. You and your totally wonderful Web page deserve it.

Chapter 5

ABCs of Making a Great Web Page

In This Chapter

▶ Discovering what HTML is and how it works behind the scenes

▶ Checking out essential features that make a Web page complete

▶ Following practices that make a Web page understandable to all

*Y*our communication and language skills began pretty much with cooing and howling. Eventually, you learned your ABCs and how to spell, read, and write. As you developed all these skills, you began to express yourself to more and more people — first to your parents and family, then to your friends, and then to your teachers and classmates. In this chapter, you discover a new way of communicating with a *really* wide range of people via the Web.

You start with the language of making a Web page, which involves a set of formatting instructions called *HTML*, and some terms that describe basic elements common to every Web page. The terms are easy-to-understand words like *headings, titles, body text,* and *links.*

Note: To get the end result as easily as possible, you can just glance over the section about HTML and move on to the essentials of family welcome pages.

This chapter shows you how to take what you want to say (which you develop in Chapters 2 and 3) and present those words and images so they can be seen on a Web page. You also find out how to make your Web page complete and understandable. After you have this basic knowledge, You'll be able to create pages that will impress your friends, your teachers, and lots of people on the Web that you haven't even met.

Before you start making a Web page, you need to get your materials (as well as your thoughts) together. Here's a rundown of what you need to get started:

____ Ideas for what you want to do (see Chapter 2)

____ Subjects to talk about (see Chapter 3)

____ A plan for how the page works with other related pages you want to make (see Chapter 4)

___ A word-processing program to create a text document

___ A Web browser that allows you to preview your page before you publish it on the Web (see Chapter 6)

Unless you plan to enter HTML instructions one by one (and most people don't), you'll also need software programs referred to as HTML editors or Web page authoring tools. These programs automatically add HTML formatting to your documents. They let you format text by specifying the purpose you want a word, phrase, sentence, or paragraph to serve on a Web page. You just click on familiar computer software features like toolbar buttons and menu options. Instead of typing a techie-looking series of symbols to make a word bold, for example, you click on a button with a bold letter or choose a menu item called Bold. Some of these programs are described in Chapter 6; also see Appendix B. For more details about the inner workings of HTML, refer to Chapter 14.

All You Need Is HTML

HTML is a standardized way of *marking up* documents so that all computers (Macs, PCs, whatever) can read them, whether they're on one network within a single building or on a giant series (*web*) of networks like the Internet.

Finding out how HTML works

HTML was developed in the early 1990s by people who were associated with a research organization in Switzerland called CERN (the European Laboratory for Particle Physics). CERN had many different computers connected by a network, but the computers all *spoke* different languages. If one person sent a file to a colleague's computer, the colleague might not be able to make heads or tails of it. HTML resolved that problem by providing a *standardized* way of creating documents so that all computers can read them.

However, to actually *display* documents created with HTML, those Swiss computer geniuses had to invent one more thing: a program called a *Web browser*. Web browsers are computer programs that recognize and display the instructions in HTML documents.

Using Web browsers and HTML tags

All Web browsers are set up so that they recognize standard HTML instructions called *tags*. These instructions work in the background — much like a busy Mom or Dad setting up and then running a birthday party — telling a browser things like, "This phrase is a level 1 heading," This phrase is italic," or "Put this image here." You never see the instructions unless the person who created the HTML made a mistake in writing them. You see only the results on a computer screen. (Don't let the sight of HTML frighten you; it is explained in Chapter 14.)

Make a simple HTML file

Be adventurous; turn on your computer and start up a word-processing program right now. Try entering the exact words shown in Step 2. That way, you can get used to creating your own HTML documents. At the very least, you'll become familiar with seeing HTML instructions. It's easy; just follow these steps:

1. **Windows 95 users: Select Start⇨Programs⇨Accessories⇨Notepad.**

   Mac users: Double-click on the icon for a program called SimpleText (the earlier version, TeachText, is fine, too), and then double-click on the icon to start the program.

   Whether you're working on a PC or a Mac, you see a blank window with a text cursor (a blinking vertical line), ready and waiting for you to start typing.

2. **Type the following HTML text, pressing Return or Enter at the end of every line, so that the contents of your word-processing file look *exactly* the same as the following example.**

   ```
   <HTML>
   <HEAD>
   <TITLE>Lucy's Playhouse</TITLE>
   </HEAD>
   <BODY>
   <H1>Hi! I'm Lucy</H1>
   <IMG SRC="lucy.gif">
   <I>Welcome to my place. Come and play with me!</I>
   </BODY>
   </HTML>
   ```

   Breaking the lines this way will enable you to read your HTML instructions more clearly and help you if you edit them later on. HTML doesn't actually recognize line breaks caused by pressing Return or Enter. (To find out how to make real line breaks that show up on a Web page, see Chapter 14.)

   Note that the text contained between <TITLE> and </TITLE> is the title for a Web page. This title does not actually appear in the body of the Web page itself. Instead, the title appears in the bar at the top of the Web browser window in which the page is being displayed (see Figure 5-1).

Title of Web page

Figure 5-1:
HTML
commands
work in the
background
to identify
titles,
headings,
text, and
images.

Lucy's Playhouse - Netscape

File Edit View Go Window Help

Bookmarks: Location: file:///C|/Kids' Book/ch02Lucypa   N.

Hi! I'm Lucy.

Welcome to my place. Come in and play with me!

Netscape

3. Select File⇨Save.

A dialog box called Save appears.

4. Enter a name for your file.

If you are on a PC, name the file `test.htm`. If you are on a Mac, name it `test.html`.

You must give a file the right kind of name so that the computer software you are using can recognize the file and know what to do with it. You do this by adding an *extension* to the filename. An extension is a three- or four-letter code that comes after the filename. The extension is separated from the filename by a period. In the preceding Step 4, `.htm` and `.html` are both extensions.

Preview your file in a Web browser

If you followed the preceding steps and typed your own word-processing file, you can understand better that an HTML file is a text document. It contains text that is intended to actually appear on a Web page, along with some HTML instructions. The file is saved in text-only or plain-text format and given the filename extension `.htm` or `.html`. When it is displayed by a word-processing program, the HTML instructions and the page's contents ("Hi! My name Is Lucy," and so on) are just words on a screen.

When seen in a Web browser, however, the file undergoes a transformation. You no longer see the HTML instructions, which are enclosed by the less than (<) and greater than (>) symbols. You see only the page's contents.

After you save your file, the next step is to preview it in a Web browser. Before you begin, make sure a Web browser such as Microsoft Internet Explorer or Netscape Navigator is installed on your computer. Double-click on your browser's icon, and your browser screen opens with a blank window. (You don't need to be connected to the Internet to preview a file that resides on your computer's hard disk. If the software you use to connect to the Internet presents you with a dialog box asking you to connect, just click on the Stop or Cancel button — unless you *want* to connect to the Internet, that is. In that case, click on Connect or OK.) Now, you just follow these steps:

1. **Select File⇨Open File if you are using Netscape Navigator; if you are using Internet Explorer, select File⇨Open.**

   The Open dialog box appears.

2. **Locate the file (`test.htm` or `test.html`), click on it once to select it, and then click on Open.**

   The File opens in your browser window. If you typed all the HTML correctly, your screen should look like Figure 5.1. (If it doesn't, check your word-processing document to make sure all the less than and greater than symbols are entered.) If you make a correction, select File⇨Save to save the changes in your word processor. Then return to your Web browser, and select View⇨Reload. This step reloads the page with the corrections you just made.

A neat way to preview HTML files in a Web browser is by dragging the HTML file's icon right on top of the icon for your Web browser. You can do this with either a Mac or Windows 95. Just click on an HTML document's icon, drag it atop the icon for your Web browser, and release your mouse button. The browser launches, and your HTML document is displayed in the browser window.

Deciding What You Want Your Page to Do

It's a thrill to put something online, especially something about yourself and your nearest and dearest. It's such a thrill, in fact, that you can easily lose sight of the reason you were making the page in the first place. The best way to begin creating a Web page is to take stock of what you want to achieve.

Setting a goal

Remember that the best Web pages really convey something worthwhile and interesting. Start by identifying the goal of your project. Be sure to think about why people might want to visit your page and read what you have to say. What do you most want people to know about you and your family?

Perhaps you can let people know how cool you all are. Tell them about the wild and crazy house you live in or the awesome scenery right outside your door. Maybe you want to keep in touch with distant relatives, or meet people online and find families in other countries that share your interests, or maybe you want to get credit for a homework assignment!

Each family is different, and each Web page is different, too. Some families celebrate their ethnic backgrounds. Some describe what's special about where they live. Even if it seems like your family members don't have anything in common, that's okay. In that case, your Web pages can be about a family full of people who are creative in all kinds of ways and who are a bunch of real individuals.

Even if fulfilling a homework assignment is your only reason for making a family Web site, your pages will still be more interesting and coherent if you can establish a theme, an activity, or an area of interest that will tie your Web pages together. And you'll get a better grade, too.

Making a good impression

To be a good communicator, you need to be aware of the *impression* you're making. So when you think you're ready to put something on the Web, take an extra moment to imagine that you're the viewer, the person looking at your page on his or her computer monitor.

Do you want your pages to be amusing? Do you want them to give the viewer something to think about? Do you want them to present various topics so that viewers with different interests can find something they are interested in, too — and maybe write back to you? Do you want viewers to be impressed by the sheer number of things you and your family do? Your pages will be more engaging and share more of your unique personality if you visualize beforehand the effect you want to create.

Don't just let your Web page sit there passively, waiting for visitors to talk back to you: Give them a way to send you their comments, suggestions, or thoughts about your page. Go to some pages where kids do this well. Ayal's Home Page (http://agdec1.technion.ac.il/ayal.html) includes a form visitors can fill out to send him feedback. Katie's Kewl Page (http://www.blinn.com/katie/), by 12-year-old Katie Blinn, includes a survey that visitors can complete. See Chapters 7 and 18 for more ideas on how to let your visitors "talk back."

Do just one thing at a time

Do you ever recall getting sick because you ate too much of too many different kinds of foods? When people navigate a Web site, it's like they're flipping through the pages of a book. And like good books, good Web pages give their viewers just a little at a time to digest. So you're better off covering one subject per page and then moving on to another subject on the next page. That way you might have a site with six short Web pages instead of a site with two or three very long ones. Why do this? Shorter documents are easier to read on a computer screen. You don't want to stuff too much on any one page. It makes your eyes — and your brain — hurt.

Good Web pages are short

Keep it short and sweet. Although the World Wide Web police aren't going to give you a ticket if you make a page too long, a good rule of thumb (or click of the finger) is that a Web page should be no more than $1^1/_2$ or, at most, two *computer screens* in length. That is, the reader shouldn't have to scroll down the page more than two or three times in order to reach the end of the page.

Note: There aren't any real "Web police," other than your parents and other authority figures. The company that hosts your Web page (see Chapter 6) might pull your page off the Internet if you put out obscure or unacceptable content, however.

Including Must-Have Web Page Elements

When you're all excited about beginning something new, it's hard to wait. I know you have a hilarious joke and totally cool graphic and just can't help plopping down that clever idea you had last night. But, please, try to hold on. You first need to consider some basic elements that are essential for every successful Web page (remember all those bullets I included at the beginning of the chapter). After you have the basics down, you can add the things that give your Web page personality — that would be *your* special personality. This section tells you what welcome pages can't do without.

Giving your page a title

If your family has ever worked (or struggled) together to figure out what to call your cute little puppy or kitty, you've had some practice in agreeing upon a name, which you can now put to good use in creating your Web page title. Every good Web page has a title displayed at the top of the browser window. You place the title between these two HTML tags: `<TITLE>` and `</TITLE>`, like this:

```
<TITLE>Clare's Star Wars Page</TITLE>
```

Titles should be short, and while it's good to be specific, don't stretch your title out too much, like this:

```
Greg's Stupendous and Amazing Tricks to Do with Chewing Gum
Wrappers Page
```

A title that long may not fit in the browser window. If the current page is just one of many family pages, you can emphasize that fact by using the name of the site consistently in the title, like this:

```
The Johnson Family: Kyle's Home Page
The Johnson Family: Our Photo Album
```

Did you ever yell, "Home, Spot!," out your back door and have your neighbor's Dalmatian show up? You definitely want to avoid that kind of thing with your Web pages. Try to find a title that is all yours and that describes exactly what's on the screen beneath it. Remember that your title may show up on a list of *search results* (see Chapter 1) on one of the search services like Infoseek or Excite. Someone may access one of your pages randomly without coming through the front door (that is, welcome page) of your family Web site. And any page may be included as a link on someone else's page. (Links were introduced in Chapter 1, so flip back there if you need some quick information; for more details on *linkology,* see Chapter 15.) So don't use vague titles like these:

```
<TITLE>Smorgasbord</TITLE>
<TITLE>My Cool Hobbies</TITLE>
<TITLE>All About Us</TITLE>
```

You are wise to always use a name in your title and to describe specific contents with a word or two — again, avoid a title that's too long. Consider these examples:

```
<TITLE>Mary's Short Stories</TITLE>
<TITLE>Janacek Family Genealogy</TITLE>
```

A well-designed title is important not only for your readers but also because the titles often show up in lists of links to other Web pages. (Kids often list links to Web sites that they especially like.) Other kids (and older visitors, such as yours truly) can click on the links and check out the pages for themselves.

Creating headings

Heads, titles, headings: It's hard to sort them all out. A Web page's headings are different than its titles. The title of a Web page appears in the browser's title bar; headings appear in the main content area.

You can find dull to really dull headings and good to really good headings. Of course, *you* want to make a really good one. A heading like "My Welcome Page" is a only label: It just sits there, static, and doesn't invite anyone to read farther down the page.

Headings help organize a Web page in much the same way that an outline helps you get a grip on an essay or book report. They list the topics you are going to cover in order of importance. That's why HTML contains headings organized in levels from 1 to 6. An H1 heading (for Heading 1) is the biggest and most important heading size, and it almost always goes at the top of a Web page. An H1 heading is followed (usually) by subheadings of lower levels: H2, H3, and so on. Heading 2 is supposed to name the most important topic, Heading 3 the next. Organize your topics in their order of importance, and you're sure to have a well-arranged welcome page. Do something like this:

```
<H1>Maryann's Trip to Outer Space</H1>
    <H2>My Host Family, the Skywalkers</H2>
        <H3>The Little Planet Where I Stayed</H3>
            <H4>Shopping with Princess Leia</H4>
                <H5>Luke's Crazy Friends, Han and Chewie</H5>
                    <H6>Han's Cool Spaceship</H6>
```

To really get ahead of the game, use subheads to avoid filling a Web page with type; they help break up the text and direct your readers' eyes to where you want them. Divide a page into two or three sections whenever possible, and start each section with an H2 or H3 head. Figure 5-2 shows how a few subheadings and an occasional list break up the chapter you're reading right now, making the contents look *virtually* exciting.

Coming up with the main contents

After you create a title and organize your topics, what do you say? Do some brainstorming and research. Get ideas from family members and other people. Ask them what they share (or would like to share) about themselves on their Web pages. What kinds of things do they like to do?

Figure 5-2:
On the left:
This
chapter
looks boring
(though it's
not) with
only a
single
heading at
the top. On
the right:
Add a few
subheadings
and the
page is
more
interesting
and easier
to read.

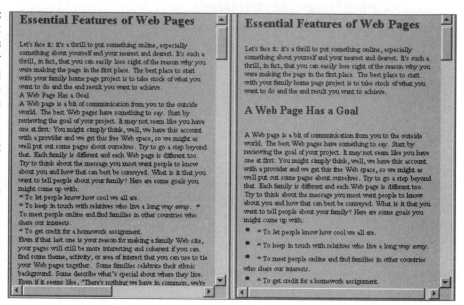

Whatever you do, don't panic and don't be taken in by the idea that your parents, brothers, sisters, or any of your other acquaintances are too boring. Just because they *seem* boring (often translates to: *"They don't do the same things I do"*), doesn't mean they *are* boring.

Ask your parents, for example, about the time before you were born. Believe it or not, they were once your age. Where were they born? What did *they* do when they were kids? What kinds of places did they travel to — or want to travel to?

If you keep your eyes and ears (and mind) open, you'll discover that everyone has a story to tell. In addition to what they do in everyday life, you'll find out about their feelings, thoughts, and imaginations. Take my word for it, sharing the hopes and dreams of those you live with will never be boring.

Focusing on your topic

Always start the opening page (the welcome page) of your Web site, or even an individual page, with a *topic sentence*. The first sentence on the page is the topic sentence. The rest of the paragraph serves as a sort of topic paragraph for the page. Your topic sentence and paragraph condense the entire contents of your site into just a few words. You may not find all this easy to do, especially if you're still working on a project and don't know how it's going to turn out. But the results are worth the effort: A short summary, such as the following one, at the beginning of a page lets people see in a flash what the page is about and, hopefully, interests the viewer enough to read on.

```
People always say my family is so crazy that we ought to
have our own TV show. Until one of the big networks becomes
interested in us, I thought I'd do the next best thing:
create a Web site so that I can tell everyone about the
people I live with. Inside you'll find pages about our
family history, our hobbies, some trips we've taken, and
links to our favorite Web sites. Welcome to our world!
```

That's a pretty generic summary, but you get the idea. Give it a try, and see if you can inject some of your goals, as well as a sense of what you want the reader to discover about your family.

Does all this talk about identifying goals, coming up with topic sentences, and writing great titles and headings sound familiar? These are the same kinds of skills you use when you're writing an essay or report as a school assignment. When you finish creating a terrific, well-organized Web page, you can do the same thing to get a great grade on your next homework assignment.

Some providers will let you run a business from your Web space (for example, America Online lets you do this from a site called MyPlace; see Chapter 6). However, providers are very grouchy when it comes to content that they consider offensive, obscene, or otherwise not nice. Some providers will give you 2MB or so of space to put up your own personal pages, but they'll change extra if you are running a for-profit business. It's not unusual for kids to start their own businesses preparing Web pages. After you get good at using HTML, you might consider this option yourself. Be sure you talk to a customer service representative and find out exactly what you can do — and how much it will cost.

Setting the table (of contents, that is)

When you're going on a trip to unfamiliar territory, you take along a road map, right? Well, a common element on the welcome page for many Web sites is a table of contents that serves the same purpose. It's a set of links to other parts of the site that reveals the contents to your readers and suggests in a glance what they might find and where they might find it. The Cross Family Home page (http://www.etsleeds.demon.co.uk/index.html) uses the table of contents as the welcome page to its Web site (see Figure 5-3).

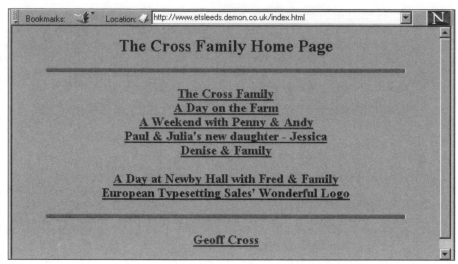

Figure 5-3:
A welcome
page
doesn't
need to be
flashy; your
page can
function as
a table of
contents,
such as
this one.

Another kind of table of contents is a set of links that leads people to specific spots elsewhere on the same page. This set of *internal links* is useful if your document is rather long and complicated, which, of course, I hope it isn't.

You may not be able to create a table of contents for your site until after you create all the pages. But when you're done, remember to go back to the original page and add the table of contents. If, for example, your Web page is broken into three sections that are marked by the subheadings "My Family," "Where I Live," and "My Hometown's History," you might have links at the top of the page that look like this:

My Family

Where I Live

My Hometown's History

Each link, when clicked, leads your visitor to the heading farther down the page. You can check out Web page template #1 in Chapter 8 and Figure 8-1 to see a Web page with a set of internal links.

Making your own logo

Before you could even talk, you probably started to wave your arms and jabber in your little car seat when your mom drove by McDonald's. Why? You knew that those big golden arches meant Happy Meals. All the big corporations use their logos on packages, advertisements, not to mention

Web sites. So why shouldn't your family have one, too? You aren't a business entity, but you are a group, and you are together. A logo would provide a way to tie you all together and give you a visual identity. Some families use their coat of arms to represent themselves online. Others draw an original logo. Besides the identity thing, a logo is a great way to anchor the top of a Web page and direct the reader's eye to the main heading, as shown in Figure 5-4.

Now's the time to do some research about your family history in the school library. Lots of family names are associated with coats of arms or other flourishes. If you come from another country, look up its flag; the flag might make a nice addition to your family welcome page.

Figure 5-4:
Use a logo that represents you or your family in a single image. You might use a coat of arms, as the Penzar family did on this page.

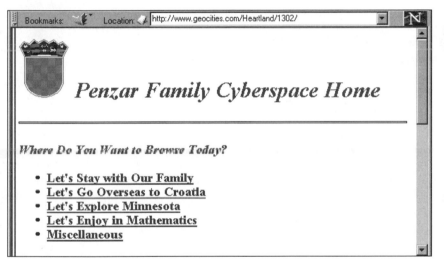

Keeping track with lists

Lists are useful for more than arranging a series of steps to follow or a bunch of things to buy at the grocery store. On a Web page, lists can serve some important visual and organizational purposes. Like subheadings, they break up the text and make a page much more readable.

HTML gives you three kinds of lists: a numbered list, a bulleted list, and a definition (or glossary) list. The one you're most likely to use is the bulleted list, which is a great all-purpose way to show a group of separate items without having to worry about the order in which they appear. Figure 5-5 shows how Hillside Elementary School used a bulleted list to present student projects by grade.

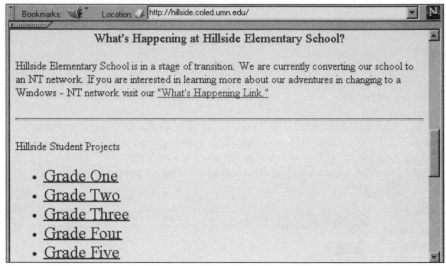

Figure 5-5:
A bulleted list organizes, calls attention to a series of items, and creates white space. What more could you ask for on a Web page?

Extending your Web with links

Anyone who surfs the Web at all has almost certainly clicked on a *link*. As I've mentioned, links — which you might see referred to as *hot links, hyperlinks,* or *clickable links* — connect a document to others that you've created or to other sites on the Web. The actual item your visitor sees on a Web page representing ½ a link is the text, phrase, or graphic that your visitor clicks on. The other part of the link is the part that your reader doesn't normally see — the URL that your visitor is taken to after clicking on the link.

Links allow you to weave your own web of information. When you begin to create your Web pages, you can make these kinds of links:

✔ A link to a word or phrase within a single document on your Web site

✔ A link to a word or phrase in another document on your Web site

✔ A link to another page on the Internet

✔ A link that automatically causes a software application to download on your computer (that is, copies the application across the Internet from the computer on which the program is stored to your computer's hard drive)

✔ A link to an external graphics file that may be too big or detailed to show in large format on your Web page (the graphic opens on its own Web page)

You may want to turn to Chapter 15 for a more in-depth discussion of links.

Opening your visitors' eyes with images

Why is the Web so cool? Images are one of the things (along with the hyperlinks you just read about) that make the World Wide Web special. The rest of the Internet, for the most part at least, isn't used to present colors or graphics, but to transfer messages, files, or documents from one place to another. The Web is a wonderfully visual place, and you may want to contribute to that richness as much as possible.

Inline graphics accompany your text

Most of the images associated with Web pages are *inline graphics;* that is, the images occur either above, below, or on the same line as the text on a given page. Sometimes an image can literally appear on the same line as a line of text. Usually, bigger images such as photos, appear on a line of their own.

External graphics reside on their own page

An *external graphic* is contained in a document of its own, and a reference is made to it in the original Web page. That reference can take the form of a hyperlink or *a thumbnail,* which is a very small version of an image. Clicking on the link or the thumbnail image causes the full-size image to open on its own Web page. Heather's Happy Holidaze Page (http://ww.shadeslanding.com/hms/), by 7-ycar-old Heather Shade, uses lots of thumbnails (see Figure 5-6).

Figure 5-6: Thumbnails like these let you give your visitors a preview of the full-size images they are linked to.

If you like the story of *Thumbelina,* you will love thumbnails. Thumbnails are a user-friendly feature of many Web pages. They provide the viewer with a version of an image that doesn't take long to appear on-screen. With a thumbnail, the viewer gets an idea of what the image contains and can then decide whether to click on the thumbnail and go to the actual image. Extra friendly thumbnails tell you the actual size of the image. A photo that is 30K or 40K can take a long time to appear on screen, so such an advance warning is a nice courtesy to offer your audience.

Wallpapering your page's backgrounds

Gray is a no-no. By default, the background of a Web page (that is, the area on which the images and words appear) is gray. These days, a Web page that uses a default gray background is a warning sign that the page's author is not very adept at design or, worse, that the Web page or perhaps the whole Web site is going to be boring. Blanket statements in this book are rare, but here comes one of them: A*lways* change the background color of your Web pages.

Here, as elsewhere, HTML authoring programs (see Appendix B) let you easily assign a color to a background, usually by letting you select a shade from a palette full of colors. Here are some general rules regarding backgrounds:

- ✔ Don't choose a background that makes your type unreadable (magenta type on a green background for example).
- ✔ If you choose a dark color for the page background, such as black, be sure to make the type light enough to be readable.
- ✔ When in doubt, choose white for a background. You'll seldom go wrong with it.

You can also use an image in the background of your page, but don't use anything so vivid that it distracts from the contents. Chapter 8 explains more about choosing colors and images for Web page backgrounds.

Ending your page with footer information

Keep looking down! Some of the most important information on a Web page occurs not at the top but at the bottom, in the *footer* section of the document. The footer is often set apart from the main body of a page with a horizontal rule. The following sections cover some of the things you can include in your own Web page footer.

Copyright notice

When you hear the word *copyright,* you may think of off-putting official documents, but this concept is not just for legal beagles. Current U.S. copyright law does not require you to put a copyright notice on your work in order to protect it: Anything you publish is automatically covered by copyright. Nevertheless, adding a copyright notice does give you an additional measure of protection, if only to show people that you care enough about the content of your Web pages to copyright it. A copyright notice usually takes this form:

```
Copyright 1997 [Your Name]. All rights reserved.
```

If you have created original art or software, you should add the copyright notice. Some Web site authors invite others to copy their graphics in exchange for sending the authors an e-mail or putting a link to the authors' pages on the borrowers' own sites. This course can be a good way to get more attention on the Internet.

Date of last update

The Web is a happening place, and most people think that, unlike cheese or bananas, a welcome page doesn't improve with age. In fact, an old Web site is called a "cobWeb site." If your site hasn't been updated for a long time, it can lose much of its credibility. Often, a "last updated" line is included in the footer of a Web site's welcome page, like this:

```
Web site last updated 1/30/97
```

On the other hand, family Web pages generally don't contain a lot of time-sensitive information and might do without a "last updated" date. It's up to you to decide whether you want to add such a date. If you *do* include a date, be sure you update your pages on a regular basis so the site doesn't seem out of it — even if it's not.

Return address

Don't forget to write! A link to an e-mail address is an essential part of most, if not all, Web pages. Links like these give the reader a chance to contact the *Webmaster* — the person who created or authored the site (Hey! That's *you!*), so they can get more information.

A return address also serves another purpose: It can give people the name of the organization or person to which a site belongs, in case someone gets access to the page directly without following a path to it from the main welcome page. Such an address might look like this:

```
Webmaster@Smith family Web site
```

Tips for Good Web Page Design

Now it's time to give those rules of good Web page design. Some of these were mentioned earlier: For example, keep Web pages short, try to accomplish only one thing on a given page, and break up text with rules, subheadings, and lists. The following sections offer some more things to consider.

Think small: Keep graphics files simple

Complex graphics files are a common problem on Web sites. So for graphics on the Web, less is more. Most users connect to the Internet from home using relatively slow modem connections. As a result, photos that require a lot of memory can take a long time to download and can contain more visual information than the average computer screen can display.

Here are some suggestions for how to keep image files small so your visitors can see them more quickly:

- ✔ Crop out backgrounds and other unimportant parts of images so that only the most important contents are included.
- ✔ Include only two or three photos on a given page.
- ✔ After you scan a photo, open the file in a graphics program like Paint Shop Pro or Photoshop. (See Chapter 10 for tips on scanning images.)
- ✔ Make sure the image resolution is 72 dpi (dots per inch), not 150 dpi. Most computer screens display only 72 dpi, so anything more detailed wastes disk space.

Keeping files small is important. If the photos in your family photo album take too long to appear, impatient viewers may turn the image display off and end up not seeing any of your great graphics anyway; worse, they may leave your site and go off to visit another one.

Provide a way back home

All pages on the Web are linked by hypertext. People using these links can enter a Web site through any number of "back doors" or "side doors," as opposed to the welcome page as the designer intended. In fact, any page that has links can be the first one that a visitor sees on your site, so *always* provide a trail of crumbs — in other words, a link — back to your welcome page so that people can go there and find out who you are and what your site is all about.

The best organized Web sites provide visitors with ways to jump from the page they are currently viewing to other important parts of the site. The sites do this by providing a series of buttons or links at the bottom of each page. These links or buttons lead to the welcome page or to other documents in the sequence. Here is a typical series of links:

Table of Contents   Previous   Back   Home

Keep a worldwide audience in mind

Remember: People from all over the world are browsing Web sites, including, perhaps, yours! One of the really exciting moments in your career as a home page author comes when you start to get feedback, particularly when that feedback comes as e-mail messages from people around the world and have been nice enough to visit *your* welcome page and *smart* enough to like it!

It's amazing to consider that your Web pages are available to everyone in the world who has a computer and a connection to the Internet. With that in mind, don't say, "I live in the Chicago area" or I live on a farm," and leave it at that. Tell people something about the town, state, or country where you live because Web addresses don't tell them where you come from. Monika Bough's father is an officer in the U.S. Navy and has been stationed at naval bases around the world. So Monika has lived on five different continents. Monika has a page (http://www.whidbey.net/~irvbough/live.htm) in which she writes about all the places she has lived. A 16-year-old boy named Daniel Warsaw tells everyone about his hometown of Christchurch, New Zealand, on his Daniel Warsaw on the Internet Web page at http://www.geocities.com/Heartland/1065/.

A Web page is a great way to make new friends from around the block or around the world. But there's a downside, too. Giving out too much personal information can attract attention from people on the Internet who aren't so nice. Be cautious and use common sense when you're talking about yourself and your family. Don't tell people any more than you really need to.

One kid's opinion

I live in Canada and don't travel all that much, but now because of the Web, I have friends all over the world. While at first, our shared interests might be our favorite movies or bands, we usually find that we have much more in common. I have learned a lot from my friends in places like Australia and England. I have even written to people who know hardly any English.

I usually put my e-mail address on Web pages only where I really want people to respond to me, like pages where I ask people to fill out a quiz. I do try to use the same things on my pages so they look like they all come from the same place. I've been trying to use the same background for each of the pages and a similar title at the top of each page. Then I put a link called "Go Back to the Main Page" right at the bottom of each page. I think people are more likely to click on a link to somewhere else on your site when they're at the bottom of the page.

Chapter 6

Putting Your Pages on the Web

• •

In This Chapter

▶ Checking for obstacles and breaks in your chain of pages

▶ Publishing new pages on GeoCities

▶ Publishing your pages on America Online

▶ Publishing your pages with an Internet Service Provider

• •

After you create your own Web pages, you're bound to be eager to get them online. The good news is that getting them out and into the world of cyberspace is really quite easy. You can be your own publisher in just a matter of minutes: Just check your work one last time and avoid certain little obstacles. This chapter explains how you can successfully move your pages from your computer to a place on the Web where they can be enjoyed by everyone.

Note: Before you begin this chapter, you may want to refer to Chapter 1, where you actually create a Web page, and Chapter 4, where you organize a group of pages into a Web site.

Get Those "Gotchas"

The prospect of getting your pages online is pretty exciting. Think about it: In only a matter of minutes, the world will be able to see a whole Web site devoted to *you,* your friends, your schoolmates, and all the things that are important to your "nearest and dearest." But please resist the temptation to shove your pages out the door before they're ready.

You want to fully create and double-check your pages on your computer before putting them online. It's a little like making sure your shoelaces are tied before you go shopping: You don't want to fall on your face in front of everyone. And believe me, it's better to find your own mistakes than to get e-mail from complete strangers who point out your boo-boos and gotchas.

How do you do all this? Open each of the Web pages you are planning to publish and look at them in a Web browser just as your visitors are going to do. If you're using a Mac, you can drag the icon for your Web page file right on top of the icon for your Web browser, and the file will open right away. Otherwise, you need to open the browser first. Then choose File⇨Open. Navigate to the name of the page you want to open, select the file, and then click on Open to view your page in the browser window. Then do the following:

- ✔ **Test your pages.** Be sure to read the words and catch any misspellings or any stray HTML instructions. Those often show up because you forgot to type the correct (<) or (>) symbol.

- ✔ **Test your links.** Click on each of your links, and make sure they take folks where they're supposed to.

- ✔ **Test your graphics:** Make sure your images appear on your pages where you want them to. Make your browser window narrower to ensure that photos or other images don't appear distorted.

- ✔ **Choose the best service provider:** If you haven't done it yet, now's the time to choose a good Web service provider.

If you've been working on your pages a lot, you may be staring right at some misspellings or other gotchas without even seeing them. Do you have a brother who loves to point out the spinach between your teeth or a friend you trust to tell you if your new haircut looks good or not? This is a good time to call on one of them for help. Ask them to carefully read your pages to make sure everything is okay. Make a game out of it and read the text backwards; this is an old proofreader's trick.

Fix those broken images

"Houston, we've got a problem," as the astronauts say. If an image on one of your pages doesn't work, you don't see flashing lights on the panel of your spacecraft (translate that to on the screen of your computer). Instead, in place of the image you want, you see an icon that's broken in two pieces (which means the link to the image doesn't work and the browser can't display the image) or the question mark icon shown in Figure 6-1.

Rejoin those broken links

Broken images are only one thing that can go wrong on a Web page. You may also come upon text that's highlighted as a clickable link, but upon clicking, you find that it doesn't take you where you want to go. These links can be links to other Web sites or to other pages on your Web site.

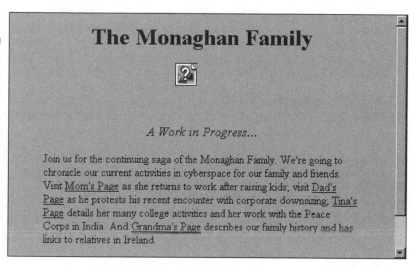

Figure 6-1:
A question
mark icon
such as this
one means
your Web
browser
can't locate
an image.
Better
check your
link and
revise it.

Click on all the links you added to your pages to make sure they refer to the right pages or Web sites. If you click on a link and see the error message shown in Figure 6-2, it means you have to remake that link.

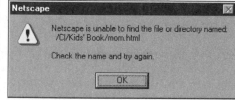

Figure 6-2:
Unless you
enter a link
just right,
you'll get an
error
message
like
this one.

If your link fails with flying colors, don't have a cow. Go back to your Web page editor and check the link for the document that contains the broken link (see the sections on "Absolute addresses" and "Relative addresses" in Chapter 15). Usually, the problem occurs when you forget to type a filename exactly right. Remember, if the file is `grandpa.html`, you can't type `grandpa.htm` or `grandp.html` and expect your link to work. Another classic mistake is using two dots instead of one (`grandpa..html`) or adding a blank space (`grandpa .html`). A Web page is pretty much like a robot in this respect: You have to type all the required characters in a filename just right, or it will let you down.

The software programs PageMill, World Wide Web Weaver, HomeSite, HotDog, Claris Home Page, and Web Workshop, all of which have versions included on the CD-ROM that comes with this book, let you preview your files before you send them to your ISP. When you use one of these programs and you see that all the images and links work correctly on your computer, chances are they'll work fine when your ISP posts them on a Web server.

When you are sure everything works, don't move your files from folder to folder like a fussy mom rearranging the furniture just before your birthday party guests arrive. Remember that all your pages are linked together. If you have an image on a document named `home.htm` and you make a link to it on another document, moving the image into another folder at the last minute will break the link. For example, if you make a link on your Web page to a file named `sofa.gif`, that link will not continue to work if you move the file `sofa.gif` from its present directory to another one. If you really want to move this file to a new directory, you must rewrite the HTML coding in the document that contains the link — you have to make the link reference the new location for `sofa.gif`. You find out more about making links in Chapter 15.

Getting Published

What, exactly, does *getting published* mean? In the world of books, magazines, and other printed stuff, it means you find someone who will distribute your work so others can enjoy it. In the wide, wide world of the Web, getting published means that you send your images and carefully prepared HTML files across the Internet via a computer called a Web server.

HTML, which stands for *HyperText Markup Language,* is the language, called *code,* that all word processors and text editors use. This code tells your browser just what to show on a computer screen. Every Web page that you create is actually an HTML file, plus the GIF and JPEG (graphics) files that you include in your page. You may want to check out Chapter 14 for information about HTML and Appendix B about Web authoring programs.

A *Web server* is like a friendly waiter who never goes off-duty. It's a computer that is connected to the Internet 24 hours a day and that can communicate with different kinds of Web browsers. The server's job is to store and maintain your Web files so that people around the world can see them anytime they want, day or night. Quite a task, isn't it? Actually, these tasks are carried out by someone called a Webmaster. A *Webmaster* is the person who makes sure that all the files on a Web server are up-to-date and the computer and the connection to the Internet are humming along without a hitch.

Posting your files on a Web server

When you pack up and label your files the right way, it's time to call in the *Internet moving van* — a software program that uses File Transfer Protocol (FTP) to transfer files from your computer to your Web server.

A protocol is a language that computers use to transfer information on the Internet. FTP is similar to HTTP (HyperText Transport Protocol, a communications language that lets you use your computer to transfer text, graphics, and other information displayed on Web pages), except that FTP enables you to transfer files from your computer to another computer (that is, a site on the Internet) and store them on the other site so that other people can go to that site and download the stored files.

You have several models of FTP *moving van* programs from which to choose, depending on the kind of service provider you select. In this chapter, you look at the following options for publishing your Web pages:

✔ **Free Web space services:** These services are those like GeoCities, which — at least for now — lets you publish Web pages for free. These services usually supply you with software that will move your Web pages from your computer to the Web server.

✔ **Internet Service Provider (ISP):** An ISP is a company that, for a fee, gives customers a way to connect to the Internet, send and receive e-mail, and publish Web pages. They give you access to the Internet, but, unlike some online services, ISPs leave it up to you to find your own discussion groups (also called newsgroups and news services) on the Internet. ISPs put some of the burden on you to find what you want. But, in return, you generally get a wider set of online information than you do with online services such as AOL and CompuServe. Some ISPs are nationwide companies such as Earthlink, Mindspan, and AT&T WorldNet Service, which is on the CD with this book. Others are local businesses with customers within a particular city or region.

✔ **Online services:** These are the well-known online businesses that come with America Online (AOL), CompuServe, Prodigy, and the Microsoft Network programs. You pay online companies a monthly fee and, in return, they give you a way to connect to the Web. The account usually comes with an e-mail address and space on a Web server, too, for the same rate. You can use the software they provide to create your pages and get them online. Many of these services give you lots of chat rooms, discussion forums, and news services, as well as access to the Internet. *Note:* The difference between commercial online services and ISPs is becoming less distinct.

Calling in the Internet moving van

Online services, ISPs and free space providers, including those like GeoCities, let you publish your pages using FTP. The difference is in where you get the FTP software that you need to do the transferring and how easy it is to use. An ISP doesn't provide such programs. An ISP requires that you download FTP programs from sites on the Web. In contrast, services like GeoCities and AOL enable, you to connect to their sites on the Web and use programs that reside on their sites' computers. The FTP programs these services provide are generally easier to use than the ones you download yourself from the Web. You read more about the kinds of FTP programs you use with an ISP later in this chapter.

Online services versus ISPs: Which is better?

All commercial online services (the main ones are AOL, CompuServe, and Prodigy, sometimes called the *Big Three*) started out by offering only the content and activities provided on their particular site. For example, if you used AOL and wanted to get news reports or join a chat room, you were limited to AOL for these services.

However, these online services became more flexible as the Web became more popular and as people began switching to ISPs — because although ISPs didn't (and still don't) provide flashy content or nice user interfaces, they did charge flat monthly fees for access to the Internet, and they let their customers use powerful Web browsers such as Netscape Navigator and Microsoft Internet Explorer.

Today, all the online services offer their customers access to the Web, as well as space where their customers can publish their own home pages. The *Big Three* have their pros and cons. Here are some:

✔ **Pro — Extra help:** Online services give you plenty of tutorials, online support, and software to help you create and publish your pages.

✔ **Pro — Free publishing:** You don't have to spend extra money to publish your Web pages.

✔ **Pro — Ready-made content:** Because of the online services' GUIs (graphical user interfaces), you don't have to search very far to find things you're interested in. (You can check out AOL's GUI in the figure in this sidebar.) Online services have plenty of other ready-made content, for example, news services, discussion forums, and chat rooms.

✔ **Con — Connectivity:** An ISP typically gives you a wider range of local phone numbers you can call over your modem to connect to the Internet. So you get fewer busy signals than you do with, say, "America Almost-Always-Online."

✔ **Con — Lack of flexibility:** Online services sometimes require you to use software that you might not choose because it doesn't meet your needs or is difficult to use. With ISPs, you select the software yourself and you can usually do a lot more with the Web pages you publish on an ISP's server.

✔ **Con — Popularity:** AOL is so popular that many of its customers are finding it difficult to connect at certain times during the day or week.

✔ **Con — Reliability and technical support:** Unlike ISPs, online services aren't quick to fix equipment or provide tech support, and they don't have backup systems in place in case of trouble with the network. ISPs often have people on call providing tech support seven days a week, day or night.

The bottom line is this: If you're happy with your online service and know how to use its resources, there's no reason to move to another service. Each one of the online services has its own way of letting its customers create Web pages and publish them on a Web server. If you get really serious about maintaining a Web site and maybe even start a business, you're better off switching from one of the online services to an ISP.

If you want to sign on with an online service just to post Web pages and occasionally send and receive e-mail, you don't need to pay a flat monthly fee for unlimited access. You might save a few bucks by opting for an hourly fee — typically, you get five free hours of connection time each month and pay a few dollars for every hour thereafter. But this won't be an advantage, if you have a son or daughter who's likely to be connected for many hours each day.

Windows users will find a program called WS_FTP on this book's CD. You might start by calling your provider's customer service representative or reading any online documentation that explains how to get space on a Web server. Usually, the process works like this: You are assigned a username and a password (generally, the same username and password you enter when you connect to the Internet), so only *you* have access to your files on the server. Your provider will tell you whether you need to name your files a certain way (whether your Web page documents should end in .htm or .html, for example).

Each of the services described in this chapter provides software that you can use to create your Web pages. These services also give you other software programs that act as moving vans.

Publishing with GeoCities

In Chapter 1, you find out how to get a simple Web page on GeoCities' free Web page service by using its Web page creation software. Now you find out how to publish a whole suite of files on your *homestead* (the place where your Web page files reside) in your GeoCities *neighborhood* (an area set aside for Web publishers with similar interests). You accomplish this task by using GeoCities software packages that enable you to publish files on the Web and organize them after they are online.

GeoCities isn't the only free Web page service around. If you use Web Workshop to create a page (as described later in this chapter), you can send your pages to the VividPost Web site run by the company that makes Web Workshop, Vividus Corporation (http://www.vividpost.com/). You can access this service only if you use Web Workshop to create a Web page and click on Web Workshop's Publish button. Web Workshop connects you to the VividPost Web site and provides you with instructions about how to publish your Web page.

If you are concerned about mounting phone bills brought about by family members calling into the Internet several times a day to work on their Web pages or to check e-mail, ask your telephone company if there's a way to reduce the charges. Ameritech, for example, has instituted "Call Packs" that allow you to pay a set fee for phone calls. Currently I pay $10 a month for 200 local phone calls: That's five cents per call, and it doesn't matter how long I am connected. I pay five cents whether I am connected five minutes or five hours. Ask your telephone company if it has a similar arrangement.

Using the GeoCities File Manager

After you create one or more Web pages and publish them on GeoCities, you can add more pages or revise your existing work by using the GeoCities File Manager. You can get to the File Manager directly by pointing your Web browser to the URL http://www.GeoCities.com/homestead/ file_manager.html.

Note: See Chapter 1 for a detailed description of how to create a Web page and publish it on GeoCities.

Scroll down the page and enter your GeoCities member name and password. (Don't worry about the checkboxes that ask you about showing files with extensions like .gif, .jpg, and .html. Leave them all checked for now.) Then click on Submit. The File Manager page appears with your GeoCities member name and the URL for the Web page you created and published on GeoCities at the top of the page.

Now that you have connected to the GeoCities File Manager page, you can take new Web pages and publish them — that is, you can use the File Manager page to move them from your computer to the GeoCities site. To do this, scroll down the File Manager page to the section labeled EZ File Upload. The options in this part of that page are described in the following section.

Move 'em out with EZ File Upload

EZ File Upload is GeoCities' version of the Web file moving van that I referred to earlier in this chapter. Its job is not to create Web pages (files) but to move the pages to the directory or folder that has been set up on your Web server. You pack 'em up, label 'em correctly, and EZ File Upload moves 'em out.

Note: The word *upload* is computer-speak. It's the opposite of *download,* which, of course, is copying files from a Web server to your own computer. Instead of downloading a file or a computer program from a Web site to your computer, you upload a file from your computer to a location on the Web, in this case to your Web service provider's site.

Your Web browser should be displaying the EZ File Upload section of the GeoCities File Manager page. *Note:* The first checkbox in the EZ File Upload section offers some help in changing your Web page filenames to lowercase. The case of the filenames is important for some kinds of Web servers, particularly those that use the UNIX operating system. If you think you may have made such a mistake in linking one page to another or in inserting an image on a page, click on the box next to Automatically convert filenames to lowercase (see Figure 6-3). Otherwise, leave it unchecked. Because you've already checked your pages, this isn't a problem . . . right?

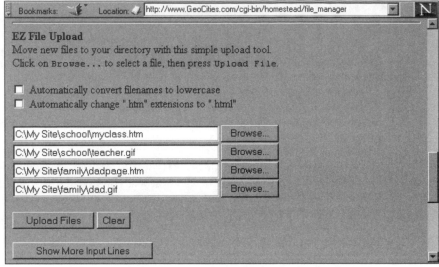

Figure 6-3:
Check the
names of
your Web
site files,
enter the
filenames
here, and
EZ File
Upload
moves 'em
to your
space on
one of
GeoCities'
neighbor-
hoods.

The following steps explain how to use EZ File Upload to do some uploading to your spot on GeoCities:

1. **If your Web page documents end with** `.html`, **check the box next to Automatically change "**`.htm`**" extensions to "**`.html`**."**

   GeoCities' Web server apparently recognizes only Web page files that end in `.html`, so it helps users by automatically changing the filenames to the form it prefers.

2. **If you have several files to upload, click on the Show More Input Lines button.**

   Keep in mind that *every* object and file, including image files, sound files, and Web pages must be uploaded separately. Image filenames end in `.gif`, `.jpg`, or `.jpeg`. I suggest that you keep track of what you've uploaded by including a text box for each file.

3. **If you know the *exact* names of your files, enter the filenames in the text boxes (beside the Browse buttons).**

   Remember, though, that you must type everything just right My advice is to click on the Browse button to access your hard drive and locate the file you want. Then double-click on the filename to enter it in a text box.

4. **When your files are entered, click on Upload Files.**

   After a few seconds, the File Manager screen reloads in your Web browser and reports what was uploaded.

5. **Select File⇨Open Location, enter the URL for your Web site, and click on Open to see your page on the Web.**

   Congratulations on a successful move!

Free Web sites are great, but remember that you're a homesteader; that is, you're occupying Web space for free, with no guarantee that this service will be free forever. So at some point, you may want to move your files to another location on the Web. The rest of this chapter examines your publishing options with a commercial online service and ISPs.

Publishing with America Online

AOL is a pretty good service to use for creating and publishing your Web pages. Like GeoCities, AOL provides its members with a tool called My Home Page (not available to Mac users) for creating simple home pages . AOL also gives members free Web server space where you can post Web pages that you created with a program other than My Home Page. These pages can be for business or personal use. AOL also provides its members with Frequently Asked Questions and step-by-step tutorials that lead you through the process of creating and publishing Web pages (something GeoCities doesn't provide).

Here are some important resources that AOL provides for Web publishers:

- ✔ **My Home Page:** My Home Page is an easy-to-use tool that lets you create simple Web pages and post them on one of AOL's Web servers. AOL gives you the option of choosing who will actually see the information you enter using My Home Page: only you, only other AOL members, or anyone on the Web.

- ✔ **My Place:** If you have an account with AOL, you can prepare your Web files using a Web page authoring program like World Wide Web Weaver (which is available for the Mac) or HomeSite (for Windows users) and upload them to a directory (which will have the same name as your *screen name*) that AOL sets aside for your Web pages: Each AOL screen name has a directory with 2MB of free space on which you can post your documents.

- ✔ **EZScan:** If you don't have access to a scanner and want to put photos on your Web page, AOL will do it for you for a fee of $2.50 per photo (at least, that was the rate when this book was written).

AOL provides 2MB of Web server space for each member based on his or her screen name. Two megabytes is a lot of disk space and should be enough to hold at least a dozen or more Web pages and their associated graphics. However, if you need more space, you can create up to four additional screen names for yourself, publish 2MB of Web files for each screen name, and then link the pages together. (Just don't tell AOL I told you to do this!)

World Wide Web Weaver, HomeSite, and other programs such as PageMill, Claris Home Page, and HotDog are included on the CD that accompanies this book. Some of these programs are tryout versions that you can use for a limited period of time or have some features disabled. Others are fully functioning versions. See Appendix D for more details.

AOL has an easy Web page publishing program called Personal Publisher that's a rough equivalent of the GeoCities Basic Home Page Editor. You must use Personal Publisher to get your files on AOL; you can't use any other kind of "moving van" software. AOL, as I mentioned, also gives you Frequently Asked Questions, tutorials, and lots of other helpful support along with the Web page creation tool.

Using My Home Page

To get into My Home Page, follow these steps:

1. **Sign onto AOL by double-clicking on the icon for AOL's software, entering your password, and clicking on Sign On.**

   When you are connected, the AOL welcome page window appears.

2. **Press Ctrl+K (for Keyword).**

   The Keyword dialog box appears.

3. **Type** Personal Publisher, **and click on Go.**

   AOL may have you download some Personal Publisher software at this point, which takes a minute or so. The Personal Publisher welcome page appears.

4. **Scroll through the list of options, and double-click on the option To Access Personal Publisher.**

   The Personal Publisher page appears (see Figure 6-4).

5. **Click on the button Create/Edit My Home Page.**

   A screen entitled (surprise, surprise!) Create/Edit My Home Page appears.

6. **Scroll to the bottom of the Create/Edit My Home Page screen, and click on Create.**

Figure 6-4:
Follow along with the characters Roger and Byte, who will help you create a Web page on AOL.

Entering your personal information

With My Home Page, Windows users can quickly create a page that appears only to other AOL members or to everyone on the Web. You can format this page with headings and graphics as you do any Web page, but there's a catch. AOL requires you to include some private information — for example, your birth date (you kids may not be bothered about this, but some of you parents may), your AOL screen name, and other member information, all of which can look really ugly when it's attached to the rest of My Home Page. If you want to avoid this member section, you can always create your page with another Web page editor (which I cover later in this chapter) and then upload it to AOL (see "Uploading to My Place").

Consider keeping an eye on your kids as they fill out the personal information on My Home Page. In case you're squeamish about having them provide a potentially wide audience of strangers with their age, sex, and other details, you can tell them to leave some spaces blank.

If you get to Create/Edit My Home Page and see the member information for one of your parents, don't alter the information. You want to be creating your own new My Home Page, not editing someone else's. Instead, get your own screen name, *free* of charge. That way, you can have your own My Home Page, password, and e-mail address, too. And it's this easy to do:

Begin filling out the fields under the heading Enter Information About Me.

Anything you enter automatically updates your Profile in your AOL Member Directory. You don't have to fill out all of these fields. The fields you fill out include the following:

✔ **Screen name:** Your AOL screen name.

This name is the name that AOL will use to direct mail to your account. Your screen name is part of your AOL e-mail address, which has the form screenname@aol.com.

✔ **Member name:** This is the name you want visitors to know, as opposed to your AOL screen name. You can't be as creative here as with your screen name. You can use your real name or an alias; be sure to choose a name that's easy for you and your visitors to remember.

- **Location:** Where you live.

- **Birth date:** Yup, you get to tell the world how old you are.

- **Sex:** Male or female, that is (which you can leave blank, if you wish).

- **Marital status:** Why do you want to tell strangers about this? Beats me. Leave it blank.

- **Computers:** What kind of computer you use.

- **Hobbies:** People might actually use this field to contact you or look at your pages, so enter something interesting here.

- **Occupation:** When in doubt, enter **Webmaster**.

- **Quote:** A snappy phrase you like or that you just made up.

- **Searchable by:** This lets you specify who can see your home page — AOL users and Internet users, AOL members only, or only you.

Designating that only you will be able to see your home page gives you the chance to review and correct the information. When you're ready, you can change this option to give only AOL members or all Internet users access to your information.

Creating your home page

After you go through these fields, you actually begin to create your home page, as follows:

1. **Click on the Add button at the bottom of the screen.**

   The heading at the top of the Create/Edit My Home Page window changes from Information about me to Adding to Home Page for [your AOL member name]. In this window, you can add text and graphics to your home page.

2. **Scroll down to the Add Text area of the Adding to Home Page window, and type the text you want to enter, or copy it from a word-processing file and paste it in this area.**

3. **To add a link, scroll a little farther down the same page to the Add Link area.**

   See Chapter 15 for more about links and how they work.

4. **To select the kind of link you want to add, click on the arrow next to the box labeled Select the type of link you want to add (a Web URL, an Inline Image URL, or an AOL keyword).**

   An inline image URL is a link to a graphics file, such as `photo.gif`. An AOL keyword is the name of a keyword leading to another location on AOL.

5. **Enter the URL or keyword in the text box labeled Type in Web URL or AOL keyword in box.**

6. **Type a description in the text box labeled Type in a description about this place.**

   You can help your readers by including information about why you provide a link to a particular location and why they might like to visit this location.

7. **Click on Save Changes.**

8. **Click on Edit to make changes to information you entered, click on Add to continue adding to your home page, or on Save Changes if you're done.**

   When you click on Save Changes, your home page is saved. AOL then tells you your home page address, which is pretty easy to remember, for example:

   ```
   http://members.aol.com/<screen name>
   ```

If you want to add some images to your page, close the Personal Publisher window by clicking in the *X* in the upper-right corner of the page. Click on the button Home Page Graphics to go to the Home Page Graphics window. There you can find some clip art to add to your page, as well as an intriguing service called PicturePlace that allows you to send up to two photos, slides, or drawings to AOL to be scanned for free. You can then add the scanned files to your Web pages. AOL provides the exact steps you need to follow to download the clip art or send your images to PicturePlace.

Using My Place

Whether you use Personal Publisher or another Web page tool to create your Web pages, you move your pages to your Web site on AOL by using software called My Place. In fact when moving pages to AOL, you *must* use this software, which is provided for free by AOL, to upload your files; you can't use other programs. You don't have to copy the software to your computer; you connect to AOL and then use it. Here's how to do it:

1. **Write the *exact* names of the files you are going to upload on a piece of paper.**

   This step is very important and will come in handy when you get to Step 8.

2. **Connect to AOL as described in Step 1 in the section "Using My Home Page."**

3. **Select <u>G</u>o To⇨Keyword.**

   The Keyword dialog box appears.

4. **Enter the keywords** My Place.

5. **Click on Go.**

   The My Place window opens.

6. **Click on the icon with the caption Go to My Place.**

   A window with a techie-looking title (`members.aol.com/[your AOL screen name`)opens. This is the name of the directory in which your Web page documents will reside after you transfer them. This window contains a list showing the contents of your directory (see an example in Figure 6-5).

Figure 6-5:
It's not very pretty, but this set of directories is soon to be home sweet home for your Web page files on one of AOL's Web servers.

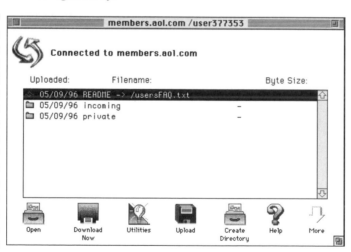

7. **Click on the Upload icon at the bottom of the dialog box.**

   A dialog box entitled `members.aol.com` appears containing a single large text box labeled Remote filename in which you enter the name of the file you want to send to the server.

8. **Enter the *exact* name of the file you want to send to the server.**

   If you are uploading a text file (which ends in `.html` or `.htm`), make sure you click on the ASCII (text documents) button. If you are uploading an image file (which may end in .gif or .jpeg, for example), make sure you click on the Binary (programs and graphics) button.

9. **Click on Continue.**

The Upload File dialog box appears.

10. **Click on Select file.**

A standard Windows file selection dialog box entitled Attach File appears. This dialog box lists the contents of your hard drive. The directories in your hard drive are in the right half of the dialog box. The files contained in a selected directory appear in the left half of the dialog box.

11. **To navigate to the file you want to upload, select a disk drive letter and a directory name in the right half of the Attach file dialog box, and then click on the filename in the left half of the Attach File dialog box to select the file.**

You're looking for the filename that you just entered. The filename is still visible in the members.aol.com dialog box mentioned in Step 7. To see the filename more easily, click on the title bar of the Attach File dialog box, and drag it to the side of your screen.

12. **Click on OK.**

The Attach File dialog box closes. The Upload File dialog box now contains the name of the file you just selected, in the text box labeled File (see Figure 6-6).

Figure 6-6:
After you enter the name of a file you want to publish on My Place, you must select it on your hard disk in this dialog box.

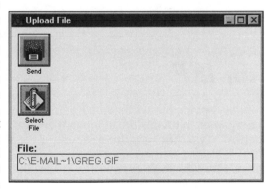

13. **Click on the Send button in the Upload File dialog box.**

    This step uploads the file to AOL. When the transfer is complete, a dialog box appears informing you of that fact. If you have sound turned on, a voice says, "File's done!"

14. **Click on OK.**

    You return to the `members.aol.com/[your AOL screen name]` dialog box mentioned in Step 6 showing the file you just added to your directory on AOL's Web server.

    If you want to upload another file, click on the Upload icon again, and repeat Steps 8 through 14. You have to upload each file one at a time.

15. **After you upload all of your files, close the `members.aol.com/[your AOL screen name]` dialog box by clicking on the Close box in the upper-right corner of the dialog box.**

    You return to the My Place window.

16. **Close the My Place window by clicking on the Close box in the upper-right corner.**

    You return to the main AOL screen.

17. **Click on Internet Connection to open AOL's Internet Connection window.**

18. **Click on World Wide Web to launch AOL's Web browser.**

19. **Enter the URL for your Web site in the browser window, and go to your site so that you can check to see if all the files appear the way you want.**

Voilà! You've uploaded, and you're on AOL. Congratulations!

Publishing with an ISP

An ISP is much like an online service but with some notable differences. So before continuing, you may want to review the sidebar "Online services versus ISPs: Which is better?" Two other big differences are the following:

> ✔ **Limited content provided:** You don't get all the content that an online service provides, such as the service's bulletin boards, forums, clubs, and so on. So although you have the whole Internet at your disposal, you have to surf around on your own and find the groups and sites that get your juices flowing.

> ✔ **No GUI provided:** In other words, an ISP doesn't have a graphical user interface that makes it easy to find things. An ISP's main purpose is to give you an Internet connection. The Web browser you choose is your GUI gateway to the Web.

Plenty of lists on the Web can help you find Internet providers in your area. Of course, you must already be on the Internet in order to read those lists, but you might be able to find a list at school or at your local library. One list called (guess what?) The List, which presents the names of providers sorted by area code or region of the country, is at `http://thelist.com/`. Another list, POCIA (Providers of Commercial Internet Access), is at `http://www.celestin.com/pocia/index.html`. Remember, too, you can get connected via AT&T WorldNet Service, which is on the CD-ROM that comes with this book.

Creating a Web page with an ISP

When it comes to creating your Web page, if you or your parents have an account with an ISP, you can use any Web page authoring tool you want. That's a nice way of saying that it's up to you to install and locate a tool to work with. You can find a list of Web page authoring tools in Appendix B, and several different sample/demo versions of easy-to-use programs are on the CD that comes with this book. You will use Web Workshop in this section.

Getting started with Web Workshop

Web Workshop, by Vividus Corporation, is tailored especially to young Web page authors. After you install the program from the CD, double-click on the Web Workshop icon to start up the program. (See Appendix D for information about installing and starting up the program.) You see a *splash screen* (an initial screen that appears only a few seconds) reminding you that this program is only a 30-day trial version. Click on Start to open a blank Untitled Page so you can begin working.

Note: The graphics in this example (see Figure 6-7) were taken on a Macintosh, but Web Workshop is available for Windows 95 users, too.

You should now have Web Workshop's window open on your screen. The title bar at the top of the window says Trial:Untitled Page because you haven't started working. Notice that when you click on any of the items in the purple boxes on the left side of your screen, the options at the top of the Untitled Page change in order to give you more ways to add graphics, work with links, and open pages.

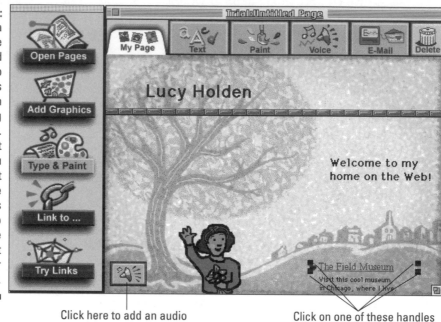

Figure 6-7:
Here's a page created with Web Workshop's built-in drawing software. Refer to it as you check out how to use this software to create colorful art for your Web pages.

Click here to add an audio greeting to your page

Click on one of these handles to resize a text block

1. **Click on the button Open Pages, which is one of the five icons at the left of the Untitled Page.**

   Four tabs run across the top of the window. My Page is where you create your Web page.

2. **Click on Samples.**

   You see a stamp-sized version of a completed Web page. Click on the miniature Web page; it fills the screen enabling you to see it better.

To create a new page, do the following:

1. **After you check out the sample completed Web page to get an idea of what you can do with Web Workshop, start creating your own page by clicking on the New Page button.**

   A blank Untitled Page appears. Don't let the empty space frighten you!

2. **Click on the Type & Paint button.**

   A new set of buttons appears at the top of the window. These buttons (Text, Paint, Voice, and E-Mail) let you add text and images to your page.

3. **Click on the Text button.**

   The text button turns a darker color to indicate that it has been selected.

4. **Move your mouse into the blank part of the window, and click anywhere near the top of the window.**

   A text box appears with a text cursor (a short vertical line) blinking within the box.

5. **Type a title for your home page.**

   The Text menu option (which only appears when you click on the Text button) contains choices for selecting particular fonts and changing font size and styles (for example, from normal to bold or italics).

6. **Click anywhere on the blank page to delete the text box.**

7. **Click on the text you typed in Step 5, and handles appear around the words you typed.**

   You can use these handles to drag the text around the window and place it anywhere you want. If you click on one of the handles, press on your mouse button, and drag, you can resize the text box so that it's narrower or wider. Try it!

To add some *eye candy,* you do the following:

1. **Viewing your Untitled Page, which contains the title text you just typed, click on the Add Graphics button.**

   A new set of options appears at the top of the window: three tabs called Backgrounds, Dividers, and Pictures. Clicking on Backgrounds presents you with some nice background designs that you can use on your page; Dividers lets you select a line that runs horizontally across the screen; Pictures gives you some simple clip art that you can add.

2. **Click on Backgrounds.**

   The Backgrounds page jumps to the front of the Web Workshop window. It has 15 small rectangles, each containing a different background pattern.

3. **Select a background pattern by clicking on its small rectangle.**

   If you don't like the one you selected, click on Background again and select a different one.

4. **Click on Dividers if you want to add a line under your page title.**

   The Dividers page jumps to the front of the Web Workshop window with ten small rectangles, each containing a different divider. You don't have to add a divider if you don't want to.

5. **Click on Pictures to select a drawing for your page.**

   The Pictures page jumps to the front of the Web Workshop window containing lots of small rectangles, with a different image for each one. When you click on one of these images, a little "stamp pad" tool appears on your window; click where you'd like the image to go. (You can click on the image later and move it somewhere else.) Part of the fun of Web Workshop is that you can construct your own drawing and make text and pictures go wherever you want.

Linking your page to other Web sites

If you want to make a link, do the following:

1. **Click on the Link to button on the left side of the Web Workshop window.**

   Four new tabs appear at the top of the Web Workshop window (called My Project, Yahooligans!, Cool Sites, and Kids Clubs).

2. **Click on the three rightmost tabs, one after another.**

   Each time you click on a tab, its page jumps to the front of the Web Workshop window. Each page contains a series of rectangles. Each of these rectangles represents a link to a site on the Internet.

3. **If you see a link you want to include on your page, click anywhere in the rectangle that contains the link.**

   When you click on a link's rectangle, two things happen: Your mouse arrow turns into a little stamp pad icon, and your Web page-in-progress jumps to the Web Workshop window.

4. **Click anywhere within your page's window to add the link to your page.**

Do you have a microphone installed on your computer? If so, do the following to make your page *speak:*

1. **Click on the Type & Paint button on the left side of the Web Workshop window.**

   Four buttons (Text, Paint, Voice, and E-Mail) appear at the top of the Web Workshop window.

2. **Click on the Voice button.**

   A dialog box appears enabling you record a two-second audio message that will be "attached" to your page. Give it a try:

   1. **Click on the Record button, and start talking.**

   2. **When you finish talking, click on Stop.**

   3. **To hear your message, click on Play.**

   4. **If you're happy with the message, click on Save. If you're not happy, click on Record to record another message.**

> 5. **Then click somewhere on your Web page to add the sound icon visitors can click on to hear your message (refer to Figure 6-7).**

3. **When you're done, select Publish from the Web Workshop File menu.**

   A dialog box appears asking you to name your file (see Chapter 5 for information about naming files).

4. **If this is to be your home page, name the file** index, **and click on Save.**

   Web Workshop stores your files in a folder called Trial until you're ready to put them on the Web. Web Workshop gives you the option of publishing your files for free on the VividPost Web site. If you want to do this, you just need to get an account name and password with VividPost. To find out how to do this, you can go to Vividus Corporation's online Web Workshop Manual (http://www.vividus.com/help/manual/toc.htm). Scroll down the table of contents page and click on the link under Chapter 4 labeled Publishing on VividPost. You'll be taken to a page that contains detailed instructions on how to publish your page.

5. **To send your files to your existing ISP, click on Cancel.**

Uploading your files with ISPs

To get your page on the Web where everyone can see it, you must have a way to move the page and all graphics on that page from your computer to a Web server. The Web space services discussed earlier in this chapter, GeoCities and AOL, provide you with a way of moving your files to their Web servers. As you may recall, you don't have to download a special program to move the files; you use programs that are contained on GeoCities' and AOL's computers. The GeoCities program is EZ File Upload, and the AOL program is My Place. (Because these services transfer files via FTP, even though they don't really use the term FTP — they're trying to be user-friendly — you may want to refer to the earlier sections in this chapter about FTP, EZ File Upload and My Place.)

As noted earlier, if you sign up for an account with an ISP that is not one of the commercial online services like AOL, you gain a lot of freedom and flexibility. You can use whatever software you want to browse the Web and send or receive e-mail, for example. If you want to publish your Web pages on your ISP's Web server, you need to find a program that transfers the files using FTP. Sometimes your ISP will provide the software. Otherwise, you can download a program yourself from the Web. FTP is a relatively easy way to move files from one computer to another. Although using an FTP program may be new to you, it's pretty easy to do (see the sidebar " Transferring files with FTP").

Macintosh users can use a program called Fetch and will have no problem finding it. It's a very popular program and is available on a shareware basis (you can try the program out for free, but must pay a $25 fee to keep it) at many sites on the Internet that offer Macintosh software. Fetch was developed at Dartmouth University. You can download it by opening your Web browser, selecting File⇨Open or File⇨Open Location, and entering the address `ftp://ftp.dartmouth.edu/pub/mac/`. You'll see a long list of files. The name of each file is underlined. Click on any one of the files that begins with the word "Fetch." The program automatically downloads to your computer as soon as you click on the filename. Fetch, like virtually all software programs that you download from sites on the Internet, is made available in a compressed format so the computer file takes up less room and downloads more quickly. In order to open Fetch and begin working with the program, you need an application called StuffIt Expander which decompresses the application. (See Chapter 9 for more on working with compressed files that you download from the Internet.)

Transferring files with FTP

After you install Fetch or WS_FTP on your computer, you can use the program to easily transfer files to a Web server. The key thing is to get the following information: your username, your password, the hostname of your Web server, and the name of your directory on that server. The first two items are easy: You choose a username and password when you first sign up for an account. The server hostname and directory name may be contained in the READ ME files that come with the software your ISP gave you when you first signed up. The easiest thing may be to call your ISP and ask its support personnel for instructions.

The address of your Web server may look like this: `homepage.interaccess.com`. (Even though a Web server is connected to the Web, it doesn't have to begin with the characters `www`.) Many directory names begin with a character called a tilde (~) followed by your username, like this: `~gholden`.

After you have this information, here's how to connect to your server and upload your files.

Note: The following steps are specifically written to work with Fetch, but they apply to other FTP programs as well.

1. **Connect to the Internet.**

2. **Start your FTP program.**

   A connection dialog box appears (in Fetch, this dialog box is called New Connection).

3. **Enter the hostname.**

   In Fetch, you enter this in the Host text box. This is the hostname of the Web server that will hold your Web pages. Often, hostnames begin with `ftp`, as in `ftp.mysite.com`.

4. **Enter your user name.**

   In Fetch, you enter this name in the User ID text box.

5. **Enter your password.**

   This word goes in the Password text box.

6. **Enter the directory into which you want to transfer your files.**

   You can also go to the correct directory after you connect, but the process works more quickly if you enter the directory name up front.

7. **After you are connected, click on one of the three options for the files you want to transfer.**

   If you are transferring HTML text documents, select Text. For graphics and multimedia files, select Binary (see the figure in this sidebar). If you are sending a combination of both types, select Automatic, and the server will try to figure out which is which. ***Note:*** Your files will transfer more reliably if you transfer your files one at a time, however.

8. **Click on Put File to start the process of transferring your file.**

   Other FTP programs may call this something else (Send, for example).

9. **In the dialog box that appears, locate the file you want to send by finding its directory on your hard disk, and single-click on the name of the file you want to transfer.**

10. **Click on OK.**

    The file is transferred. You see a cute little dog icon running in place as your file is sent on its way.

11. **Repeat Steps 7 through 10 for each file you want to transfer.**

12. **When you're done, select Quit from the File menu to quit using Fetch.**

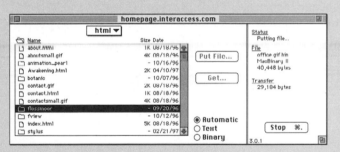

After you have put your files online, don't forget to test your pages to make sure all the links work and all your graphics show up correctly, as mentioned in Chapter 5. Tell your friends, and pat yourself on the back: You're a Web publisher. But this is by no means the end of your publishing experience; the fact is, it's probably just the beginning. Chances are that before long you'll be revising your Web pages and transferring more graphics and HTML files from your computer to your Web server. That's what Web publishing is all about: You can make corrections and improve your work at any time to reflect your new interests, new activities, and your growing expertise. Look at your Web page publishing efforts as work in progress: Get feedback from your family and friends, and keep on growing!

One kid's opinion

I made my first Web page about a year ago, when I was 13. I started creating Web pages because my friends had their own pages, and I wanted to have one, too. Most of my friends learn how to put things on their pages by looking around the Web for a while. If they find something they like, they make a note of it so that they can do something similar. I had a lot of stuff about myself that I wanted to put on the Web, like my stories and poems and my *Star Wars* information. I want to be a writer, and I thought this would be a way to get helpful criticism about my work.

I use Netscape Navigator as my browser, and I usually use an FTP program (Fetch) to send my files to GeoCities. Sometimes I also use GeoCities' program called EZ File Upload so they can get the files on the server hassle-free. It works just fine!

I've been getting feedback on my stories, but it's not criticism — mostly it's from people wanting to know when the next installment of my "Star Wars" story is coming out! Sometimes people suggest things I can put on my Web pages. They'll ask me, "Have you ever thought about putting your stories online? It would be really cool."

The other day I had the ultimate thrill: I was surfing around the Web, and I found a Web page by a person I had never heard of, and that page had a link to my own page! I thought, "Wow, this is really cool. People are actually making links to my page; my page is actually going somewhere." I've had 350 visitors on my page so far.

Part III
Cool Things You Can Do with Your Web Pages

The 5th Wave   By Rich Tennant

"YOU KNOW KIDS—YOU CAN'T BUY THEM JUST ANY WEB AUTHORING SOFTWARE."

In this part . . .

After you have your well-organized and interesting pages on the Web, don't stop there and rest on your laurels. One of the wonderful things about Web publishing is that you can revise and improve your work any time you want. Part III describes some bells and whistles that can make your Web pages come alive with color, sound, animation, and more.

Another way to improve a simple Web page is to redesign it. You learn about some design techniques the professionals use. After you read about how basic page designs work, you can grab a template from the CD that comes with this book and put your contents into that template's basic design.

Who could ask for more? Actually, there is more. And it's all free. Part III also provides keys to treasure chests of amazing free clip art for your Web pages. To avoid getting caught with your hand inside the cookie jar, you can check out important information about copyrights. With this information, you'll be sure you're helping yourself *only* to what's legitimately free for the taking.

Chapter 7

Secrets of Web Page Special Effects

● ●

In This Chapter

▶ Finding free GeoCities counters and guestbooks

▶ Making the right moves: Using animation

▶ Tracking down sound (tracks): Using audio

▶ Checking out how cyberspace kids find and use advanced features

● ●

*N*ot many people can resist peeking behind the curtain to discover how a special effect is created. You probably remember just such a moment at the end of the movie, *The Wizard of Oz,* when Dorothy's dog, Toto, pulls back the curtain, the Wizard is revealed as just an old man pushing buttons and pulling levers. The good news is that, once you understand how they work and how to access them, you can create eye-popping images or spine-tingling sounds in your Web pages — and get a standing ovation from your audience.

The best place to start is the Web itself. While browsing the Web, you've probably found a few sites that made you shout things like "Wow!" and "Cool!" Here's a little quiz: How do you think the people who achieved those effects on their own Web pages started out? My guess is that, like you, their first step was probably to say "Wow!" and "Cool!" while gaping at someone else's page. So the next time you see Web page animation or artwork that impresses you, ask yourself, "How can I do that?"

Often, you don't have to do too much fancy programming, drawing, or recording to get cool effects on your home page. You might have to add a line or two to the HyperText Markup Language (HTML) instructions that are used to format the text and images on your Web page. (See Chapter 14 for more information about how to use HTML.) Usually, though, this is pretty painless: Your Internet Service Provider (ISP) may include some utilities that you can use (for example, counters and computer programs that let you display the current date and time) and provide some instructions on how to use them. The best place to start is with the organization that hosts your Web page, for example, GeoCities, America Online, or an ISP such as Earthlink.

This chapter pulls back the curtain and explains some of the cool Web page effects seen on many kids' and families' Web pages. It explains what the effects are, how they work, and suggests ways to add some of the effects to your own pages. Chapters 11, 12, and 13 explain how you can create effects with animations, sound, and graphics. So, it's time to get rolling!

Testing GeoCities' Member Features

If you're a member of GeoCities and have set up your own Web page in one of its neighborhoods, as described in Chapter 1, you're in luck. GeoCities provides a pretty good assortment of Web page add-ons for its members. Add-ons are software programs or multimedia files that you can add to a Web page to make it more entertaining. Go to the Member Features page shown in Figure 7-1 (`http://www.geocities.com/Utilities/ features.html`), and check out the current list.

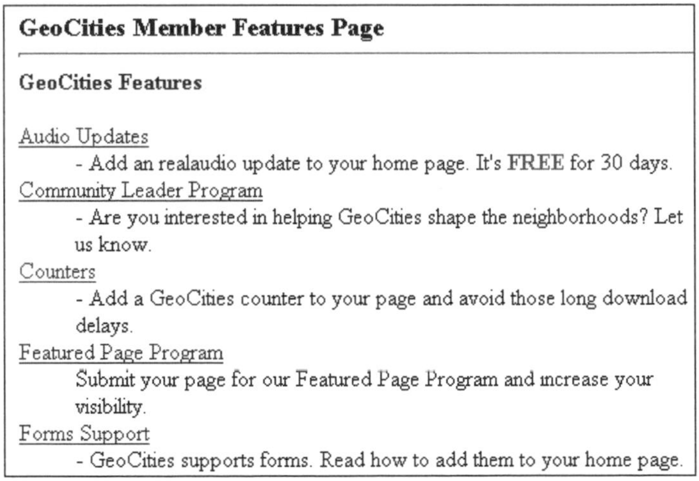

Figure 7-1:
You find cool utilities to add to your Web page at the GeoCities Member Features page. Scroll down the page to see more offerings.

GeoCities Member Features Page

GeoCities Features

Audio Updates
    - Add an realaudio update to your home page. It's FREE for 30 days.
Community Leader Program
    - Are you interested in helping GeoCities shape the neighborhoods? Let us know.
Counters
    - Add a GeoCities counter to your page and avoid those long download delays.
Featured Page Program
    Submit your page for our Featured Page Program and increase your visibility.
Forms Support
    - GeoCities supports forms. Read how to add them to your home page.

Making a counter with a-one, a-two, a-three

What's the single most popular cool effect that people add to their Web pages? A counter would get my vote. A *counter* is a utility that records the number of visits that are made to a Web page — that is, how many times the files on your page are accessed. This utility resides on the Web server, which is the computer that holds your Web pages.

You don't have to create the counter itself; instead, you include a hypertext reference to it. Here's how:

1. **Connect to the Internet, and start your Web browser.**

2. **Select File⇨Open Location.**

   The Open Location dialog box appears.

3. **Type** `http://www.geocities.com/cgi-bin/counter/member.password` **in the text box.**

   The `member.password` at the end of the address isn't supposed to include the term `member.password`. Instead, that's a *placeholder* where you type *your* GeoCities member name and password. To do that, just press the period key on your keyboard, and then type your GeoCities password. If your member name, for example, is maryjones and your password is rtzfdx, you type `http://www.geocities.com/cgi-bin/counter/maryjones.rtzfdx` in the text box.

4. **Click on Open.**

   The dialog box closes, and your browser takes you to the Web site with the Web address you just entered. If you entered your GeoCities member name and password — correctly, of course — you see the image of your counter set at the number 1, as shown in Figure 7-2. You haven't actually installed this counter yet; you have just connected to a page on one of GeoCities' Web servers where the counter is contained.

5. **To enable this counter to appear on your page, add a reference to the counter in the HTML instructions for your page, as follows (see Chapter 14 for more information about using HTML):**

   ```
   <IMG SRC="/cgi-bin/counter/your-member-name">
   ```

   Remember: Don't actually type `your member name`: Type your GeoCities member name. Don't add *any* blank spaces in this line of HTML. Type everything exactly as you see it here.

   Also, be sure to position this line exactly on your Web page where you want it to appear. When in doubt, put it at the bottom of the page, but before the two HTML instructions `</BODY>` and `</HTML>`.

Figure 7-2:
As this
figure
shows, the
counter
registers
you as
visitor
number 1.

6. **Save your HTML document by selecting File⇨Save.**

   A dialog box appears in which you enter a name for your file and add the extension `.htm` (or, for Mac users, `.html`) to identify this file as an HTML document.

7. **Go to your Web browser, and open your Web page in the browser window.**

   Your new counter should appear. If it doesn't, try selecting View⇨Reload (for Netscape Navigator) or View⇨Refresh (for Microsoft Internet Explorer) to reload the page.

Things like URLs and lines of HTML must be entered exactly right or they don't work. For example, in the HTML in the preceding steps, you need a blank space between IMG and SRC, and you need to add those quotation marks (") after the equals sign and just before the greater than (>) symbol at the end. It's usually easier to go to the GeoCities Member Features page and copy the code you need to enter. To do that, click just before the text you want to copy, hold down your mouse button, and scroll across the text. Then select Edit⇨Copy (press ⌘+C on a Mac). You can then paste what you've copied by selecting Edit⇨Paste (press ⌘+V on a Mac).

Modifying your Web page's HTML

In order to add counters, clocks, or other cool things to your Web page, you often have to add a line or two to the HTML instructions for that page (see Chapter 14). When using a Web page authoring program, such as HomeSite or PageMill (which most of you probably do), HTML isn't something you have to worry about too much. Your program will ensure that the text you want to appear as the main heading appears in the correct type size, that the text you want to appear in boldface appears in bold, and so on. What the program is actually doing is creating an HTML document for the page. The HTML commands (or instructions) that identify images, some text as a heading and some as bold is there — you just don't see. You may want to check out Appendix B for more information about Web authoring programs.

Every Web page has a set of these HTML instructions working in the background. When you're browsing Web pages, you can see the HTML easily enough by selecting View⇨ Document Source in the Web browser you're using. (Whether you're using Netscape Navigator or Microsoft Internet Explorer, the menu commands are mostly the same.) When you do this, a text file appears with some complicated-looking instructions. That's the HTML for the page you're viewing.

You can add HTML to your Web page to include a counter. If you have a free page on GeoCities, just follow these steps:

1. **Go to the GeoCities File Manager page** (`http://www.geocities.com/homestead/file_manager.html`).

    The page appears with text boxes where you enter your member name and password.

2. **Enter your GeoCities member name and password, and click on Submit.**

    The GeoCities File Manager page appears.

3. **Check the box next to the filename of the Web page you want to view. Then scroll down the screen, and choose Advanced HTML Editor by clicking on the arrow next to the Choose Your Editor box.**

4. **Click on Edit.**

    The Advanced Home Page Editor opens.

5. **Scroll down to see the HTML instructions for your own home page.**

    You can paste or type the HTML for your counter, guestbook, or other Web page add-on wherever you want, but it's usually best to add it at the bottom of the HTML, as shown in the figure in this sidebar.

```
<!--LINK2-->
<IMG SRC=/pictures/whiteball.gif> <A HREF =
http://http://www.disney.com/>Disney Home Page</a><br>
<p>

<!--LINE3-->

<p>

<!--FOOT-->

<!--LINE4-->

<p>

<p>
<hr>
<p>
<center><b>
This page hosted by <a href="/"><img src=/pictures/gc_icon.gif
align=middle alt="GeoCities" border=0></a>
Get your own <a href="/">Free Home Page</a></b></center>
<br><br>

<IMG SRC="/cgi-bin/counter/brianwolf">
```

Paste your HTML here, after the GeoCities link.

6. **Click on Save near the bottom of the Advanced Home Page Editor window to save the changes to your HTML, or click Preview (the button next to Save) if you want to preview your page with the new goodies.**

    If you click Save, you return to the File Manager page, where you can work on another document. If you click Preview, your page opens in your browser window.

If you're not a member of GeoCities and you want to add a counter to your own page, don't despair. Go the Web Counter Web site (`http://www.digits.com/`), where you can download a counter. America Online also provides a free counter to its members, which you can access by scrolling down the list of options included in the welcome page at AOL's Personal Publisher site (see Chapter 6).

Kilroy signed my guestbook

A *guestbook* on a Web page performs roughly the same function as a guestbook in a hotel or at a museum: It keeps a record of who has been there. You can put a guestbook on your Web page. The guestbook will provide a place for you to type messages and post them for everyone to see and a place where others visiting that site can respond.

If you were to set up your own Web page guestbook from scratch, you'd have to do all sorts of complicated things, such as create a form, write a script (fairly complicated code that tells a computer what to do), test things, and so on.

However, GeoCities provides a link on its Member Features page (called <u>Guestbooks</u>) to a free guestbook service run by another organization on the Web called Lpage. If you register with Lpage, you can have your own guestbook right away with no fuss. (Actually, Lpage created the guestbook program, which resides on one of Lpage's Web servers; you just add the text-entry portion to your own page.) Here's how to do it:

1. **Go to the GeoCities Member Features page (**`http://www.geocities.com/Utilities/features.html`**), and click on the link <u>Guestbook</u>.**

   This step takes you to Lpage's World Famous Guestbook Server page (`http://www.lpage.com/wguestbk/`), shown in Figure 7-3.

Figure 7-3:
If you register with Lpage, you can add a free guestbook to your own Web page.

2. **Click on the Register button.**

   This step takes you to a registration page where you are asked to think up a snappy name for your guestbook. (***Hint:*** If your name is Brian, you might just call it "briansfriends" or something similar.)

3. Enter your name, and click on Submit.

This step takes you to a page where you are asked to click on one of a lists of links that is presented on the Lpage registration page. You are supposed to click on a link that describes your site. Unfortunately, there aren't any categories like Personal or Fun. You might click on Entertainment or Recreation/Sports.

4. Click on a link for a major topic.

This step takes you to a page with another series of links — pick the one that describes the contents of your Web site most closely (when in doubt, choose the always helpful *miscellaneous*).

5. Click on a link for a minor topic.

A page appears reporting the categories you just selected.

6. Click on Next.

This step takes you to the New World Famous Guestbook User page, where you have to fill out a form that asks for the following information:

- The URL and the title of your Web page

- Your e-mail address

- An alphanumeric password for your guestbook (*Alphanumeric* means that this password needs to contain both letters and numerals. Remember to write this password down in a place where you'll be able to find it later.)

- Some keywords that describe your site

  (Skip the text box about the banner ad; this is only for commercial Web sites.)

- Your city, state, and country

7. When you're all done, click on Register.

You now see a page notifying you that registration was successful and presenting you with some scary-looking HTML code. You have to copy and paste this code into the HTML in your own Web page before you can actually install your guestbook. Later, you'll receive an e-mail message containing instructions on how to add the HTML to your page.

If you want to preview your guestbook, scroll down the page a little bit, and click on the link <u>View your homepage with the guestbook installed . . . yes your homepage!</u> Unfortunately, this is only a preview; it doesn't actually install your guestbook for you.

8. To select the HTML code that you need for your guestbook, click just before the first line of code, which begins `<a href=`, and drag your mouse right across the following lines of code:

```
<a href=http://www.Lpage.com/wgb/
wgbsign.dbm?owner=Brianfriends>Sign My Guestbook</a>
<a href=http://www.Lpage.com/wgb/
wgbview.dbm?owner=Brianfriends>View My Guestbook</a>
<a href=http://www.Lpage.com/wguestbk><img src=http://
www.Lpage.com/gif/lpagebutton.gif height=31 width=88
alt="Guestbook by Lpage"></a><p>
```

The selected HTML code is now highlighted.

9. **Leave the HTML selected, and press <u>E</u>dit⇨<u>C</u>opy.**

The selected text is now copied into your computer's memory; you can now paste it in the HTML for your Web page.

10. **Open the HTML for your home page (see the sidebar "Modifying your Web page's HTML"), scroll down to the bottom of the page, and position your text cursor just before the following lines of HTML:**

```
</BODY>
</HTML>
```

11. **To paste the HTML you copied in Step 9, select <u>E</u>dit⇨<u>P</u>aste (press ⌘+V on a Mac).**

Voilà! The code that you need to install your guestbook is now added to the HTML in your Web page.

12. **Save your HTML document by selecting <u>F</u>ile⇨<u>S</u>ave.**

13. **Go to your Web browser, open your Web page in your browser window, and scroll to the bottom of the page to see the reference to your guestbook, which is a clickable link called <u>Sign My Guestbook</u> (see Figure 7-4).**

14. **Click on the link <u>Sign My Guestbook</u>, and you see the guestbook that your visitors can fill out (see Figure 7-5).**

Figure 7-4:
Here's what you see at the bottom of your Web page after you install a free Lpage guestbook.

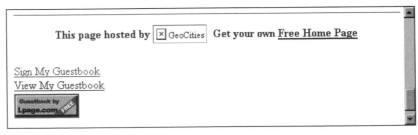

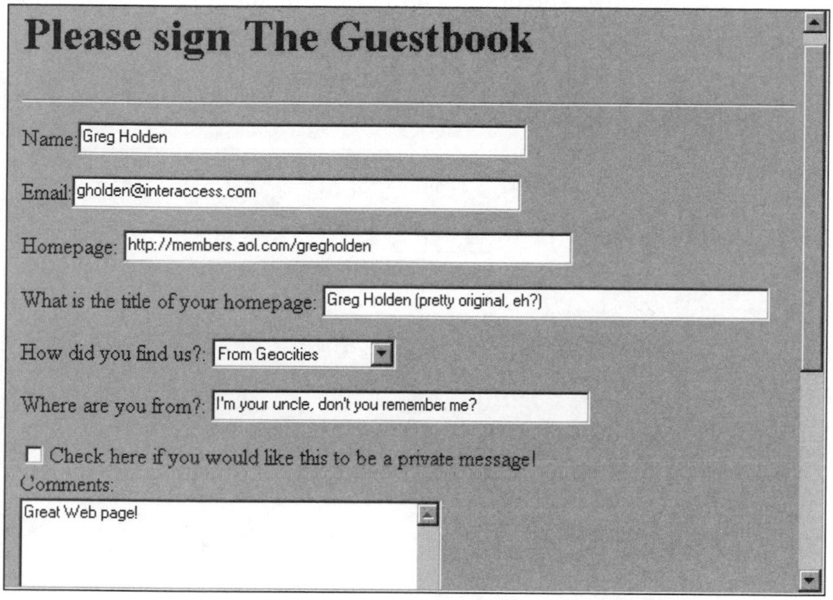

Figure 7-5:
Your
guestbook
contains
spaces
where
visitors can
type
information
about
themselves,
including
the address
for their
Web pages,
and make
comments
about your
page.

Please sign The Guestbook

Name: Greg Holden

Email: gholden@interaccess.com

Homepage: http://members.aol.com/gregholden

What is the title of your homepage: Greg Holden (pretty original, eh?)

How did you find us?: From Geocities

Where are you from?: I'm your uncle, don't you remember me?

☐ Check here if you would like this to be a private message!
Comments:

Great Web page!

Getting in Motion with Animation

By now, you've probably visited Web pages that include graphics that *move* — a little animal runs across the page or an image seems to spin around. Maybe you'd like some action of your own and want to know where to begin.

The moving pictures you often see in Web pages are called *animated* GIF images. *GIF* stands for *Graphics Interchange Format,* one of the two graphics formats (along with *JPEG,* which stands for *Joint Photographic Experts Group)* that can be viewed on Web pages. An animated GIF is a special kind of GIF image that consists of a sequence of several separate images. Each one of the images is a little different than the one before it. When the images play together in sequence, they seem to be moving. It's a little like those "flip books" of images you may have seen: If you turn the pages quickly enough, a lady in an old-fashioned dress might seem to be jumping over a chair. An animated GIF works pretty much the same way.

In Figure 7-6, you can see a simple example of animation. When this animation appears on-screen, a bunch of stars seem to be spinning around. Actually, one star is drawn and made to rotate by using a graphics program. Every time the image rotates a little bit, it is saved as a separate GIF document. After a series of images is assembled, the designer uses a special software program, such as GIF Construction, to put the separate image files together so that they play in sequence (they spin around), like frames in a movie. That's how you create an animated GIF.

Figure 7-6 shows the first six frames of an animated 21 star sequence.

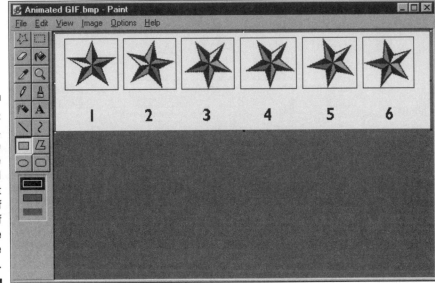

Figure 7-6:
You, too,
can create
a simple
animated
GIF that
consists of
a series of
separate
images like
this.

In Chapter 11, you discover how to create some simple animated GIFs. You can, of course, use someone else's animated GIFs that are available as clip art. See Chapter 9 for some suggestions on where to find these and other types of art that you can put on your Web pages.

Using Audio to Sound Off

Some Web pages are quiet as a mouse; they let their images and words do the talking. Other Web pages come complete with their own musical accompaniment. Sometimes, an electric piano plays in the background while you view the page. Why do some pages have sound while others are silent?

Playing your song

Whether you play the kazoo or the violin, you may want to know about something called MIDI, which is one of many kinds of sounds you can use on a Web page and one of the easiest to produce. *MIDI* stands for *Musical Instrument Digital Interface*. MIDI provides a way for electronic instruments and computers to talk to one another. MIDI musical instruments put out sounds that can be captured in a format that a computer can recognize and play. That's because MIDI sounds are in *digital* format: They consist of zeroes and ones, just like computer files. The background sounds you hear on Web pages have been created by someone playing such an instrument (usually, a MIDI keyboard).

Copying sound clips

In your journeys around the Web, you may have run across the clip art that I mentioned earlier in this chapter. Clip art images are available many places on the Internet, and they can be downloaded for free. Along with clip art, you're likely to also find *free sounds* (sometimes called sound bites). These are *short audio files* that someone has recorded and saved in a format that a computer can play. Often, the audio clips you hear on a Web page aren't an original performance by the page's author but one of these free sound bites that the author has copied.

If you want to check out free sounds that you can play on you Web page, go to Yahoo!'s site (`http://www.yahoo.com/`), and search for the keywords "sound clip." Yahoo! will present you with more than 600 links to television shows, movies, rock bands, and other groups that have put out sound files you can copy. Also, check out Yahoo!'s sound archive page at `http://www.yahoo.com/Computers_and_Internet/Multimedia/Sound/Archives/`.

Background sounds sound good

Whether you create your own music or copy a sound file from somewhere on the Web, you must take some special steps in order to include the sound file on your Web page. You do that by adding a few key instructions to the HTML instructions for your Web page. (Go to Chapter 14 for information about using HTML.) There's no way around this: You have to get techie for a little while and enter some HTML commands yourself. You need to add the following lines of HTML (substitute your filename for `sound.mid`):

```
<EMBED SRC="sound.mid" autoplay="true" hidden="true">
```

Note: The EMBED tag is recognized by Netscape Navigator (but not by other browsers). Autoplay tells the visitor's browser to play the sound automatically upon connecting to your page. `hidden=true` means that your visitor won't be presented with a sound control panel with stop and play buttons so as to control the sound. This panel will be "hidden."

```
<BGSOUND SRC"sound.mid" loop="10">
```

Note: The BGSOUND tag is recognized by Microsoft Internet Explorer and may not be interpreted correctly by other browsers.

Taking the bite out of your sound bite using audio

Lots of Web pages have audio greetings that the authors or their friends have recorded. If you have a microphone and a sound card (see Chapter 12 for more about system requirements), it's amazingly easy to record your own audio greeting, too. Windows 95 comes with a built-in utility called Sound Recorder that makes this a piece of cake. To start up and use Sound Recorder, just follow these steps (**Mac users:** See the steps for using the Sound control panel in Chapter 12):

1. **Click on the Start button in the Windows 95 taskbar, and select <u>P</u>rograms⇨Accessories⇨Multimedia⇨Sound Recorder.**

   The Sound Recorder dialog box opens.

2. **Important: Pick up your microphone. Clear your throat. Take a drink of water. (You get the message.)**

3. **Click on the button in the lower-right corner (the red circle), and start talking.**

   As you speak, the slider in the middle of the Sound Recorder dialog box moves to the right, and audio signals make the green line dance.

4. **When you're done, click on the Stop button (the black square at the bottom of the Sound Recorder dialog box).**

   It's best to keep your message short; sound files can get very big very fast.

5. **To hear what you recorded, click on the Play button (the arrows pointing to the right).**

6. **To save your message, select <u>F</u>ile⇨<u>S</u>ave.**

   The Save dialog box appears with the Save As option preset to Sounds (.wav). Leave this setting as is.

7. **Give your file a simple name, and click on Save.**

After you create your file, it will have the file extension `.wav`, as in `greetings.wav`. You can now add this sound file to your Web page as you do any GIF or JPEG image: by making a link to it. Add the following line of HTML to the HTML instructions for your Web page (see the sidebar "Modifying your Web page's HTML"):

```
<A HREF="greetings.wav"> Greetings from me! </A>
```

The words `Greetings from me!` appear as a highlighted link on your page. (Feel free to change this link to something more clever or original.) Be sure to change the filename, `greetings.wav`, to your own filename.

As I mentioned earlier, the images you see on Web pages are in file formats called GIF and JPEG. In order to be played on the Web, sound files have to be in certain formats, too. The most common ones are WAV, MID, AU, and AIFF. If you encounter a file on a sound archive called `music.mid`, `voice.au`, or `greetings.aiff`, you'll know it's an audio file. These files can be played by most Web browsers, but you or your visitors may also need special applications called plug-ins that work with a browser and enable that browser to play sound or other multimedia files it wouldn't be able to process otherwise.

Adding a tick-tock clock

Everyone knows *time is of the essence.* In order to help your visitors keep track of time, why not put a clock on your page that shows the current time — and not just any clock but the U.S. Naval Observatory's (USNO) Master Clock, the country's official timekeeper? To do this, once again, you must add a line of HTML to the instructions for your Web page. This line makes a reference to the USNO's clock that results in an image of the clock appearing on your page. Find out how to add this clock at `http://tycho.usno.navy.mil/what.html`.

Don't be late for a very important date. Some Internet Service Providers (ISPs) provide a way for you include HTML on your Web page instructions that causes the current date and time to appear on your Web page. You don't have to do a lot of programming to get the information to appear; you only have to make a reference to a program on one of their computers. This program (the techie name is a *server-side include*) provides you with the current date and time. Ask your provider if it provides such a program.

Grab all the goodies you can get

Some companies that give you access to the Internet also make it relatively easy for you to add advanced Web page features to your own Web pages. These are the kinds of things that would be pretty complex if you undertook to create them on your own. But GeoCities, AOL, and ISPs give you the code and installation instructions. All you do is follow the steps. Here are some examples of advanced goodies that you can find and add to your own pages:

✔ **Sign on dotted lines with fill-out forms.** Forms are areas of a Web page that let a visitor to that page enter information that can then be submitted to the owner of the Web page. Usually, forms consist of text boxes (where text can be typed), checkboxes (boxes that can be clicked on and selected), radio buttons (buttons that can be clicked on and selected), and drop-down menus (with options that can be clicked on and selected). After the visitor fills out the form, the visitor usually clicks on a button called Submit, and the data entered is sent to another computer where the owner of the Web page can read it.

(continued)

(continued)

GeoCities lets you add forms to your own page that visitors can fill out and send back to you by e-mail. Go to the GeoCities Member Features page (http:// www.geocities. com/Utilities/ features.html), and click on the link for Interactive Forms to find out how the GeoCities form works.

Note: Forms can be pretty complicated if you add the HTML instructions yourself. Find a good Web authoring program that helps you create forms, for example, PageMill, World Wide Web Weaver, or HomeSite (all with versions on the CD at the back of this book).

✔ **Map it out with imagemaps.** Imagemaps are Web page graphics that are divided into two or more clickable regions. When you click within one of these regions, you are sent to a related Web page. Imagemaps aren't for beginners, but if you want to find out how to create your own,

you can fine a nice explanation of imagemaps at the Webheads Web site (http://www.pitt.edu ~webheads/MAPCLASS/imagemaps. html). Mac users can also try Felipe's Clickable Gif Map Tutorial-Mac at http://edb518ea.edb.utexas. edu/html/gifmap.html.

✔ **Search utilities — where are you?** If you're on GeoCities, you can add a search box that lets visitors search for someone else on the GeoCities Web site. Your visitors may want to do this if you make references to other GeoCities Web sites on your page. Click on the link <u>GeoCities Search Feature</u> on the Member Features page, or go directly to the GeoCities Search page (http://www.geo-cities.com/ BHI/search.html). Scroll down the page, and copy the lengthy bit of HTML. Paste it into the HTML for your own Web page, as explained in the sidebar "Modifying your Web page's HTML."

The more goodies you add to your Web page, the slower it will appear on your visitors' screens. Use animations, audio, and sounds sparingly so your page doesn't get too bloated. Think about why you want to use one of these features — other than the fact that they're cool, of course. The most effective features complement your page's contents and make your page more useful. That way people will want to visit your Web site again and again.

Other Kewl Tools for Web Pages

After you add a few sound and animation goodies like the ones listed in this chapter, you may just say to yourself, "Hey, I'm getting the hang of this Web page thing. What other cool things can I add?" Here are a few other advanced features that will help you use your Web page to get your message out there in cyberspace or to connect with more visitors.

▶▶

Training words to scroll

On most Web pages, the words just sit on the screen, waiting patiently for you to read them. On a few pages, some words can scroll across the screen. They either move in the main part of the browser window or in the *status bar* at the bottom of the browser below the main contents of the page.

You can achieve this effect in a couple of ways. If you're pretty good with HTML, you can use the <MARQUEE> tag to mark the text you want to appear to be scrolling, like this:

```
<MARQUEE> This text will scroll across the screen.
Yippee! </MARQUEE>
```

The downside is that this particular HTML command was invented by Microsoft, and only visitors who come to your page by using Microsoft Internet Explorer can see the effect.

Another way that is more widely supported is to add a JavaScript scroller to the HTML for your page. (JavaScript is a programming language created by Netscape that is rapidly becoming a standard language on the Web. JavaScript commands can be added directly to the HTML for a Web page, and the effects are seen in a Web browser window.) A *scroller* is a word or phrase that moves from right to left in the bar at the bottom of your browser screen. A scroller lets you send a special greeting or important notice to your Web page visitors. To make the scroller work, you must add some additional code in the JavaScript language to the HTML instructions for your page.

Some authors of this JavaScript code have made it freely available to anyone who wants to copy it. Then all you have to do is create the text that you want to march across the browser status bar. You can see an example of text *marching* across a status bar on Kelly's home page (http:/www.toptown.com/ centralpark/Kel/index.htm).

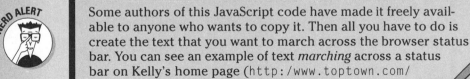

You can find a great introduction to JavaScript at http:/ www.freqgrafx.com/411/. Click on the link Library to find the Scrolling Status Bar script that you can add it to your own HTML.

Linking to a chat site

Chatting is one of the coolest things you can do online, but usually you have to go to a special *chat site* (a site on the Internet where you can connect to other online computer users and communicate in real time by typing messages to one another). You need special chat software to actually exchange messages with other chat users. But wouldn't it be great if you could make a link to a chat line from your own Web page so your visitors could type messages to you right after they visit your site (provided you happen to be online at the time)?

Sarah Gravelines, 13, of Manitoba, Canada, has done just that. Sarah loves to chat online and has included a link to a chat program she uses and a chat site that she likes on her Web page called Sarah's Trés Cool Homepage (http://www.angelfire. com/wv/sarpage/index.html). Her page boasts many of the cool features listed in this chapter: a guestbook, a counter, a simple form, a link to a search utility, and lots of other links. It's a must-see for young Web page authors.

Having a PowWow on the Web

One way for kids to chat safely on the Web is by downloading a Windows shareware program (software you can try out for a time and then pay a fee to keep) called *PowWow for Kids* by Tribal Voice. It comes with password security and even profanity filters to keep out naughty words. PowWow allows up to seven kids to chat, send and receive files, and cruise the World Wide Web as a group. Best of all, a version of PowWow is on the CD that comes with this book. Find out more about how PowWow works at http://www.tribal.com/kids/.

One kid's opinion

I personally like special effects, in moderation. An animation can be a nice addition to a Web page. But going overboard can make a page too flashy and hard to view and load. I have a counter on my page, and it's great. It gives me and my visitors a chance to see how popular my page is. Sounds are cool on a page, too. I'd rather download sounds than just listen to them on the page. But that's just me. I am in the process on putting an animation on the index of one of my pages.

Chapter 8

Getting Plain or Fancy with Templates

● ●

In This Chapter

▶ Checking out Web page designs that professionals use

▶ Organizing your Web page with design templates

▶ Using lots of images without getting jumbled

▶ Making a page interactive with frames

▶ Presenting lots of contents with tables

● ●

Do you have two aunts like my Aunt Jane and Aunt Zelda? Aunt Jane wears gray suits with white blouses and puts a silver stick pin in her lapel. She would have a plain old garden-variety Web page. But you can barely see my Aunt Zelda for the layers of hot pink ruffles and bright silk scarves. Her Web page would sing, jump, glow, and do everything but whistle "Dixie" to try to knock your socks off.

Whether you like to be plain or fancy, to make your page stand out from the crowd, you've gotta *design* it. As I mention in earlier chapters, before you begin to design your Web page, you need to think about the material you want to include and envision the effect you want to create. Then the idea is to arrange the words, images, and colors so that they all work together to produce that effect.

This chapter discusses five design templates that you can use to set up your pages like a pro. *Templates* are previously prepared designs. They're sort of like the classified ads that newspapers sell for Valentine's Day in which you can decide whether you want your message to be inside a big heart or a flower border. Your part in the process is to fill in the blanks with your own words and pictures. You can take your pick of either a simple or a compli-cated template. Then you plunk in your contents, and presto, you've quickly designed your own pages.

If you followed the exercises described in Chapter 1, you already know something about working with a Web page template. That chapter explains how to use GeoCities' Basic HTML Editor to create a page. The Basic HTML Editor provides you with a page template in which you fill in a series of text boxes to create the content of your page. But the templates described in this chapter are different; they let you see how a page might look beforehand, and they don't provide text boxes that are easy to fill in. You must delete the words and images that come with each template and replace them with your own Web page contents. The advantage of templates is that they save you time and trouble. You don't have to think out every detail for designing a page, and the HTML is already entered for you.

Each of the templates described in this chapter is included on the CD-ROM that comes with this book. The filenames of the templates are given in the sections that follow. After you read about how the basic page designs work in this chapter, you can go to the CD and select the design you want to use on your own page. Just install the disk in your computer's CD-ROM drive. Be sure to copy the folder containing the template you want to your hard disk. Open the template in your Web editing program. Then you just change the title and the text as you like, insert your own images, and you're on your way! (See the last page of this book for information on installing the CD and Appendix D for information on using the templates. See Appendix B for information on Web editing programs.)

In all the steps in this chapter, I use Netscape Composer, Netscape's Web page editing program, which is freeware (free for you to use). Netscape Composer isn't included in the version of Netscape Navigator that is on this book's CD, but Appendix B tells you how to download from the Web. You can use other programs on the CD to open these templates and edit them, however.

Note: At the time of this writing, I was able to download either Netscape Navigator Gold 3.0 or the newer version called Netscape Communicator (from the Netscape Web site at `http://home.netscape.com/`), both of which contain a group of tools, including a Web page editing tool.

Template #1: Simple Is Classy

Template 1 (named `simple.htm` on the CD with this book) helps you create a simple Web page that uses a series of introductory links, an introductory paragraph, a main heading, and a few subsections, each of which is introduced by its own subhead.

Take a look at an ad in a magazine for a really expensive item. I bet you'll find a design that is *plain,* yet sophisticated and distinctive. Sometimes, simpler really *is* better. On the Web, you have no trouble finding Web pages that try to accomplish too many things at once; the result is that they look too crowded. You may want to make your page stand out from all the others by keeping it uncluttered and *minimal.* A minimal design contains the following elements, arranged in a single column that runs horizontally across a Web page:

- ✔ A set of clickable links that serves as a table of contents for the page

- ✔ A main heading (called H1 in HTML, or Heading 1 in some HTML editing programs)

- ✔ An introductory paragraph, which can be formatted as a blockquote (that is, indented on both the left and right margins)

- ✔ Horizontal rules to divide the main body of the page from the introductory paragraph and *footer* at the bottom of the page

- ✔ Main contents that are broken into paragraphs (You may decide to divide your contents into subtopics, in which case, you create H2 headings or Heading 2. You may also choose to use bulleted or numbered lists to break up the page.)

Clare Moseley's page, which I put together, is probably a little longer than Web pages should be, but I include it as the first template because it's a good example of a Web page simplified by the minimal use of design elements (see Figure 8-1). Clare introduces the subject of her page (herself, that is) in a paragraph that's formatted as a *blockquote.* Because Clare has a lot to say about herself (just kidding, Clare!), her page is more than four computer screens in length. As I say elsewhere in this book, it's best to keep each of your Web pages to 1 or 1 1/2 screens in length. Other contents can be included on separate pages. But sometimes when you've got a lot to say about a particular topic, it's hard to break your message into smaller chunks. When a Web page gets several screens long, it's often helpful to include a table of contents at the beginning of the page. The *table of contents* is actually a series of links at the top of a Web page (the underlined words in Figure 8-1). Each one of the links is an internal link to a spot farther down the same page.

Note: "Clare" will let you borrow the layout of her Web pages as long as you change the contents to reflect your interests rather than hers. Again, you can find this page in the file named `simple.htm` on the CD.

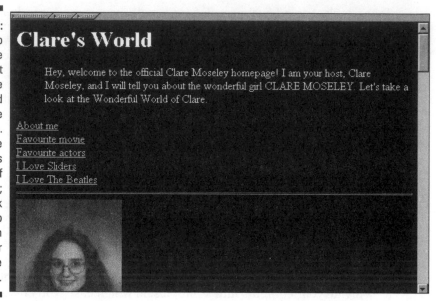

Figure 8-1:
Your Web
page
doesn't
have to be
complicated
to be
effective.
This simple
design uses
a table of
contents;
each link
takes you to
a location
farther
down the
same page.

Serving up a table of contents

Have you ever been to a buffet and found so many different kinds of foods you couldn't tell what was what? To keep your Web page from being like that, you can create a table of contents. This feature will help your viewers find their way around your page and make sure they get to sample all your tasty morsels. Creating a series of internal links that serves as a table of contents for a Web page is easy if you have a good Web page editor. The following steps tell you how to create a set of table of contents links using Netscape Composer.

1. **In the Composer window, open the Web page you want to edit.**

   For this first template, open the file `simple.htm`, which is in the folder called simple (see Appendix D for information about accessing the folder). Composer lets you edit text right in the main content window. Three sets of bars appear at the top of your page. The Character Format toolbar (which is the middle of the three toolbars shown in Figure 8-2) lets you add links quickly by clicking on the Link button. A dialog box named Properties appears in which you enter the URL for the file or page you want to link to. Click on OK, and the link is made (the process of making links with the Netscape Web page editing software is described in greater detail in Chapter 15). By clicking on the buttons in the formatting bar, you can make selected text bigger or smaller, add emphasis by making text bold, italic, or monospace, or even assign a color to text.

Link button ┐   ┌Composer's Insert Target button

Figure 8-2:
Like many
Web
authoring
programs,
Netscape
Composer
gives you
lots of
toolbar
buttons to
click on and
format your
Web page
contents.

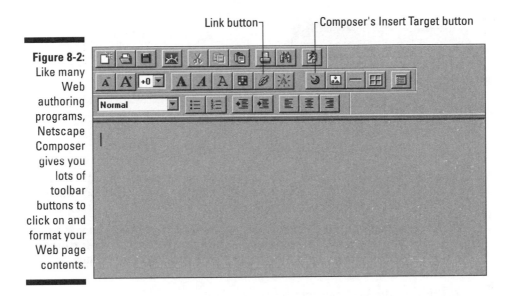

You begin by identifying the main sections of your Web page. These sections are the *destinations* for the links you're going to make.

You should see the document `simple.htm`, as displayed in Composer or whatever Web authoring tool you are using to edit the template. The title bar at the top of the page is "Clare Moseley's Page on Clare Moseley." Near the top of this page, and below the blockquote paragraph, is a series of five underlined links.

2. **Select each one of the five links, and type some replacement text. The text you type will serve a starting point for a link to a destination elsewhere on this page.**

   Clare's page contains these links: <u>About me</u>, <u>Favourite movie</u>, <u>Favourite actors</u>, <u>I Love Sliders</u>, and <u>I Love The Beatles</u> (refer to Figure 8-1). You need to replace each of these links, but first, you need to identify the destination for your first link.

3. **Scroll down the "Clare Moseley's Page" document. Position your cursor at a spot farther down your page, where you want to create the *destination* for your first link. Click on the Insert Target button in the Composer toolbar (refer to the toolbar in Figure 8-2).**

   The Target Properties dialog box appears (see Figure 8-3).

4. **In the text box in the dialog box, enter a name or number for this target.**

   You must give your target a name so that you can make a link to it later on. Often, it's simplest to give your target a number; since this is the first link in your table of contents, just type the number 1. (Named targets are case-sensitive, which means if you enter a name that uses all lowercase letters, when you make a link to that target later on you must use lowercase letters.)

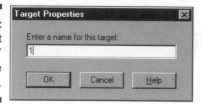

Figure 8-3:
This target
is "named"
the
number 1.

5. Click on OK.

The Target Properties dialog box closes, and a target icon appears at the spot that will be destination number 1. The target icon looks like a target with a little red arrow pointing to it.

6. Scroll back to the top of the page, and select the words you want to be the starting point for this link — in other words, the underlined text your visitors will click on to go to the destination you just targeted.

7. Click on the Link button.

The Character Properties dialog box appears (see Figure 8-4). The bottom half of the Character Properties dialog box displays all targeted destinations you've made in your Web page.

8. Click on the number 1.

The characters #1 automatically appear in the text box marked Link to a page location or local file.

9. Click on OK.

The Character Properties dialog box closes, and the words you selected (in this case, About me) appear underlined because they're now linked to the target you identified in Step 3.

10. Repeat Steps 3 through 7 for each of the other internal links in your Web page table of contents.

Template #2: A Web Page that Divides and Conquers

Template 2 (sections.htm on the CD) helps you create a Web page that briefly covers several different topics. Each topic has its own section and is divided from other sections by horizontal rules.

Figure 8-4:
To make an internal link, highlight the text you want to serve as the anchor, click on the Link button, and then select the target in the Character Properties dialog box.

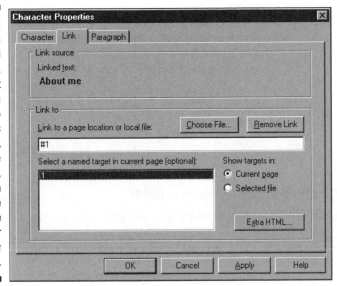

Do you have friends who get a lot of attention because they can get their point across quickly (maybe by teasing) but others who are boring because they go on and on and on? Web pages can be like people in those respects: Some are interesting teasers; some are boring gabbers. The best Web pages (the kind you want to create) are effective because they introduce a subject with just enough information to entice visitors. Immediately after the introduction, these pages provide links to another destination (see Template #1, earlier in this chapter) on the page or to a separate page on the site where the topic is discussed more fully. That way, nobody gets bored (or frustrated).

But what if you have a lot of subjects to talk about on a single Web page? In that case, you will probably want to divide your subjects into sections. Generally, you do this by including *horizontal rules.* Horizontal rules are lines that run from left to right across a Web page and divide one element from another. Generally, horizontal rules are a good way to divide sections of a Web page, but plenty of well-organized pages don't use them at all.

Note: You can use sections.htm (another one of Clare's pages) on the CD to follow the steps in the next section and create a Web page divided into sections. See Appendix D for information on accessing this file.

Horizontal rules that rule

Imagine that you want to include a number of horizontal rules on your Web page, but you want to do it in interesting and uncluttered ways. In other words, you want to ensure that your Web page really does get attention like your interesting friends do. One way to do that is by varying the way the rules appear. Some Web page editors let you easily match your rule to your frame of mind. Shorter? Centered? Aligned against the left or right margin? No problem. In Netscape Composer, just follow these steps:

1. **Open the Web page you want to edit in Netscape Composer.**

2. **Insert a horizontal rule (which Netscape calls a horizontal line) by clicking on the Horizontal Line button in Composer's toolbar, or select Insert➪Horizontal Line.**

   The plain old *default* horizontal rule appears on your Web page: This rule is 2 pixels wide and stretches across the entire width of your Web page.

3. **Click on the horizontal rule to select it.**

4. **With the rule selected, select Format➪Object Properties.**

   Because you've already selected a horizontal line, Composer displays the Horizontal Line Properties dialog box (see Figure 8-5).

5. **Change the settings to make the line appear differently.**

   To make the rule thicker than 2 pixels, change the number in the Height text box. To make the line shorter than the full width of the screen, change 100 to a smaller number (such as 50, or 75, or whatever) in the Width text box.

   To align the rules, you can click on the Left (for left margin), Right (for right margin), or Center radio buttons. (You can select Center only if the rule is less than the full width of the screen, however.) Check the 3-D shading box if you want the rule to be shaded rather than solid black. Check the Save settings as default box if you want to save these settings for other rules you plan to add.

Figure 8-5:
Break the rules —
horizontal rules, that
is — by changing
the settings in
Composer's Horizontal Line Properties dialog box.

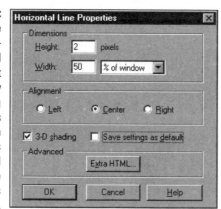

Template #3: Attack of the Shutter Bug

Template 3 (photos.htm on the CD) helps you create a Web page that uses a number of photos. See Appendix D for information on accessing this file.

If one photo is good and several are great, then lots and lots are fantastic, right? We love it when you can make your text flow around the photos. However, if you aren't careful, your page can quickly get jumbled up. Photos can bump up against other photos, text can get squished in between other photos, and then you (and your visitors!) have a real mess on your hands.

When you want several photos to appear close to one another on the page, you can prevent page clutter by allowing enough empty space around each of the photos. But this can be hard to do when the text doesn't extend the full length of the image. To include enough space, use your Web authoring software to insert a special line break after the paragraph. In this type of line break (Netscape calls it "Break Below Image(s)." the space below the paragraph will be clear until the bottom of the image is reached. Then the next paragraph won't appear until after the bottom edge of the image.

In Netscape Composer, it's easy to insert a clear space below an image by following these steps:

1. **Position your text cursor *after* the paragraph that you want to appear next to the image.**

   Your text cursor should be positioned right after the last period in the paragraph.

2. **Select Insert⇨Break Below Image(s).**

   This step tells a browser to break the text until the bottom of the image is reached. You will not see any change in Composer when you do this. You must preview your page in the browser window to see the effect.

3. **Select File⇨Browse Page.**

   A dialog box appears asking whether you want to save the document.

4. **Click on OK.**

   The page opens in the browser window, and the photos and text are separated.

If you're using HTML to edit a Web page (for example, GeoCities Advanced HTML Editor — see Chapter 6), you enter one of the following tags (commands) under the text that appears next to the image:

- ✔ `<BR CLEAR=LEFT>`: This tag breaks the text until the left margin of your Web page is clear. Use this tag when your photo is on the left side of your page.

- ✔ `<BR CLEAR=RIGHT>`: This tag breaks the text until the right margin of your Web page is clear. Use this tag when your photo is on the right side of your page.

- ✔ `<BR CLEAR=ALL>`: This tag breaks the text until both the right and left margins are clear. Use this tag when you have photos close to one another on both the right and left margins.

For more information about using HTML tags, check out Chapter 14.

Template #4: One Perfect Column

Template 4 (`index.htm` on the CD; see Appendix D) helps you create a clean and professional-looking Web page with its contents in a single vertical column.

When it comes to Web pages, sometimes less is more. At least that's what some designers think. It's not at all unusual to encounter a page with its contents arranged in a single column down the center, with plenty of white space on both the left and right sides.

Version 1: Simply indent

The easiest way to create a single column of text and images is to center and indent everything. Format each paragraph of text as a *blockquote,* which, as I mentioned earlier in the chapter, is indented on both the right and left sides. Try to keep all photos only as wide as the text.

In order to format text, you can select Format➪Indent One Level. To indent the text as far as you want, you may have to perform this step two or three times.

Remember that in this single-column layout, all horizontal rules must be centered and made shorter than the full width of the page.

Version 2: Use tables

A better, though more difficult, way to create a single column is to use tables. Tables are a feature of HTML that allows you to present information in columns and rows. A border around the table can be used to separate lots of different information on a page into cells. *Cells* are rectangles that contain the words and images in a table. You create these cells yourself using a Web page tool like the ones on this book's CD or by adding the appropriate HTML tag for cells. The contents of each cell are contained within the `<TD>` and `</TD>` commands, like this:

```
<TD>Welcome to my Web page.</TD>
```

You can also use tables in a hidden way to arrange an entire page in columns. Many Web page authoring tools let you do this. Every program has its own particular menu commands for creating tables and dividing them into cells, but here are the general principles:

- ✔ Set the table border to 0 (this makes the table outline invisible; the viewer sees only the contents).
- ✔ Fill some table cells with blank space so that they act as empty columns that add more white space to a page.

Stylus Media uses this approach on its own home page (`http://homepage.interaccess.com/~gholden/stylus/`). A duplicate of Stylus's home page is included on the CD (see Figure 8-6). It's called `index.htm` and is located in the `Column` folder (see Appendix D). As owner of Stylus, I grant you permission to copy the page and replace the contents with your own.

Figure 8-6:
You can make your Web page uncluttered and elegant by borrowing the HTML from this page and substituting your own text and images.

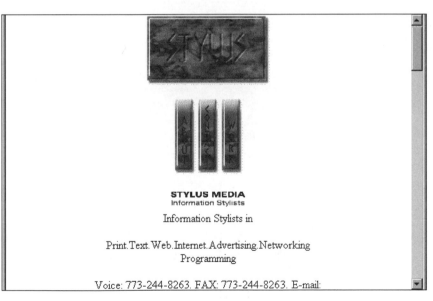

STYLUS MEDIA
Information Stylists

Information Stylists in

Print. Text. Web. Internet. Advertising. Networking
Programming

Voice: 773-244-8263. FAX: 773-244-8263. E-mail:

As explained in Step 1 for Template 1, you copy this Web page layout by installing this book's CD in your computer's CD-ROM drive. Then you open your Web page authoring tool and select File⇨Open. When the Open dialog box appears (this may be called Open Page or Open Location, depending on the software you are using, locate the index.htm document, which is in the Column folder (see Appendix D).

Feel free to delete the contents and substitute your own text in the single column. The text you need to select and delete begins after the second <TD> tag. The following excerpt of the HTML for this page indicates where you should delete Stylus's contents and substitute your own:

```
<!DOCTYPE HTML PUBLIC "-//IETF//DTD HTML 3.2//EN">
<HTML>
<HEAD>
   <TITLE>Welcome to STYLUS</TITLE>
```

Be sure to change the title "Welcome to STYLUS" to your own title (for example, "Welcome to my home page").

```
<META NAME="GENERATOR" CONTENT="User-Agent: Mozilla
3.0b5Gold (Macintosh; I; PPC)">
</HEAD>
<BODY BGCOLOR="#FFFFFF">
```

Delete all of the following lines of HTML:

```
<CENTER><P><IMG SRC="stylusred4.gif"><p>
<a href="about.html"><img alt="about" border=0
src="about.gif"></a><a href="contact.html"><img
alt="contact" src="contact.gif" border=0></a><a
href="work/work.html"><img border=0 alt="work"
src="work.gif"></a><p>
</CENTER>
```

Stop deleting!

```
<TABLE border=0>
<TR>
<TD  width=30%></TD>
<TD width=40%>
```

Delete everything after this tag and before the next </TD> tag, which is near the bottom of the page. Paste your own contents in between these two tags (between <TD width=30%> and </TD>).

The advantage of using tables to create a single column is that you are certain everything will line up. You don't have to center headings (unless you want to) or use blockquotes, which never seem to align the right side of a paragraph with the other paragraphs above or below it. The HTML for tables might be a little scary, but you don't have to work with the HTML yourself; after all, that's what templates like this one are for.

Template #5: Cell-abrate with a Newsletter

Template 5 (`tables.htm` on the CD; see Appendix D) helps you create a Web page that uses a feature called a *table* to present lots of separate text and photographic elements in rectangular containers called cells.

Sometimes you just can't help yourself. You have a lot of different things to say, and you can't hold back from saying it all at once. Luckily, restraint is not necessary. A great way to say a lot about your favorite subjects (like yourself) is to divide the contents into individual cells using a Web page table. Figure 8-7 shows an example of a newsletter that I made about a real kid named Noah.

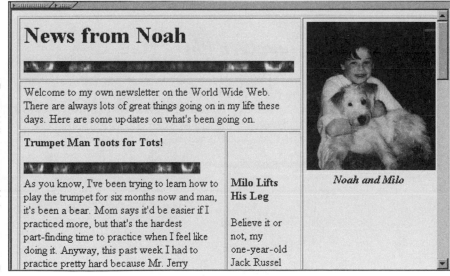

Figure 8-7: You can get a lot of headings, stories, and photos into a compact space by using a Web page table.

OPEN

Other Sources of Design Templates

The templates included with this book aren't the only ones you can find. Here are some sources on the Web that you can check out if you want to explore even more design options.

Netscape's Web page starter site

If you use Netscape Gold or Netscape Composer, you can use Netscape's page templates, which are part of its Web Page Starter Site (`http://home.netscape.com/home/starter.html`). Click on the link for <u>Web page templates</u>. You'll find sample pages for yourself, your family, or clubs, as well as JavaScript utilities, such as a calculator.

Web page builder site

A good resource for Web page *newbies,* this site (`http:www.infomediacom.com/preview.htm`) contains page templates, clip art, and other resources.

Just for fun: Web libs

Okay, this isn't a Web page template as such, but it's a language template, and it's fun. Go to `http://wt.k12.pa.us/~cnm/cgi-bin/weblibs.pl`. Fill out the form with some words of your choice. Submit the form, and Web Libs returns a text document with your words filled in, often in funny places.

Time for a change of table cells

In order to adapt this table to your own contents, you need to change the contents of each of the table cells. You may recall that a cell is a rectangle that contains the words and images in a table. Netscape Composer makes editing tables a snap. You simply click right in the cell, press Backspace or Delete to erase the contents, and then enter your own words.

If you don't have Composer or another editor that lets you work with tables, you can change the contents of a cell directly in HTML. Just remember that the contents of each cell are contained within the <TD> and </TD> commands, like this:

```
<TD>Welcome to my Web page.</TD>
```

Just delete the words Welcome to my Web page, substitute your own text, and you're on your way.

CLARE DECLARES

One kid's opinion

I came up with the plan for the page that's being used as the first template in this chapter (the document called `simple.htm` on the CD that comes with this book). The design of this page is fairly basic and is good for beginners. A good way to start this kind of Web page is with a main heading and then an introduction. I did this by writing a short paragraph about me. Then I put a horizontal line to separate it from the rest of the information. I then put a picture on the page, aligned at the left margin. Next to this image, I put some facts and figures about me. After you provide a good, clear introduction like this on your Web page, you can put anything that is important to you, like your favorite TV show, movie, actor or actress — anything that you want to tell people about.

Chapter 9

Grabbing Goodies: The Great Graphics Giveaway

*Y*ou know how your Aunt Millie feels about garage sales? She just loves pretty things, and the only thing that gets her more excited than finding the perfect vase for her hall table is getting it really cheap. Well your Web page should be colorful and fun, but it shouldn't cost an arm and a leg, either. Lots of the graphics you can use to furnish your Web pages are absolutely free — you don't have to draw them yourself, and you don't have to pay for them, either. You only have to make sure the icons, buttons, and other images you copy are being made available on the Web as *copyright free clip art*.

So put on your pith helmet and grab your binoculars Web page explorers. In this chapter, you're going to hunt down sources of great clip art illustrations that you can use on your Web pages.

Using Your Friendly Neighborhood Search Service

Coming and getting it on the Web isn't as easy as ordering from the menu at your favorite fast food restaurant. Luckily, you have a way to find *menus* that you can use to *order* things on the Web. The Web contains so many kinds of information scattered across so many Web sites around the world that simply finding what's out there has become a business in itself. So, don't leave your home page without one. Several companies called *Internet search services* have made it their job to keep track of what's on Web pages and find what you need. See the section "Searching for the searchers" for a list of popular search services.

Spiders and worms and robots, oh my!

Detectives need clues, and search services need words. The search services work by using special computer programs that go from Web site to Web site, making a list of the titles of Web pages, the most important headings on Web pages, and other keywords and phrases. These programs do their work automatically, often at night and on weekends when the Internet is less busy. They go by a variety of different names: worms, spiders, wanderers, or robots, for example. The programs send their lists of contents back to the search services, which store the information in huge lists called *indexes*.

Goin' on a keyword hunt

When you want to look for something on the Web, you go to one of these services' Web sites and enter *keywords*. Keywords is just a fancy name for a word or phrase that you want the search service to locate on a Web page. You'll see a simple text box somewhere on the home page. You enter one or more keywords that describe what you're looking for (some sites let you enter an entire phrase, for example, "clip art icon of houses." You click a button that's usually called Search or Submit. This click sends your keywords to the service. The service, in turn, searches its index of Web sites and reports back to you with a list of Web pages that contain the keywords.

Searching for the searchers

Each one of the Internet search services has its own address. Here are just a few of the better known ones:

- ✔ AltaVista (http://altavista.digital.com/)
- ✔ Excite (http://www.excite.com/)
- ✔ InfoSeek (http://www.infoseek.com/)
- ✔ Yahoo! (http://www.yahoo.com/)

The rights (and lefts) of copyright law

You've probably seen those mysterious words included in tiny type at the bottom of many Web pages: Copyright 1997 Jane Doe Enterprises, or the like. Don't copy any graphics or other contents from these pages without asking permission from the author beforehand. This sort of notice basically means that the author has the right to copy the material and other people can use the material only if the author agrees that they can do so. One funny thing about current copyright law in the U.S. is that all material published on the Web is protected by copyright whether a notice is included on the page or not. So, unless you get permission, you want to copy *only* material that is described as clip art. Even if the images on a Web page are labeled as clip art, that doesn't *always* mean that the author intends for you to use the images free of charge. Read the terms of use carefully. Don't be reluctant to ask to borrow a graphic, though — the author may be flattered to know that you like his or her work and give you the right to copy it on your own page.

Usually, you don't even have to look up the addresses. Your Web browser probably includes an option in one of its menus that will help you find these services. All you do is the following:

- ✔ In Netscape Navigator 3.0, select Directory⇨Internet Search.
- ✔ In Internet Explorer 3.0, select Go⇨Search the Web.

Both options take you to a page that collects links to many search services. Figure 9-1 shows an example of Netscape's Net Search page.

Figure 9-1:
Search services can help you find clip art. To connect to a service that enables you to search for keywords, click on one of the links on this page.

Yahoo! Where are you?

Yahoo! is one of the best resources on the Web for just about anything, including free art and graphics that you can use on your Web pages. The art isn't contained on Yahoo!'s site; it's in an index that provides you with links to sites that contain the resources you're looking for. Here's how to find art on Yahoo!:

1. **If you are using Netscape Navigator or Microsoft Internet Explorer, select File⇨Open.**

   A dialog box appears in which you enter the URL (Web address) for the site you want to go to.

2. **Enter this URL for Yahoo!:** `http://www.yahoo.com/`

   Yahoo!'s home page appears. This page gives you a good idea of the kinds of things you can find on Yahoo!

3. **Click on the link <u>Computers and Internet</u>.**

   Now you're at the page that contains links for all the information on Yahoo!'s site relating to computers and the Internet.

4. **Scroll down the page, and click on the link <u>Graphics</u>.**

   Now you've burrowed one level deeper into Yahoo! The page you're looking at (shown in Figure 9-2) has all the graphics information contained on Yahoo!

Figure 9-2:
Yahoo!'s pages contain lists of links like this one. Each link takes you to a graphics site somewhere on the Internet.

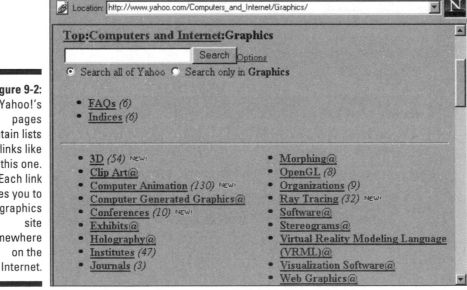

5. You might want to explore some of the links listed on the Computers and Internet: Graphics page, but because the subject at hand is Clip Art, scroll down the page, and click on the link <u>Clip Art@</u>.

The @ symbol means that this category is located in more than one place in Yahoo!'s web of information. This click takes you to Yahoo!'s clip art page. Each link on this page connects you to a site on the Internet that offers free art that you can download and use. Click on a link, and start exploring. After you've visited a site, come back to the Yahoo! clip art index page, and find another clip art site to visit.

Because you're likely to need graphics more than once as you create your Web pages, it's a good idea to save this page as a Bookmark (Netscape) or a Favorite (Internet Explorer). Navigator lets you do this by selecting <u>B</u>ookmarks⇨<u>A</u>dd Bookmark. In Internet Explorer, select F<u>a</u>vorites⇨<u>A</u>dd Page to Favorites.

One of the best clip art sites for kids is one that was created (surprise, surprise) by a kid himself. Twelve-year-old Matthew Arends loves to draw and has made some of his work available to kids just like you. He charges $5 for his collection. Check it out at `http://www.geocities.com/SoHo/4112/`.

Clip art is yours for the picking

Yahoo! is an index to the contents of the Internet. Yahoo!'s Web site presents you with lists of links to pages on the Web and other parts of the Internet. The links are organized according to the contents of the entire page. An Internet search service is different. It lets you search for keywords. You submit a word or phrase to the site, and the service returns pages that contain those words.

When you search for clip art using one of the search services like Magellan or Lycos, you have to do things a little differently. As you learned earlier, you enter a keyword or phrase that you want to search for, and the search service returns results. This kind of search is much less focused than "burrowing" through Yahoo!, but it can turn up some resources that Yahoo! might not be able to find. Here are a couple of ways to focus your searches and make them more successful.

Trick #1: Combining search keywords

By combining words and using conjunctions such as "and" and "or," you can make your search more focused, and you're more likely to find what you want. Instead of simply entering the words "clip art," tell the service what type of drawings you want to find, as in this example, using Netscape Navigator:

1. **Select** <u>D</u>irectory⇨Internet <u>S</u>earch.

   The Netscape Internet Search window appears. The layout of this page changes often; at the time this book was written, the top of the search window included buttons that let you search five services (Lycos, Webcrawler, Excite, Yahoo!, and InfoSeek).

2. **Click on InfoSeek.**

   The InfoSeek search page appears.

3. **Click in the text box, and enter the keywords** clip art for kids of houses and pets.

4. **Click on Seek.**

   The service does its thing, and in a few seconds, a page appears showing a list of links. Each link is connected to a page somewhere on the Web that contains the words you just told InfoSeek to find.

   The second and third links are to the following sites:

   Randy's Icon and Image Bazaar (`http://www.iconbazaar.com/others/`)

   ZIA Education ASCII, Clip Art, and Icons Page (`http://204.30.30.10/kids/art/kclip.htm`)

5. **Click on the link <u>ZIA Education</u>.**

   Your browser transports you to Zia's Art Links page, which contains links to all sorts of free art resources. By telling a search service to search for a combination of words, you can quickly turn up great clip art resources like Zia's Art Links page.

Trick #2: Search for GIFs and JPEGs

Search services are like eager bloodhounds. They'll search for just about any text you want. If you're looking for a specific drawing such as a kite, try entering one of the following in any search service's text box:

    ✔ `kite.gif`

    ✔ `kite.jpg`

    ✔ `kite.jpeg`

The service will scour its millions of Web sites, looking for all pages that contain files called `kite.gif`, `kite.jpg`, or `kite.jpeg`. Simple clip art images are most likely to be saved in GIF format, so try filenames with the `.gif` extension first. Click around and see if you find one you like.

Searching for filenames is neat, but the graphics you'll come up with are probably not going to be free clip art. Rather, they're likely to be original drawings whose owners hold copyrights to them. Instead of just downloading the graphics and putting them on your page, be sure to send an e-mail message to the owner of the page requesting permission to use the image.

Other Places to Find Clip Art

Don't overlook the fact that the best Web page resources can be right in your own backyard. Check with your Internet Service Provider to see whether free graphics are available on one of that company's Web pages. GeoCities (`http://www.geocities.com/`), which hosts the free Web page you create in Chapter 1, contains lots of cool resources for Web publishers. You can scour GeoCities for free graphics as well.

The BUTNZ site created by Douglas Vess (`http://www.geocities.com/SoHo/8885/`) provides lots of different clip art buttons you can add to your own pages to make links to other locations.

Software is where it's at

Sometimes, the software programs that you download and use to create Web pages or to work with graphics contain clip art images that you can add to your pages.

The Web Workshop program, which is described in Chapter 6 and included on this book's CD-ROM, comes with its own assortment of free dividers, backgrounds, and pictures, and it also lets you add images right in your Web pages.

Start by searching on your own computer. Look in the folder or directory on your hard drive that contains a graphics or Web page authoring program, and look around for a folder entitled clip art. Better yet, search your whole hard drive. In Windows 95, follow these steps:

1. **Select Start⇨Find.**

   A drop-down menu list appears containing options for the file or folder you want to find.

2. **Select Files or Folders.**

   The Find: All Files dialog box appears.

3. **Enter** clip art **in the Named text box, select the disk drive you want to search, and click on Find Now.**

   Windows scours your hard disk for any folders or files containing the words *clip art*. Any matches appear in the bottom half of the Find: All Files dialog box.

On the Macintosh, you search for files like this:

1. **Click on the Mac desktop to make sure you are in the Finder. Select File⇨Find.**

   The Find File dialog box appears.

2. **Click on the uppermost drop-down menu, and tell the Finder where you want to search.**

   Usually, on local disks is good enough.

3. **In the text box on the right of the Find File dialog box, enter** clip art.

4. **Click on Find.**

   An Items Found window appears. It presents all folders or files that contain the words clip art.

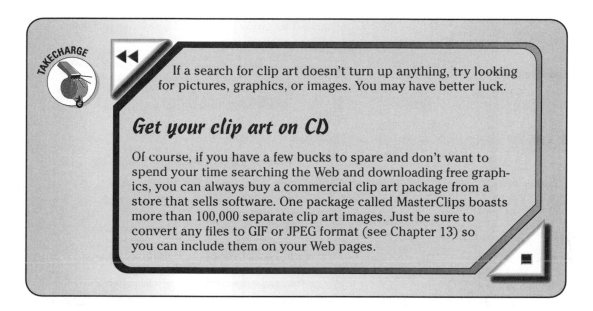

If a search for clip art doesn't turn up anything, try looking for pictures, graphics, or images. You may have better luck.

Get your clip art on CD

Of course, if you have a few bucks to spare and don't want to spend your time searching the Web and downloading free graphics, you can always buy a commercial clip art package from a store that sells software. One package called MasterClips boasts more than 100,000 separate clip art images. Just be sure to convert any files to GIF or JPEG format (see Chapter 13) so you can include them on your Web pages.

Speaking of clip art and CDs, you've got a source of free images right in your hands. The CD at the back of this book contains 14 images created by Stylus Media's developer designer John Casler. You can copy them and add them to your own Web pages. See Appendix D for instructions on how to copy and use these images.

Copy Cat Ways to Get Graphics

When you find a clip art image you want to use, you have several ways to get it on your computer. The following examples use the BUTNZ site at GeoCities. If you want to follow along, go to the site now by directing your Web browser to `http://www.geocities.com/SoHo/8885/`. The BUTNZ home page appears (see Figure 9-3).

Let your mouse do the browsing

Web browsers like Netscape Navigator and Microsoft Internet Explorer make copying an image a snap — or, more accurately, a mouse click. Both browsers let you copy or save an image file simply by doing the following:

Click on a button like this one, and copy it with your mouse

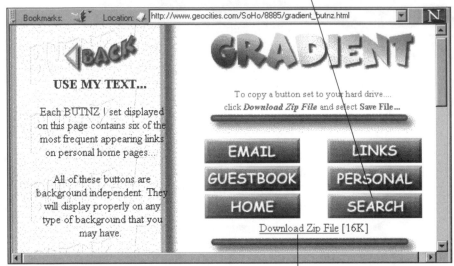

Figure 9-3:
The BUTNZ
site lets you
copy clip
art with
your
mouse, do
drag-and-
drop, or
download
a ZIP
archive to
your
hard disk.

Click on the underlined text to download a compressed ZIP archive

Copying with Windows 95

1. **Position your mouse arrow over the image you want — for example, one of the buttons on the BUTNZ page.**

2. **Click and release (right-click) your right mouse button.**

    A drop-down menu appears.

3. **Select Save Picture As (Microsoft Internet Explorer) or Save Image As (Netscape Navigator).**

    A dialog box appears with the name of the image file entered.

4. **Assign a location for the file, and click on Save.**

Copying with a Mac

1. **Position your mouse arrow over the image you want — for example, one of the buttons on the BUTNZ page.**

2. **If you are using Microsoft Internet Explorer, click and hold down your mouse button. If you are using Netscape Navigator, click and hold down your right mouse button.**

    A drop-down menu appears.

3. **Select Download Image to Disk (Microsoft Internet Explorer) or Save this Image as (Netscape Navigator).**

   A dialog box appears with the name of the image file entered.

4. **Assign a location for the file, and click on Save.**

You Mac users can have an additional thrill when it comes to copying graphics. You can act like a caveman and drag the image from its home on a Web page and deposit it right on your desktop. If you're really organized, you can drag the image right into a Web page you're working on or to a folder where you want the file to reside.

Downloading archived files

The third way to copy graphics from Web pages is to click on a *compressed file archive*. An archive is a single file that contains several different files. The single file not only conveniently stores lots of documents in one bundle, but it also compresses all the files it contains. The archive takes up less disk space than the files would if you downloaded and stored them separately. However, to open an archive and work with the files it contains, you sometimes need to install special utilities. This process is explained in the next section.

Unpacking Archived Files

Archives are commonly used to store graphics files and applications because archives save space and enable you to download the files more quickly on the Web. In the BUTNZ page shown in Figure 9-3, the archive shows up as the link Download Zip File [16K]. If you click on that link, you'll download a file that contains six separate BUTNZ (er, buttons) to your hard disk.

What exactly do you do with the archive once you've downloaded it? That depends on the type of archive you have obtained. You are likely to encounter two types of archives:

   ✔ **A self-extracting or self-executing archive:** These archives end with the extensions `.sea` or `.exe`. All you have to do is double-click on the file, and it opens itself.

   ✔ **Other types of archives:** The other archives require a special application to open them. You are likely to encounter two types of formats with these archives. The most common formats are ZIP, used on Windows computers, and SIT, used on Macintosh computers.

The next two sections tell you what to do when you download ZIP or SIT files.

Zipping and unzipping on Windows 95

A ZIP archive is a file or group of files that have been packed into a single compressed bundle using applications called WinZip or PKZip. Not surprisingly, the same applications that are used to bundle the files up are also used to unbundle them, too. All you need to do is install WinZip or PKZip on your computer before you download the file. Download the file from one of the sites mentioned in the following Webventure note. Double-click on the Setup icon, and the Setup program will lead you through the rest of the process.

After the program is installed, you start it by choosing its name in your Windows 95 program menu. You open an archive by choosing File⇨Open Archive. To extract the files in an archive, click on the Extract toolbar button (see Figure 9-4).

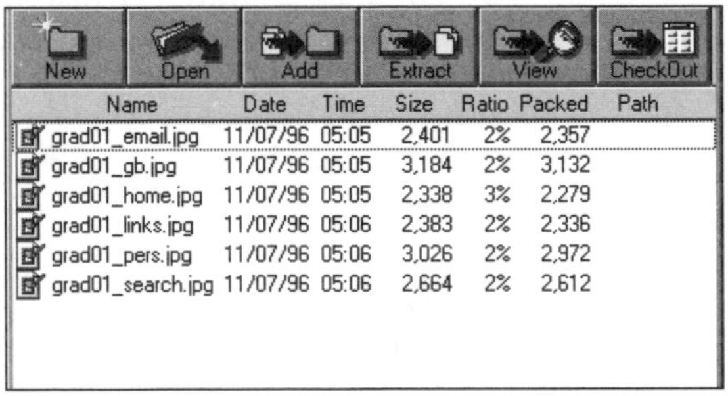

Figure 9-4:
Use a program like WinZip to open an archive, see what's inside, extract the contents, and work with them.

	Name	Date	Time	Size	Ratio	Packed	Path
	grad01_email.jpg	11/07/96	05:05	2,401	2%	2,357	
	grad01_gb.jpg	11/07/96	05:05	3,184	2%	3,132	
	grad01_home.jpg	11/07/96	05:05	2,338	3%	2,279	
	grad01_links.jpg	11/07/96	05:06	2,383	2%	2,336	
	grad01_pers.jpg	11/07/96	05:06	3,026	2%	2,972	
	grad01_search.jpg	11/07/96	05:06	2,664	2%	2,612	

Toolbar: New, Open, Add, Extract, View, CheckOut

Note: StuffIt Expander for Windows will open ZIP and SIT archives, as well as many other kinds of compressed files you might run into.

All of the programs mentioned in this section are very popular and are available as shareware: Their makers will share them with you, but they really want you to pay for the programs if you intend to keep them. WinZip is so popular that it has its own Web site (http://www.winzip.com/), where you can download an evaluation copy. Although it's available as shareware, its creators ask that you to pay them $29 if you intend to keep it. PKZip is advertised for $99 at http://www.pc-ware.com/pkzip.htm. StuffIt Expander is available as freeware — in other words, it doesn't cost you a thing. Find out more at http://www.aladdinsys.com/.

To unpack an SIT archive, use StuffIt Expander for Windows. However, because the files contained in this archive are likely to be in Macintosh format, there's no guarantee that you'll be able to read or view with them. Stick with ZIP files if possible.

Unzipping on a Macintosh

The best utility around is StuffIt Expander, which will handle almost all your unstuffing needs and is available as freeware on the Web. Download the file from Aladdin Systems' Web site or any other shareware site. Whenever you download an SIT file, it will have the extension .sit. You can open it one of two ways:

1. Drag the SIT file's icon atop the StuffIt Expander icon.

2. Double-click on StuffIt Expander to start the program.

3. Select File⇨Expand.

4. Find the SIT file you want to open, and click on Expand.

In either case, the files are extracted and placed in their own folder. Open the folder, and you can begin working with them.

What do you do with the graphics files after you've *grabbed* and stored them on your computer? You just turn to Chapter 13, which explains how to add graphics to your Web page.

One kid's opinion

I love clip art! It's one of the coolest things about being on the Web. I can't believe how people make all these drawings and then let you use them on your pages. A lot of people you meet online are really nice. I get some of my images from GeoCities. I'm a writer, not an artist, so I'd rather use a graphic created by someone who can draw, rather than try it myself.

Part IV
Advanced Web Page Techniques

The 5th Wave — By Rich Tennant

"Oh, Scarecrow! Without the database in your laptop, how will we ever find anything in Oz?"

In this part . . .

The best Web pages seem to be magical: When you connect to them, colors appear, figures move, and sounds come out of your computer's speakers. In Part IV, you find out how to pull your own rabbits out of your Web page hat.

A good photo can turn a ho-hum Web page into an eye-popping experience. You get some tips about scanning and editing photos so that they appear clearly and quickly on your viewer's computer screen. You also discover how to make your Web page colorful and draw some images to jazz up your Web page.

Animations are certain to make visitors to your Web page say "Wow!" And animations are easier to create than you might think, as long as you have the right software tools. You find out how to create your own GIF animation, which is like a miniature movie that plays on your Web page.

Web pages don't have to be silent, either. You discover how to record your own voice message and add it to your Web page. You can also add music clips that entertain your visitors while they peruse your words and images.

Chapter 10

Smile and Say Cheese!
How to Scan Photos

. . . .

. . . .

Someday, computers will be so smart that they'll be able to act like cameras that capture images and put them into electronic documents like Web pages. Until that day, you'll have to scan your photographs to get the images they contain into your computer — and once they're in your computer, you can get them on your Web page. This chapter gives you some tips on how to make great scans.

Focusing in on Photo Scanning

Scanning is a magical sort of process in which one kind of visual information is turned into another kind of information. When a movie camera records a scene, it captures a series of individual images. Each one of those images is a frame in a roll of film. The film is usually played so fast that you don't see the individual images; you only see the final effect — in other words, a motion picture. Scanning is the same sort of process: The *scanner* takes a single image and turns it into squares that are so small you normally can't see them. But each square (called a pixel) contains digital information that a computer can interpret. (To find out more about pixels and computer images, jump ahead to Chapter 13.)

Techie photographic types refer to photos as *continuous-tone* images. That means they are made up of tones in which values change continuously. Scanning is a way of turning continuous-tone images into a format that can be understood and displayed by a computer — in other words, *digital* format. Computers exchange data bits of digital information. When you scan a photo, you turn the visual information contained in that photo into a bitmap. A *bitmap* is literally a map of the image that consists of little bits of information called *pixels*.

Using Scanners to Make Web Snapshots

The good news about scanners is that their prices are going down all the time; you can now find flatbed scanners for just under $200. Four types of scanners are commonly available these days:

- ✔ **Built-in scanner:** A particular type of computer, the Hewlett-Packard Pavillion 7130P, contains a built-in scanner: You put a photo into a little slot, and a camera inside the computer box scans the image. Then your photo is returned to you. It certainly takes up less room than other options.

- ✔ **Flatbed scanner:** The name of this device reflects the fact that the bed on which the photo or other image is placed is flat. An optical device much like a camera moves under the bed and scans the photo. This is the type of scanner the pros use.

- ✔ **Hand-held scanner:** You hold this type of scanner in your hand and pass it over the image in order to turn it into a bitmap.

- ✔ **Multifunction device:** This device is a relatively new type that performs many different functions. A typical multifunction machine sends and receives faxes, scans images, acts as a laser printer, and makes copies, too. They're very practical for home use.

Which scanner should you buy? Sorry, but there's no simple answer here. It depends on your needs. The flatbed scanner is the best choice for making lots of scans, either for home or business use. However, multifunction machines give you the equivalent of many different kinds of equipment for a single price. Hand-held scanners take up less room than flatbeds; they're a little less expensive, though not much. It's up to you.

Other Scanning Resources

OPEN

You don't have to purchase a scanner to convert your glossy photos or drawings to digital computer documents. More and more organizations are popping up, ready and eager to help get your images on the Web. Here are a few suggestions.

Scanning services

If you mail photos to some friendly places in cyberspace, you will receive shortly thereafter the scanned images on a floppy disk. If you have an account with America Online, enter the keyword **PicturePlace**, and press Go.

Lots of businesses on the Web offer photo scanning services: You may want to go to Yahoo!'s index at `http://www.yahoo.com/Business_and_Economy/Companies/` and click on the link <u>Communications and Media Services</u>.

Service bureaus

Service bureaus provide lots of computer services for publishers, and one of these services is making scans. Look in the Yellow Pages under Typesetters or Service Bureaus. Call your local branch of Kinko's; many outlets provide scanning and other computer services along with the usual photocopying.

The Scanning Process

After you purchase or borrow a scanner, what do you do next? Here, without further ado, are the basic steps you need to follow.

Step 1: Pick a good image

Ever hear the phrase, "Garbage in, garbage out"? It certainly applies to photos or other images you want to put on the Web. Remember that your images won't appear in print; they'll be seen on a computer screen.

Computer monitors vary widely in quality. Some are bright, some are dark, some are sharp, others are practically murky. The best images for the Web are these:

- ✔ **High contrast:** Select images that display a clear difference between light and dark areas. A photo of your friend standing outdoors on a sunny day will work better than a candid shot taken in a dimly lit basement.

- ✔ **Relatively bright:** If you have a choice, select images that are well illuminated. You may love the subtle haziness of a landscape when it is printed on glossy paper, but when you try to put it on a computer screen you may end up with nothing but fog.

- ✔ **Small size:** Inline images (images that appear in the body of a Web page along with the text and other contents) are generally less than 7 inches wide. Often, photos are only 1 to 4 inches wide, and perhaps 1 to 5 inches tall. Snapshots are great for Web pages. If you scan an entire 8 ½ x 11-inch sheet of paper, you had better reduce the size of the image to fit on a Web page.

Step 2: Launch your software

All scanners come with some sort of software that lets you scan the images and save them in various formats. Sometimes, scanners come with programs that act as *plug-ins* (programs that work within other graphics program like Adobe Photoshop). Two examples of these plug-ins are the Macintosh applications, PlugInScan and ScanMaker. After you install the scanners following the instructions that come with your scanner, start up the program, turn on the scanner, and make a preview scan of your first image.

Step 3: Preview your scan

Virtually all scanning programs let you make a preview scan of an image. A preview scan gives you a quick idea what an image will look like after you do the actual scan. Look for the button that says Preview, such as the one in the Preferences menu in the ScanWizard window, shown in Figure 10-1.

When you press the Preview button, you hear a whirring sound as the optical device in the scanner does its stuff. A preview image appears on screen with a *marquee box* (a rectangle made up of dashes) around the image. This box lets you crop the image. *Cropping* an image means that you select the part of the image that you want to appear in the final version and leave out parts of the image that aren't essential. In Figure 10-1, for example, the marquee box is placed right around the boy and the dog; the nonessential areas around the two figures are, therefore, cropped out.

Contrast and brightness controls   Preview button   Cropping marquee box

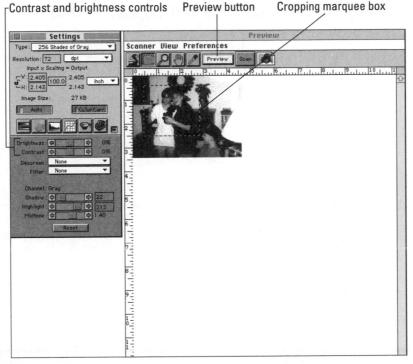

Figure 10-1:
You can
make a
preview
scan and
crop or
reduce an
image
before you
make the
actual
scan.

The importance of cropping

Cropping an image is important and you should do it whenever possible because it makes an image smaller. The smaller an image file, the quicker it appears on the Web and on your visitor's computer screen. To crop, click on the cropping button, position your mouse pointer just above and to one side of the image, and clicking and pressing your mouse button, drag your mouse down and to the opposite side of the image. Release your mouse when the subject of your photo is outlined within the marquee box. Cropping — as opposed to simply scanning the entire photo — results in a good looking and compact image for your Web page.

You don't have to crop your photo as soon as you scan it. If you have a graphics program, you can scan the image in "big" format and open it up later in the graphics program where you can crop it and change the contrast and brightness, too. If you're doing your scanning at a service center like Kinko's, you should probably crop your photos right away so you can get all of the images on a diskette.

Step 4: Decide on an input mode

After you crop your image, you have to tell the scanner how you want the visual data in the image to be captured. Choose one of the following options in your scanning program's Mode menu:

- ✔ **Color:** If you're scanning a color photo, this is the option to use.

- ✔ **Grayscale:** If you're scanning a black-and-white photo, use this option.

- ✔ **Line art:** If you're scanning black-and-white drawings, signatures, cartoons, or other art, use this setting.

What's the difference? No one's going to call the bad-scanning police if you scan a black-and-white drawing in color mode. You'll just end up with an image that's far larger than it needs to be. It'll take up more space on your hard drive, take longer to upload to your Web site, longer to appear on-screen, and so on.

Step 5: Set the resolution

Earlier in this chapter, I noted that scanned images are made up of little bits (dots) of information called pixels. Those dots are small, but they aren't always the same size. When you scan an image, you have the option of making the dots *really* small so that the image appears extra smooth. This is called setting the *resolution* of an image.

The smaller the dots, the better an image appears in a printed booklet, brochure, or flyer. The size of the dots is expressed in dots per inch (dpi). The higher the number of dots per inch, the smaller the dots and the finer the image.

In an image with 1250 dpi, the dots are so small that you can't see them at all; this level of resolution is used in printing. Many laser printers print at a resolution of 300 or 600 dpi. A resolution of 300 dpi is finer than 72 dpi. Because an image scanned at 300 dpi has much more information in it, it will take up much more computer memory than a 72 dpi version. Also, computer monitors can display no more than approximately 72 dpi, which brings one to the following conclusion: When you're just starting out, scan at 72 dpi!

If you are scanning images only to be placed on the Web, scan them at 72 dpi.

It's true that 72 dpi is a very coarse resolution; the image will appear bumpy. However, the file will be as small as possible, and that's the most important thing when it comes to scanning Web graphics. You don't accomplish anything scanning an image so that it has 300 dpi when no one will see more than 72 dpi on a computer screen. You'll be wasting valuable computer memory, and worse yet, your images will take too long to appear on the Web. Later, when you experiment with using graphics programs, you can scan at higher resolutions and reduce them to 72 dpi.

If you are scanning images that you expect to output on a laser printer, as well as publish on a Web page, scan at 150 or 300 dpi. You can use the high-resolution (300 dpi, that is) version for your paper publication. Then you can open the scanned image in a graphics program (as explained later in this chapter) and save it in a lower-resolution version (72 dpi). You can then put the 72 dpi image on your Web page.

Step 6: Adjust contrast, brightness, and size

Be patient — you're almost ready to scan. The more preparation you do now, the better your image will appear when it gets into cyberspace. You do only one more thing before you finally press the Scan button in ScanWizard: Look at the preview scan and, if the image seems dark or "muddy," adjust the brightness and contrast. In ScanWizard (refer to Figure 10-1), the brightness and contrast controls are sliders that you can move either to the left or right. Try them out and see if the image improves. If you're happy with the image as is, leave the brightness and contrast set to zero.

If you're sure the image at its present size is too large, you can do some quick math and estimate how much the image must be reduced. For example, if an image is 8 x 10 inches and you are sure it must be about 4 x 5 inches when it appears on your Web page, scan it at 50 percent of the original size.

Step 7: Ready, set, scan!

Press the Scan button. Listen to your scanner whir away as those colors turn into pixels. Because you're scanning at only 72 dpi, it shouldn't take too long to scan your image. When you're done, the image appears again in your scanning program's window.

Step 8: Save your image

Before you make more changes, save your image to disk by doing the following:

1. **From your graphics program's menu, select File⇨Save or File⇨ Save As.**

2. **In the Save (or Save As) dialog box that appears, enter a name for your file.**

   In most graphics programs (for example, Photoshop), a drop-down menu appears in this dialog box when you click on the arrow next to the Save As text box. This menu gives you options for the file format in which to save your image. Since you're scanning images to be used on the Web, your choices are simple. You save your image in either GIF (sometimes called CompuServe GIF) or JPEG (sometimes called JPEG/JFIF) format.

   Mac users: Click on the arrow next to the Format drop-down menu, and select the file format you want from the drop-down list.

   When you assign a name to your image, be sure to include the right file extension; Web browsers recognize only image files with extensions like `.gif`, `.jpg`, or `.jpeg`. If you name your image *me* and you save it in GIF format, name it `me.gif`. If you save it in JPEG format and you work on a PC, call it `me.jpg`. On a Mac, call it `me.jpeg`.

3. **To select the directory on your hard drive in which you want to save your file, in the Save dialog box, click on the arrow next to the Save in text box.**

   Mac users: Click on the arrow on the right side of the drop-down menu at the top of the dialog box, and locate the folder in which you want to save your file.

4. **When you locate the correct directory, click on Save.**

   The Save or Save As dialog box closes, and your file is saved. You can now go on to make more scans or select File⇨Exit to leave your graphics program.

   Mac users: Select Quit from the File menu to leave the graphics program.

Graphics Alphabet Soup: GIF and JPEG

GIF and JPEG are two methods of saving an image for use on the Web. Both formats compress the data into a bitmap image so that the computer file of the image takes up much less disk space. GIF and JPEG are also cross-platform formats, which is a fancy way of saying that they are recognized by lots of different types of computers and can be displayed by most Web browsers.

▶▶

Sometimes, the scanning software you use lets you save only in JPEG format and not GIF. Don't worry; either format works fine. If you have a choice of one or the other, however, the following sections explain the pros and cons of each format.

When to use GIF

GIF, which is pronounced either "JIF" or "GIF," stands for Graphics Interchange Format. The GIF format was originally developed by CompuServe to let customers with different computers send graphics files to one another. GIF compression works best with images that have well-defined edges, such as cartoons, line art, or drawings (see the star images in Chapter 13), as opposed to photos.

When to use JPEG

JPEG, which is pronounced "jay-peg," stands for Joint Photographic Experts Group, the name of the group that came up with the format. JPEG uses a different way of compressing an image than GIF does. But without getting too technical about it, with large black-and-white or color photos, JPEG works better than GIF.

GIF compresses images at only one level. However, if you save an image in JPEG format, your scanning software will probably prompt you to select a compression level you want to use. That's because JPEG has a number of different levels. After you assign a name to an image and click <u>S</u>ave, a dialog box appears like the one shown in Figure 10-2.

Figure 10-2:
JPEG lets you
choose from
four levels of
compression,
as shown in
JPEG Options.

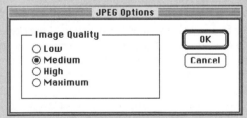

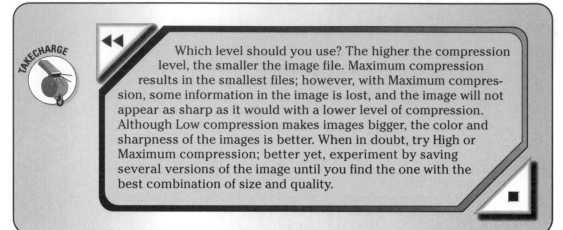

Which level should you use? The higher the compression level, the smaller the image file. Maximum compression results in the smallest files; however, with Maximum compression, some information in the image is lost, and the image will not appear as sharp as it would with a lower level of compression. Although Low compression makes images bigger, the color and sharpness of the images is better. When in doubt, try High or Maximum compression; better yet, experiment by saving several versions of the image until you find the one with the best combination of size and quality.

Cropping and Retouching Photos

After you scan an image and save it, you can still adjust it if something doesn't seem quite right. Maybe a friend did the scanning for you, and you want to crop the image more tightly or save it in a different format. In either case, you need a graphics software program that will let you work with images.

The graphics programs that most professionals use on the Web are Adobe Photoshop and Corel PhotoPaint. However, these programs are expensive and far more complex than the average kid or parent really needs to make a fun, personal Web page.

For everyday scanning and photo retouching, download a shareware program from the Web and try it out. If you like it, pay the nominal shareware fee.

A good shareware ($30) program for Windows 95 is LViewPro, which was created by Leonardo Haddad Loureiro and marketed by MMedia Research Group. It's included on the CD that accompanies this book (see Appendix D). LView Pro is used for the examples that follow. To download the latest version or get more information, go to http://www.lview.com/l.

On the Mac, Thorsten Lemke's GraphicConverter ($35) is a great shareware graphics program. You can download it from many Mac shareware sites, including http://www.hotfiles.com/macuser/software/. A Windows 95 program called Paint Shop Pro, by Jasc, Inc., is available as shareware ($69); it has more features than GraphicConverter or LView Pro. You can download a 30-day trial version at http://www.jasc.com/pspdl.html.

Note: If you want a Mac-specific program, you can also check out *Macs For Kids & Parents,* by Tom Negrino and Wendy Sharp, published by IDG Books Worldwide. It has a demo of the Claris Home Page program on the CD.

Cropping

Simply scanning an entire photo from edge to edge and putting the entire photo on your Web page usually results in an image that takes up more space than it should — in terms of height, width, and disk space (kilobytes of memory). Cropping a photo does these two things:

 ✔ Concentrates the viewer's eye on the most important area

 ✔ Makes the file size and the image size smaller

The following steps show how I reduced the file size of an image of my niece Clare. In its present state, the image is 11K in size, which isn't bad, but some adjustments in a graphics program can make it smaller. Here's how to crop the image using LView Pro in Windows 95.

1. **Open LView Pro.**

   A blank white window opens, showing LView Pro's menu options above the window.

2. **Select File⇨Open.**

   The Open Image File dialog box appears.

3. **Select the image you want to work on, and press Open.**

   The image appears, with the LView Pro toolbar either to the right or left of the image (see Figure 10-3). Clicking on the top of the toolbar makes the toolbar flip to the other side of the image.

   When you place your mouse arrow over the image, the mouse becomes a crosshair. You use this crosshair tool for cropping.

4. To draw a box around the image, click just above and to one side of the image, and pessing the mouse button, drag the mouse down and to the other side of the image.

The area contained within the bright red-and-white striped rectangle (the box you just drew) is the area that is preserved; everything else will be cropped out (see Figure 10-3). If you didn't draw the cropping area quite right the first time, click somewhere else, and draw another box. You can also adjust the shape of the box by clicking on the outline and resizing it.

Figure 10-3: When you draw a rectangle around an image like this one, be sure to leave a little space around the person's head.

5. Select Edit⇨Crop!

The image is instantly cropped. If you're not happy with the results, select Edit⇨Undo.

6. If you are satisfied, select File⇨Save or Save as.

Save as lets you save the file with a different name, so you can preserve the original version if you want to.

If you choose Save as, the Save Image as dialog box appears. Be sure to choose either JPEG or GIF from the drop-down Save as type menu at the bottom of the dialog box. Also, add the extension that corresponds to the file type: .jpg for JPEG or .gif for GIF.

By simply cropping the photo like this and saving it in JPEG format, its file size is reduced from 11K to 6K — a reduction of more than 45 percent. (*Note:* Saving in GIF format compresses the file less severely, but the file size still shrinks to 9K.)

Changing contrast and brightness

Often, the image you want to put on your Web page is poor in quality, but you really want to put it out there in cyberspace anyway. A good graphics program can't make a silk purse out of a sow's ear, but it can make a poor image a little better. Figure 10-4 shows an example of a photo that's a little dark and with poor contrast (it's also 56K in size, and can stand to be reduced, too).

You can use the following steps to make a poor image look better on your Web page. (Again, this example uses LView Pro, but you can find similar controls for contrast, brightness, hue, and other qualities in other graphics programs):

1. **Open the image in LView Pro, following Steps 1 and 2 in the preceding set of steps.**

2. **From the program's menu bar, select Retouch▷Contrast Enhance.**

   Most of the controls for changing the image can be found in the Retouch menu. Check out the dizzying array of options in Figure 10-4.

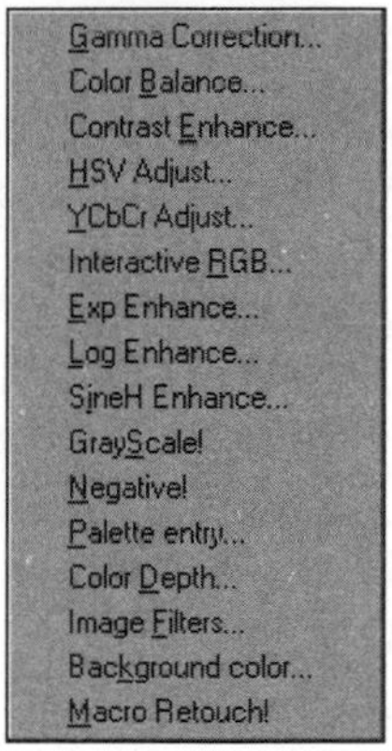

Figure 10-4: Use LView Pro, and other graphics programs to alter the appearance of a computer graphics file in many ways.

```
Gamma Correction...
Color Balance...
Contrast Enhance...
HSV Adjust...
YCbCr Adjust...
Interactive RGB...
Exp Enhance...
Log Enhance...
SineH Enhance...
GrayScale!
Negative!
Palette entry...
Color Depth...
Image Filters...
Background color...
Macro Retouch!
```

When you select Contrast Enhance, the Contrast Enhancement dialog box appears (see Figure 10-5).

Figure 10-5:
Changing
the contrast
is one of the
easiest and
most
effective
ways to
improve a
scanned
photo
image.

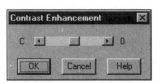

3. **Click on either the right or left arrows to see the contrast of the image change.**

   In this case, the image needs less contrast, so the setting is changed to –10.

4. **Click on OK to close the Contrast Enhancement dialog and return to the image.**

5. **Select Retouch⇨HSV Adjust.**

   The HSV Adjustment dialog box appears (see Figure 10-6).

6. **Clicking on the right arrow in the topmost of the three controls (labeled H, which stands for Hue), increase Hue as much as you want.**

   You see the effect on the photo that you are editing. In the image shown in Figure 10-6, Hue is increased to 10. Saturation (labeled S) is at zero. Value (labeled V) is increased to 10. Change the settings to suit the image you are working on.

   Hue is a way of measuring color. Saturation refers to the amount of gray in the image. Value refers to the lightness of the image.

7. **Click on OK to close the HSV Adjustment dialog box.**

   By now the image is looking better.

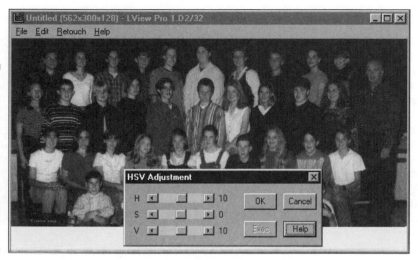

Figure 10-6:
Adjusting
Hue,
Saturation,
and Value
can make
an image
more
colorful and
brighter,
too.

8. Select Retouch⇨Log Enhance.

The Log Enhancement dialog box appears. Log stands for *logarithm*. Because it brightens dark pixels while keeping already bright ones from becoming too bright, Log Enhancement is a good way to brighten up a dark image.

9. Click on the rightmost arrow to increase the brightness as much as you want (in this case, 7).

10. Click on OK to close the Log Enhancement dialog box.

11. Select Retouch⇨Sine H Enhance, and click on the rightmost arrow to brighten the image even more.

Be careful; even clicking on the arrow once or twice can produce a dramatic effect in the image. In this example, the setting was left at 1.

These steps provide you with only the basics for retouching scanned photos. By now, the image is looking much better than before (see Figure 10-7), but it's still much bigger than it needs to be, and it's still 56K. By changing the color depth and the size of the image, you can optimize it for your Web page. If you want to play around with all of your graphics program's settings, you can do much more with your image. For example, try out the image filters and "Sharpen" utilities, if you have them in the graphics program you are using. Not all programs provide these capabilities.

Figure 10-7:
With a little
help from
your
graphics
software,
you can
make a ho-
hum image
shine and
ensure that
your Web
audience
sees all the
important
details.

Resizing

After you adjust the appearance of your photo, the next step is to reduce the image size. If you're using LView Pro, you resize by selecting Edit⇨Resize. The Resize Image dialog box appears. The numbers in the upper-left corner of the LView Pro window indicate that the image is 562 pixels wide and 300 pixels high, or roughly 7 x 4 inches. That's a really big image for a Web page. Simply using your graphics program to resize the image can help. To make the image smaller, follow these steps:

1. **Select Edit⇨Resize.**

   The Resize Image dialog box appears.

2. **In the Height and Width text boxes, enter a smaller number.**

   To keep it simple, divide one of the numbers in half. In this case, change 562 to 281 or 300 to 150, which are shown in the boxes next to "New size." These two numbers represent the height and width you want the image to be, as expressed in pixels. Make sure the "Keep aspect ratio" box is checked; this tells LView Pro to maintain the shape of the image so it doesn't get distorted. Simply click in the text box you didn't change, and LView will adjust the numbers automatically to maintain the ratio of height to width.

3. **Click on OK to close the Resize Image dialog box. The new, resized image appears on-screen, replacing the earlier version.**

   The file size is now reduced from 56K to 17K, thanks to the resizing.

4. **Select File⇨Save as, and give your file a name and extension, as explained in Step 6 under "Cropping."**

Capturing Video Images

In this high-tech, digital world, you have more options than simply scanning a photo in order to capture an image you can put on a Web page. What about all those home movies your family has been taking with its camcorder over the years? A neat little device called Snappy Video Snapshot lets you select still images from your videotapes and save them in digital format so that you can show them on your Web page.

Using Snappy Video Snapshot

Snappy Video Snapshot, by Play Incorporated is a popular software and hardware package for capturing video images and turning them into computer documents. (This program works only with a PC; sorry Mac lovers.) You plug the hardware module into your printer port, install the software, and plug your camcorder into the hardware module using the cables that come with the product. You can go to Play Incorporated's Web site (http://www.play.com/) to find out more about Snappy Video Snapshot.

After you install the hardware and software correctly, you can start up the program, turn on your camcorder, and actually play your own videotape through your computer screen. When you come to a frame you want to capture, pause your camcorder and press the Preview button in the Snappy window (see Figure 10-8).

Figure 10-8:
Use the Snappy Snapshot controls to select a videotape image and adjust it before taking a snapshot of the frame you want to capture.

Capturing an image with Snappy is pretty similar to the process of using scanning software, as explained earlier in this chapter. You take a preview of the image, which you can crop and adjust for brightness and contrast. When the image appears as you want, press the Snap button in the Snappy window, and you've got it.

Note: The only tricky thing about using Snappy to capture images for Web pages is that you need to save your image in JPEG format. Press the Save button, and select JPEG from the drop-down menu of available file formats. Be sure to add the extension `.jpg` to the filename. JPEG works better with complex color images, such as video snapshots.

One kid's opinion

I was able to borrow a scanner from my dad's office. Borrowing a scanner is good if you have only a few images that need to be scanned. But if you plan on scanning a lot, you should buy one. I did all of my scanning on my Web pages myself. The first few times, I had to scan stuff more than once. If I am unhappy with the results of an image, I will scan it again, but this time with a different scaling or contrast. Knowing how to scale and set the contrast for the pictures right is important. I've had many pictures where I have forgotten to set the contrast before doing the final scan, and when I previewed the image, it looked awful. I suggest making a couple of separate scans that have variations in brightness and contrast. Open them up in a Web browser, and then choose the version you like best.

Chapter 11
Lights, Camera, Animated GIFs!

• •

In This Chapter

▶ Making magic with animated GIFs

▶ Finding animations kids love

▶ Creating simple animations

▶ Other ways to make Web page contents move

• •

*Y*ou don't have to go to Hollywood to direct a movie or produce a cartoon show. Now that you have your own Web page, you can smell the greasepaint and listen to the roar of the crowd right in your home. All you need are some good ideas, the right software, and the instructions in this chapter on how to make animated GIF images.

Animated GIF images are a special type of image saved in the GIF format. This type of GIF image can consist of only two or a whole series of separate GIF images. The person who puts those images together can arrange or draw them so that they seem to be moving when viewed in sequence. In fact, you might say that animated GIFs are like miniature movies that play within a single image *frame*. A frame is a rectangular area that you define in the graphics program you use to create your animated GIF images. Each of the images is positioned within the same frame.

If you like your entertainment quick and easy, you can go to one of the Web sites that offer free clip art images, including animated GIFs. Copy any image you like, and add it to your own Web page (see Chapter 9). However, if your creative juices are flowing, you can make your own animations. So decide how you want to express yourself, follow the instructions in this chapter, and the rest is history.

To make animated GIFs you need the following:

___ An idea of the animations you want and what you want them to do

___ Paper and pencil to draw the images

___ A graphics program to create or edit the images

___ One of two special programs that let you assemble a series of GIF images into an animation. If you're on a PC, you might use GIF Construction Set for Windows (available as shareware for $20) from

Alchemy Mindworks, Inc. You can download it from the Alchemy Web site (`http://www.mindworkshop.com/alchemy/gifcon.html`). If you're on a Mac, you might install GIFBuilder, which is made available as freeware by its creator, Yves Piguet. You can download GIFBuilder at `http://iawww.epfl.ch/Staff/Yves_Piguet/clip2gif-home/GifBuilder.html` or from the Info-Mac archives at `ftp://ftp.amug.org/pub/info-mac/gst/grf/`.

You can find other programs that let you create GIF animations, for example, Microsoft GIF Animator, which you can learn about at `http://www.microsoft.com/imagecomposer/gifanimator/gifanin.htm`. GIF Construction Set and GIFBuilder are two popular programs that I have used. Choose the program that's right for you, and copy it to your hard drive so you can follow along with this chapter.

Note: Animated GIFs are not supported by every Web browser roaming through cyberspace. Older versions of America Online's Web browser and some other browsers show only a single "frozen" image, which is yet another good reason to upgrade to a better browser (such as Netscape Navigator 3.0 and Internet Explorer 3.0, which are included on the CD with this book).

If you need a browser or need to update yours, you'll find everything you need to get connected on the CD that comes with this book. Just install the sign-on software to AT&T WorldNet Service from the CD and get connected in minutes. (See Appendix D for more information.)

Setting the Scene: Understanding Animated GIFs

Chapter 7 introduces you to animated GIFs and describes the GIF format in general, but here's a quick recap. GIF, which stands for *Graphics Interchange Format,* is a type of image compression used to present inline or external images on Web pages. Originally developed by CompuServe, GIF is a popular format for displaying graphics on the Web because it reduces the size of an image without reducing its quality. And as you probably know, the smaller the image, the better it transmits over the Internet.

But enough of this talk. It's time for some action. If you have access to a scanner, you can scan a number of photos or drawings and turn them into a homemade animation or movie (see Chapter 10 for more about scanning). If you don't have a scanner to capture the images you want to include in your animation, you can create a *type-only* animation (more about that later in this chapter). Best of all, you can draw your own image frames to create your animated GIF movie.

Popular (and free) animated GIFs

If your notion for some motion doesn't include planning, drawing, or testing, just help yourself to the free GIF animations waiting for you right on the Web. Many image archives offer clip art images that you can easily download. Clip art images are images that their owners have made available on the Web to anyone who wants to download them; although the owners give you the right to copy the images on your own pages, some clip art images do carry use restrictions or small shareware fees. (See Chapter 9 for more about copyright.)

A great source for copyright-free animated GIFs is Rose's Animated GIFs (`http://www.wanderers.com/rose/animate2.html`). See Appendix C for other suggestions.

The following sections suggest sources for animations that will add some *sweat-free zing* to your Web page (also refer to Chapter 9 for some sources of clip art images, some of which are animated GIFs).

E-mail animations

More and more kids' Web sites are including animated images that invite visitors to respond by e-mail. Sometimes, the animation consists of an envelope being folded and unfolded; other times, a mailbox opens automatically. In either case, the message is "Send me some e-mail!" Sometimes, clicking on the animated GIF image causes an e-mail message dialog box to open, which you can use to quickly send e-mail to the owner of the Web site.

Counters, frogs, and other animations

Figure 11-1 shows other popular animated GIFs that you can use on your pages. The following list describes them from left to right:

- **A Wacky Counter:** This Web page counter, which never stops moving, is at `http://www.lookup.com/Homepages/72413/counter.gif`.

- **The Dancing Frog:** This plump fellow would make Kermit proud. This fellow can be found at `http://sciborg.uwaterloo.ca/~rarmas/pics/others/kerokero.gif`.

- **Walking the Dog:** A playful pooch dashes across your Web page. You can take it for a walk after you copy it at `http://www.morestuff.com/anima/dogrun.gif`.

- **Friendly Duke:** This little guy's name is Duke. He does a whole series of somersaults in the animated GIF you find at `http://www.triang.com.br/imag/java.gif`.

Figure 11-1:
Use these
animated
images on
your Web
page, or
shop
around for
others.

Java Applet Animations

But maybe you're the kind of movie director who prefers hiring a cast of thousands and spending millions and trillions of dollars. You want to be on the cutting edge of Web technology and add *Java applets* to your page.

Java applets (and similar objects by Microsoft called *ActiveX Controls*) are not as compact and simple as animated GIFs. *Applets* are, in fact, miniature computer programs written in a language called Java that Web browsers can interpret and execute.

An applet doesn't have to come up to you on the street and introduce itself. You'll know it when you see it. First, a gray rectangle appears on the Web page you connect to. Next, your browser displays a message (such as "applet NervousText loading") in the status bar at the bottom of the window. Then you have to wait while the browser downloads and processes the applet. Go to the fridge and get a soft drink; by the time you return, the applet will (hopefully) be on your screen.

Note: The browsers included with AT&T WorldNet Service on the CD do display Java applets, but not all browsers "do" Java. Older versions of Netscape Navigator (before version 2.0) and some other browsers don't display applets at all.

Sophie Winsley includes a pretty simple kind of applet on her Sophie's Fun Page in which letters of different colors bounce around randomly (`http://homepages.enterprise.net/ ted.hall/sophie.html`). The applet on Sophie's page is called SineLine.

Another complication is that applets vary in size and complexity. Some applets are as simple as an image of bubbles that seem to float; others perform complex tasks like displaying the current stock market prices. Whatever they do, applets take a long time to appear on a Web page. If you've stayed with me and read through all this so far, here is a little secret: Often, the benefit isn't worth the time a Web browser takes to display an applet. Try to make GIF animations whenever possible.

Creating Your Own Animation

I love reruns of certain television shows (particularly "The Simpsons"). But I also get a thrill when a new show comes out. So if being original is where you're at, don't copy someone else's images. Create your own. Put on the director's cap, and direct your own graphic movie. You don't have to be a prize-winning artist to do this, either. You can create a simple, yet effective, animation that doesn't require a lot of drawing; for example, these two kinds of animations:

- **Hand-drawn:** You can find a simple cartoon like the one that Ayal made for his Web page (`http://agdec1.technion.ac.il/ayal.html`). Check out his animation in which two figures play a game called Matkot. The ball goes back and forth, and the hands holding the paddles move, too.

- **Text-only:** An *all-type* (a series of images that consists solely of words, not drawings) animation is one that is used by many businesses on the Web.

Creating an all-type animation

In an *all-type* animation, in each image contains a different phrase. For example, the images might say, in succession, "Visit my Web site," "Send me e-mail," and "Check out the awards I've won." The following sections explain how to create such a series of images.

Do you want to take a peek behind the scenes? A great way to see how animated GIFs are put together is to copy one from the Web and open it in GIF Construction Set or GIFBuilder. That way, you can see the individual frames, one by one, and evaluate how the designer handled issues like transparent colors or color palettes.

Step 1: Install the right software

Here's a surprise: The first step is to obtain the right software for creating animated GIFs. You can download versions of GIF Construction Set for either Windows 3.1 or Windows 95. GIFBuilder requires a Macintosh with System 7 or later. Refer to the download sites for these programs near the beginning of this chapter.

After you install the right program for your computer, read the fine print that comes with the software. In both GIFBuilder and GIF Construction Set, the information about the software's features and how to use them is contained in the Documentation file. If you get stuck, GIF Construction Set has a help file that you can access from the <u>H</u>elp menu while you're working with the program.

Mac users: Select GIFBuilder Shortcuts from the AppleGuide menu. (Look for the big question mark at the right of the Mac menu bar.)

Step 2: Draw your images

Next, show me the money — uh, that is, show me the images. GIFBuilder and GIF Construction Set don't come with the tools needed to actually *create* the images that make up your animated GIF. You must draw, type, or otherwise make those with a graphics program, such as MacDraw, SuperPaint, or Photoshop.

It's also up to you to make sure the sequence of images you create varies from image to image in such a way that, when put together as a single animated GIF by your GIF animation software, the images appear to be animated. In the case of Ayal's animation mentioned earlier, he had to draw several different frames. In each frame, the ball and each of the paddles were in a different position.

A good way to start, before you even fire up your computer, is to draw the images, frame by frame, using the old-fashioned pencil and paper technique. Then you will know how many separate images you want and the order in which you want them to appear. (If you need some pointers on creating a simple drawing, even if you can't draw like a professional, see Chapter 13.)

Step 3: Create the computer graphics

Okay, this is getting pretty exciting, but you're not quite ready for prime time yet. After you know what you want to do, open the graphics program of your choice. This example will use the simplest software available: the built-in Paint program that comes with Windows 95. **Mac users:** Use MacPaint, which works pretty much the same. A more sophisticated program like CorelDRAW, Adobe Photoshop, or even LView Pro will certainly work better. You can find a version of LView Pro on the CD that comes with this book.

1. **Open Paint by selecting Start⇨Programs⇨Accessories⇨Paint.**

   The Paint window opens. You may see a white rectangle left over from the last image you or someone else worked on.

2. **Select View⇨Tool Box.**

   If the tool buttons and color palette aren't visible, select View⇨Color Box to display them.

3. **Select Image⇨Attributes.**

   The Attributes dialog box appears.

4. **Change both the width and the height to 150 pixels.**

5. **Click on OK to close this dialog box and return to the Paint window.**

   The Paint window now contains a white square.

6. **Click on the text tool (the letter A).**

   Two new icons appear under the tool buttons. Click on the lower one. This icon lets you create transparent type. Then click on a color in the palette at the bottom of the window. This action assigns a color for the text you are about to type. Pick a nice vivid primary color like green or blue, as opposed to a hard-to-read color like yellow.

7. **Type the message you want to appear in the first frame of your animation.**

   Pick a bold typeface. Position the words in the frame where you want them to appear. You need to maintain the frame size (150 x 150 pixels, which you set in Step 4), as well as the position of the words within this frame. If you don't set up the frames the same way, the images will appear to bounce. You can set up the frames any way you want. Just do it the same way for each one. Figure 11-2 shows how the first frame will look.

8. **To save the image, select File⇨Save As, and choose GIF format (or GIF89, if your graphics program includes GIF89 as an option).**

Save each frame as a separate image file, and give each one a name that'll be easy to remember: welcome1, welcome2, welcome3, for example.

Since Paint creates only bitmap (BMP) images, you won't be able to work with the image as is. You must convert it to GIF format using LView Pro (see Chapter 10) or another graphics utility. **Mac users:** Use GIFConverter, a program available as shareware ($30) by Kevin A. Mitchell, which you can download at http://www.kamit.com/ gifconverter.html.

Repeat this process for each of the frames you want in your animation. You can have as many frames as your movie director-self desires, but you won't get an Oscar if your animation contains 40 images and requires 75K of disk space. Keep your images short and simple, especially when you're starting out.

Step 4: Assemble your movie frames

Roll 'em, roll 'em, roll 'em. Keep those movie frames rollin'. After you create the individual frames, you need to put them in a movie sequence using either GIFBuilder or GIF Construction Set. Since this example uses PC software, the following steps refer to GIF Construction Set. (Don't worry, Mac users; GIFBuilder works very much the same — in fact, you have the added advantage of being able to drag-and-drop your images directly into the GIFBuilder window in order to assemble your animation.)

Each frame should be 150 x 150 pixels

Figure 11-2:
Cut! You've created and captured the first frame of your animated GIF movie.

WELCOME
TO
CLARE'S
WEB PAGE!

You might find it helpful to inspect the sample animation, called `ball.gif`, that comes with GIF Construction Set. Doing this will give you an idea of how the various image files (which are computer files called blocks — header block, loop block, control block, and image block) fit together. The various blocks are shown in the `ball.gif` image in Figure 11-3.

You've got the hang of making your own animated GIFs, and now there's no limit to ways you can use them. One project that will get valuable brownie points with Mom or Dad is an animated GIF that includes all the members of your family. You can place it on the page of your Web site that talks about your family. Start by creating a text-only frame that serves as an announcement — something along the lines of "Here's My Family!" Then include each sister and brother in their own frame. You can see an example using photos of my very own family in Figure 11-4.

You can use the example of `ball.gif` as a model for your own animated GIF. Here's what you do:

1. **Open GIF Construction Set, and select File⇨New.**

   A new GIF Construction Set window appears. A file called a header block is listed at the top of this window with a preset size. You should change this size to fit the size of the frames in your own animation.

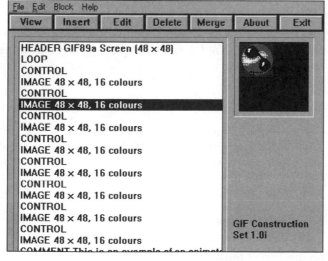

Figure 11-3: Open the sample file, `ball.gif`, in GIF Construction Set to get a look at the building blocks of a typical GIF animation.

Figure 11-4:
An
animated
GIF movie is
a great
way to
immortalize
each of the
members of
your family.

2. **Click on the Edit button at the top of the screen.**

   The Edit Header window appears.

3. **Enter the width and height of the images you created before (in this case, 150 x 150 pixels).**

   You can click on the box next to Background to select a background color. When you click on the number, a color palette appears. You can then select the color you want for the background of your animation. Leave the Global palette box checked.

4. **Click OK to close the Edit Header window.**

5. **Click on the Insert button at the top of the GIF Construction Set window.**

   The Insert Object dialog box appears. It contains the different kinds of blocks you can use to build your image (Image, Control, Comment, Plain Text, or Loop).

6. **Click on the Loop button.**

   This inserts the loop block at the beginning of your animated GIF file.

   Stop your loop when you want to get off. A *loop* occurs when all the images in an animated GIF have played and the sequence is about to start over again. There's no reason to have GIF images have to loop over and over again. Both GIFBuilder and GIF Construction Set let you specify the number of times an animation needs to loop before it stops. Often, letting the image play one, two, or three times is enough. Stopping the animation gives your graphic a more subtle and professional effect.

7. **Click on the Insert button.**

   The Insert Object dialog box appears.

8. Click on Control to insert a control block.

The control block is now added.

9. Click on the Insert button.

The Insert Object dialog box appears.

10. Click on the Image button.

The Open dialog box appears.

11. Locate and select the first image in your sequence and click on OK.

You find the image where you saved it earlier on your hard drive; in this example, it's a file called `welcome1.gif`. A dialog box appears asking which color palette you want to use for your animation.

12. Select "Use this image as the global palette," and click on OK.

For your first image, it's probably best to select this option.

After you select global palette, the color palette dialog box does not reappear. You now see a miniature version of the first image in your animation in the upper-right corner of the GIF Construction Set window.

After you follow these basic steps, continue assembling the parts of your image. After your first image block, insert a Control block, then another image block, then a control block, and so on, until all the frames in your animation are added.

13. When you are done, select File⇨Save.

Save your animation with a new name; be sure the extension `.gif` appears at the end of the filename.

Now it's time for the really fun part — that is, a sneak preview of your animation before you insert it into your Web page. Grab some popcorn, sit down, and click on the View button in the GIF Construction Set toolbar (refer to Figure 11-5). Your animation will play over and over on your computer screen. Con-gratulations! Press Escape when you want to say "Cut!" and stop the preview.

Do you want a guaranteed *A?* If you're in an art or drawing class, you can impress your classmates and your teacher by creating your own animated GIF for an assignment. Because animated GIF files are pretty small, you can copy one to a floppy disk. Take it to school so you can play it on one of the computers there. You'll probably need to copy GIFBuilder or GIF Construction Set to the disk, too, so you can play the file.

Step 5: Add the animation to your page

It's show time. After you create your animation, the *easy* part is adding the animation to your Web page. You simply add it the same way you do any other GIF or JPEG image (as explained in Chapter 13). You don't need to add special codes. If you're adding the HTML manually, you insert a reference like this one to the source code for your Web page:

```
<IMG SRC="welcome.gif">
```

The `welcome.gif` part of this line of HTML assumes that the GIF image is in the same directory as the Web page HTML document. (See Chapter 15 for tips on describing paths to images or other files that are contained in other directories.)

If you're using Adobe PageMill (a version is on the CD that accompanies this book), click on the Insert Image toolbar button, locate your file in the dialog box that appears, and click on Open to add the image to your page. If you're using Allaire HomeSite (also has a version on the CD), select Tools⇨Quick Image. In the Image dialog box that appears, click on the folder icon next to the Source text box. The Select a File dialog box appears. Locate the image you want to add on your hard drive, and click on Open. The Select a File dialog box closes. Click on OK to close the Image dialog box, and return to the main HomeSite window.

One kid's opinion

The best animated GIF I've ever seen is a cartoon-like "wormhole" opening on a page that's devoted to the TV show "Sliders". I think one good animated GIF is enough for a Web page. Any more than that takes up too much computer memory, and the page takes longer to appear. Lots of different animated GIFs on the same page can actually look kind of silly.

Chapter 12

Jazzing Up Your Pages with Sound

. . . .

In This Chapter

▶ Hardware and software for playing and adding sound on Web pages

▶ Choosing the best sounds for your Web page

▶ Presenting sound on a Web page

▶ Creating your own sounds

. . . .

*H*ave you ever seen a Charlie Chaplin movie? You might be surprised to discover that they are in black and white and silent. At that time (roughly 1900-1927), while a movie was running, a real, live person sat in the theater and played the piano to provide the sound. Then came a transition period in which some movies remained silent and some were *talkies* (they had a soundtrack, in other words). That's where the Web is now. Some pages have sound and some don't; some Web surfers can hear sounds on Web pages and others can't.

The possibility of adding sound to your Web page creates lots of new possibilities. It's another way to hook your viewers and keep their attention from wandering elsewhere. This chapter tunes you in to how audio is transmitted on the Web. You hear about the different kinds of sound files commonly included on Web pages. You get some sound advice (no pun intended) on which file formats you should use and how to keep sound files from becoming screeching megabyte monsters. Finally, you get some pointers on where to find free audio files you can use, as well as instructions on how to make your own Web recordings.

Making Your Web Page Sound Off

If you want to dance to the music, you have to pay the piper. In other words, you have to have some special equipment if you want to make your Web pages talk or sing (or if you just want to play a sound on someone else's page). So before continuing, check out what you need to get started:

___ **Sound card:** A computer card is a thin, rectangular piece of plastic that plugs into a special place inside your computer. Some computers come with a sound card installed. If yours doesn't, you must buy one, such as one of the popular Sound Blaster cards by Creative Labs, Inc., which range from $139 to $249.

___ **Speakers:** Your computer may have a speaker installed, but some computer speakers are so feeble that you can barely make out the sound across the room. Any computer store will be happy to sell you a new and improved set of speakers for as little as $20 to $30.

___ **Audio-capable browser:** Some newer Web browsers (like the ones included on the CD) have built-in software that recognizes audio files on Web pages and automatically starts to play them. If your browser has this capability, great; if not, you'll need to install the following item.

___ **Audio software:** If your browser doesn't play sound files, you need to install an application that helps your browser recognize and process sounds. You'll find some suggestions later in this chapter.

To create your own sound files for your pages, you need a sound input device, such as the following:

___ **Microphone:** If your computer has one built in, you're in luck. If not you'll have to buy one, but they aren't too expensive.

___ **MIDI or other instrument:** As explained in Chapter 7, MIDI stands for Musical Instrument Digital Interface, a music format that computers can understand. A MIDI device is a special kind of musical instrument that produces digital sound that can go directly into a computer. The sound file it produces can then be edited and added to a Web page.

___ **Sound recording software:** If you use a microphone to record an audio message (see Chapter 7), you need to use a computer program that saves your message in a format that can be added to your Web page. The easiest programs to use are Sound Recorder (which is built into Windows 95) or the Macintosh's built-in Sound control panel.

Make sure you get involved before the dollars start to fly out of your wallet. It's reasonable for kids to want equipment to create and play audio files on the Web. It's not reasonable to spend top dollar for high quality speakers and microphones if all you plan to do is create or play Web sounds. Sound transmitted on the Web is pretty limited in quality, so inexpensive equipment may be all you need.

The two standard sound formats

Sound file formats are another basic aspect of sound on Web pages that you need to understand. In order for a Web browser to play a sound "bite" (a short audio excerpt) that you have included on a Web page, that sound file has to be in a format that the browser will recognize and be able to process. Lots of sound files are on the Web, but you really need to know about only two kinds of file formats: AIFF and WAV.

I recommend that you save your sound file in one of the following two formats because they are supported by most Web browsers:

- ✔ **AIFF:** Audio Interchange File Format, a common Macintosh audio format
- ✔ **WAV:** Windows PCM waveform, the common Windows audio format

If you use a Mac, save your sound file in an AIFF format, using either the Sound control panel or a special sound application such as SoundMachine. Use the extension .aiff, as in piano.aiff. If you use a Windows PC, save your files in a WAV format with the extension .wav, as in song.wav.

Opening your ears to Web sounds

Before you rush out to the store and buy a microphone and sound card, stop and ask, "Why do I want to put sounds on my Web page?" The correct answer is, "Because I have something to say and sounds will help convey the message that's on my Web page."

Sound files seriously slow down the rest of your page. Audio works best when it supplements your words and images. You should use audio if you have a personal message you want to say or some music you want people to hear. Think about what effect you want the sound to create, and your page will have more of an impact. Classical music will make your page seem more serious. Wacky sound effects will make your page seem more playful.

One way to answer the question "Why include sound at all?" is to think about the different kinds of sounds you can include on a Web page. You have four options:

- ✔ **Spoken word:** You speak into a microphone connected to your computer, and the melodic tones of your voice go out to all your friends in cyberspace.
- ✔ **Background sounds:** A sound file can play in the background of a Web page by use of special HTML instructions like BODY<BGSOUND="music. wav">. (See Chapter 14 for information about using HTML.)

> ✔ **Sound effects:** Most computers have a bunch of sound effects. You can set your mood with anything from dripping water to blaring horns.
>
> ✔ **Sound clips:** You can find plenty of short sound clips taken from popular movies, TV shows, or musical acts. However, before you copy one of these and put it on your own page, be careful that it isn't protected by copyright. (See Chapter 9 for copyright information.)

Giving your computer a voice and ears

You need to make sure that your computer is sound-capable. After all, there's no point in thinking about creating sounds for Web pages if you can't even hear the sounds. Chances are you already have the hardware you need. Lots of computers on the market come with speakers and sound cards already built in. (You may still want or need to install an external microphone, which is much more convenient than the built-in variety. Break out the manual that came with your machine, and take stock of what you have and what you need to get.)

Just as your computer needs software that enables you to record sounds, it needs software that lets you play sounds you find on the Web. When a browser encounters a sound file it can't play, such as a MIDI file (with the extension .mid) or a Windows WAV file (.wav), it needs some help from special audio applications. You can choose from two kinds of applications: *plug-ins* and *helper applications* (helper apps).

Plug-ins and helper apps are computer programs that assist a Web browser by processing audio, video, or graphics files that the browser cannot display by itself. Plug-ins play or display a file while the browser is still showing the page on your screen. In other words, they work within the browser. Helper apps start up and run separately from the browser in order to display or play the file. They work outside the browser.

You can download plug-ins and helper apps from the Web. Often, these programs are available for free. Sometimes the manufacturers ask you to pay a nominal fee.

Audio and other plug-ins and helper apps for Web browsers are easy to find. Netscape maintains a list of plug-ins at http://home.netscape.com/comprod/products/navigator/version_2.0/plugins/index.html. Another good list, called Plug-in Plaza, is at http://browserwatch.iworld.com/plug-in.html. Netscape also has an introductory page on helper apps at http://home.mcom.com/assist/helper_apps. Each of these sites provides brief explanations of what each application does, as well as a link to a site where you can download the version you need. The plug-ins work with either Netscape Navigator or Microsoft Internet Explorer; however, not all plug-ins are available for all types of computers. You may also want to check out *Netscape Plug-Ins For Dummies,* by Chris Negus, published by IDG Books Worldwide.

If your browser already has software available to process the more common varieties of sound files (which are discussed later in this chapter), you may not need to install an audio plug-in at all. Here's how you can find out whether your Web browser can play audio files:

1. **If you use Internet Explorer on a PC, select View⇨Options. (If you use Netscape Navigator on a PC, select Help⇨About Plug-ins.)**

   The Options dialog box appears with Internet Explorer. (The About Plug-ins page appears with Netscape Navigator.) This page tells you which plug-ins are available on your computer for use with Netscape. Scroll down the page to the list of audio files. Figure 12-1 presents the About Plug-Ins page, which is showing that this copy of Netscape Navigator has a Netscape audio plug-in called Live Audio installed. The table shows the kinds of sound files that LiveAudio will play. (*Note:* If you don't have an audio plug-in, you can download it from the Netscape plug-ins page listed in the previous Webventure tip. Click on the link Audio/Video on the Netscape plug-ins page. Scroll down the page, and download the new Netscape audio/multimedia application, which is called Netscape Media Player.)

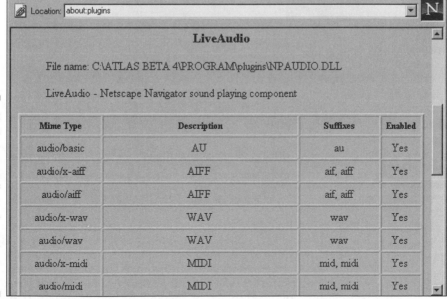

Figure 12-1: LiveAudio's about plug-ins page lists the kinds of multimedia files your Web browser can process and play.

Location: about:plugins

LiveAudio

File name: C:\ATLAS BETA 4\PROGRAM\plugins\NPAUDIO.DLL

LiveAudio - Netscape Navigator sound playing component

Mime Type	Description	Suffixes	Enabled
audio/basic	AU	au	Yes
audio/x-aiff	AIFF	aif, aiff	Yes
audio/aiff	AIFF	aif, aiff	Yes
audio/x-wav	WAV	wav	Yes
audio/wav	WAV	wav	Yes
audio/x-midi	MIDI	mid, midi	Yes
audio/midi	MIDI	mid, midi	Yes

2. **Click on the Programs tab to bring the Programs dialog box to the front, and then click on the File Types button.**

The File Types dialog box appears (see Figure 12-2). The Registered file types dialog box contains a list of the types of computer files that your copy of Internet Explorer is set up to recognize and process. You select the New Type button to tell your browser to use a helper app or plug-in you've installed.

3. **Scroll down the list to a Format Sound file type (for example, AIFF Format Sound or AU Format Sound), and click on that format to select it.**

At the bottom of the File Types dialog box, you see the message, Opens with: IEXPLORE. If this option is displayed, Internet Explorer will open and process the type of sound file you just selected. You can scroll down the list to see how many sound formats Internet Explorer will recognize and play.

Figure 12-2:
The File Types dialog box is a good place to check out how many kinds of multimedia files (audio, video, or animation) Microsoft Internet Explorer is set up to play or display.

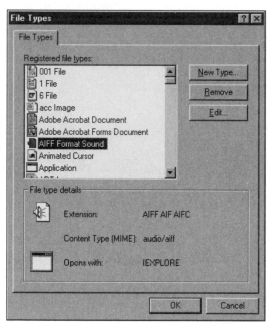

Mac users: If you are using Internet Explorer for the Mac, you can check for plug-ins by selecting Edit⇨Options and then clicking on Helpers. The Helpers dialog box appears. Click on a sound format file; the words "built-in" should appear at the bottom of the dialog box, indicating that Internet Explorer has built-in support for that format. If you don't see "built-in," you need to install a plug-in or helper app for that file type.

If you use Netscape Navigator for the Mac, select About Plug-ins from the Apple menu. The rest of the process for Navigator is the same as in Step 1 above.

Built-in support for audio and other multimedia files is one good reason to upgrade your browser to the versions of Netscape Navigator or Microsoft Internet Explorer included on the CD that accompanies this book. However, if you use an older browser or encounter an audio file that your browser can't play, you need to download a helper app or plug-in to your computer.

Every bit of information that goes on a Web page needs to be in digital format so that a computer can understand and process that information. That applies to sound, too. The sounds you hear on Web pages are bits of audio information that someone has recorded and saved in digital format on a computer. Usually, the audio signals are converted to digital form in one of two ways: by speaking or playing directly into a computer microphone or by playing the sound on a digital MIDI instrument that's plugged into the computer. (See Chapter 7 for more on getting sounds into your computer.)

Turning analog sounds into digital data

If you are a budding musician or a recording engineer, you may want to know the difference between the sounds that people speak and the sounds that computers play. For one thing, it helps you understand why you need all this hardware and software to play or record Web sounds.

The sounds in the "real world" that go into your ears or come out of your mouth are *analog* sounds. Analog means that the sounds are made up sound waves that vary greatly in pitch and volume.

Digital sounds are made by *sampling* those sound waves. Sampling means that audio software literally takes a sample of a sound wave and approximates it in digital form. Digital waves are made up of ones and zeroes that computers can understand.

Five-year-old Kaitlyn Ruth uses audio well in her Kaitlyn's Corner Web page (http://www.bayne.com/wolfbayne/kaitlyn/korner.html). Kaitlyn presents a spoken message that tells kids how to surf the Internet safely. Often, the background sounds that play when you connect to some Web pages seem intrusive. One example of a background sound that doesn't distract from the page's contents is the simple *Forrest Gump* theme on 13-year-old Nicole's home page (http://www.geocities.com/Enchanted Forest/2926/).

Check out Appendix C, for some Web sources of clip art sounds you can copy. Also, check out the Walt Disney Company Web pages (`http://www.disney.com/`), which put out sounds from popular movies that kids can copy for free.

Before you go surfing around the Web looking for exotic sounds, look in your own backyard (that is, your computer's hard disk). If you have a PC, you'll find sounds by doing the following:

1. **Select Start⇨Settings⇨Control Panel.**

   The Control Panel window appears.

2. **Double-click on the Sounds icon.**

   The Sounds Properties dialog box appears. The box Events lists all the sounds that your computer has available.

3. **Click on the name of a sound, and then click on the arrow next to Preview.**

   You should now hear the sound coming from your computer's speakers. (Obviously, you need a computer with a sound card and speakers to do this).

4. **For even more sounds, click on the arrow next to the Name text box, and select a set of sounds from the drop-down menu.**

If you want to include one of these sounds on a Web page, you need to copy it to another directory and save the file in WAV format. Follow these steps:

1. **Open Sound Recorder as described earlier, and select File⇨Open.**

   The Open dialog box appears.

2. **Navigate to the directory** `C:\Windows\Media`.

   You see a long list of built-in sounds, any one of which can be included on a Web page (that's because these sounds are in the common WAV format).

3. **Double-click on one of the sounds to open it in Sound Recorder, and then click on Sound Recorder's Play button (the arrow pointing to the right) to hear the sound.**

4. **When you find a sound you like, select File⇨Save As from the Sound Recorder menu bar.**

   The Save As dialog box appears.

5. **Navigate to the directory on your hard disk where your Web pages are located. Save the sound file in the same directory as the Web page where you want the sound to appear.**

6. **Include a reference to the sound file in the HTML for the Web page. If the sound file is** ding.wav, **include the following line:**

```
<A HREF="ding.wav"> Ding! </A>
```

In this example, the word Ding! will be underlined on your Web page because it is a link. Clicking on this link causes the sound file ding.wav to play, and your visitor should hear the "ding."

Mac users: If you have a Mac that uses System 7.1 or later, you can do essentially the same thing with the sounds built into your computer, which are called System 7 sounds. These are located in your System Folder, but you have to double-click on the System icon to find them. After you find them, you can select the icon for a file, select File⇨ Duplicate, and drag the duplicate file into the folder that contains your Web pages.

Deciding how to present Web sounds

After you find a sound you want to include, how do you present it on your Web page? The following sections describe the options available. The Nerd Alert tips explain what you need to do to add the sound feature to the HTML instructions for your Web page. Most Web page authoring tools do not include user-friendly toolbar buttons and menu options that you can click on to add a sound easily. Instead, you have to open the HTML document in a word-processing program such as SimpleText (Mac) or Notepad (Windows).

Whether you use a Mac or a PC, the process of adding a line of HTML to an existing HTML document is the same:

1. **Select File⇨Open.**

   The Open dialog box appears.

2. **Navigate to the HTML document on your hard disk, and click on Open.**

   The HTML for the Web page in which you want the sound file to appear opens the file in a word-processing window. Then add one of the HTML instructions (called *tags*). All of these examples use the generic name filename.wav. You should replace this with your own sound file (if you're on a Mac, use .aiff for the file extension.

If you're confused by all these references to HTML (see Chapter 14 for more on working with HTML).

Include invisible sounds that play in the background

Invisible sounds are background sounds that play as your page is downloading to your viewer's screen. The viewer basically has no control: If the viewer's browser supports sound, it plays the sound file. If not, the page is silent.

To have a background sound on your Web page, you need to include two separate tags in your HTML document. You need these two tags because Netscape Navigator and Microsoft Internet Explorer recognize different HTML instructions for presenting and playing a sound file in the background while the viewer is connected to a Web page. These two browsers make up more than 90 percent of all browsers used on the Web. By including both of these tags, you'll be sure that almost all, if not all, of your viewers will have the chance to hear the sound on your page.

Place the Netscape tag after the `<BODY>` tag and before the `</BODY>` tag near the end of the document. It looks like this:

```
<EMBED SRC="filename.wav">
```

The tag recognized by Microsoft Internet Explorer looks like this:

```
<BGSOUND SRC="filename.wav">
```

This step is more complicated because you have to add the attribute `BGSOUND SRC` to the existing BODY tag.

Display a sound control panel

If you add a little more HTML to the EMBED tag mentioned previously, visitors who use Netscape Navigator will see a standard sound control panel on your Web page. (This control panel isn't something you have to create; it's built into Netscape Navigator and is used with Netscape's LiveAudio plug-in.) This panel puts your visitor very much in control. The panel includes a button for stopping and playing faster, as well as a button for adjusting the volume. You can see one displayed on David Sawchak's page, shown in Figure 12-3.

To display the Sound control panel, you need to use the following commands, which work only with Netscape Navigator:

```
<EMBED SRC="filename.wav" WIDTH=[# PIXELS] HEIGHT=
[# PIXELS]>
```

The term `[# PIXELS]` in this line of HTML should be replaced with the number of pixels you want the Sound Control panel to be in height and width.

Give your visitor a link to click on

Another way to present sound on a Web page is to add it to the page as a clickable hypertext link. When your visitors click on an icon or a phrase that is underlined or highlighted, they are linked to the sound file you included on your Web site. The sound doesn't play until someone clicks on the link. It's also a good idea to include the file size of the sound file. That way, your visitors can decide whether they want to click on it.

A simple text link can be made with this line of HTML:

```
<A HREF="filename.wav"> Clickable text goes here </A>
```

Use a graphic image

You can go to one of the image archives listed in Appendix C and use an icon to represent this link. Rachel uses plenty of these on Rachel's page (`http://www.mcs.net/~kathyw/rachel.html`). In David's Grab Bag Page (`http://www.chas-source.com/sawchak/dino.htm`), 8-year-old David Sawchak presents a photo of himself as the link to a sound file, as shown in Figure 12-3.

For example, if your sound icon is `speaker.gif` and your sound file is `.wav`, your HTML will take this form:

```
<A HREF="filename.wav"><IMG SRC="speaker.gif"></A>
```

Figure 12-3:
If you use Netscape Navigator and click on David's photo, a sound control panel appears.

Sound control panel

Decide how often to repeat your sound

Each time the user clicks on the clickable text or image, the sound plays once. However, if you include one of those invisible background sounds on your page, you have a choice of how often the sound clip plays (through something called a *loop*, which is a repeated instance of a sound, video, or animation file). You can have your sound loop over and over, or if you take my advice, you'll be nice to your visitors and play the sound only once or twice.

You loop background sounds by adding an additional bit of information to both the BGSOUND and EMBED tag in HTML:

```
<BGSOUND="filename.wav" LOOP=1>
<EMBED SRC="filename.wav" LOOP=1>
```

The preceding instructions make the sound play only once. Change the number to 2, 3, or as many times as you want. To keep playing the sound over and over, you use the following instruction:

```
<BODY BGSOUND="filename.wav" LOOP=infinite>
<EMBED SRC="filename.wav" LOOP=true>
```

Creating Your Own Sounds

After you have the right hardware and software and know what kind of sound you want to add to your page, the process of actually creating the sound is surprisingly easy.

If you have a PC, you can use Sound Recorder, the built-in Windows 95 sound application mentioned earlier in this chapter. After you create some sounds and want to edit and add sound effects, you can shop around for more sophisticated software. But when you're starting out, it makes sense to use the easiest and most convenient program. Follow these steps to record with Sound Recorder:

1. **Select Start➪Programs➪Accessories➪Sound Recorder.**

   Sound Recorder's control panel appears (see Figure 12-4).

Figure 12-4:
The Sound
Recorder
application
that comes
with
Windows 95
is simple
and easy to
access.

Mac users: From the Apple menu, select Control Panels⇨Sound. The Sound control panel appears. If you are using an external microphone, select Sound In from the drop-down menu at the top of the Sound dialog box. Click on Options. The Input Source dialog box appears. Click in the little circle under Microphone. Click on OK to close the Input Source dialog box and return to the Sound control panel. Select Alert Sounds from the drop-down menu. Click on Add. A recording control panel similar to Sound Recorder's appears. Click on Record, and begin talking or playing.

2. **Pick up your microphone, and start singing or playing.**

   You see sound waves in the Sound Recorder, or *sound lines* emerging from the speaker icon in the Mac's Sound control panel, as the sound is recorded.

   If you want to record yourself playing an instrument, you might have someone work the mouse and hold the microphone so you can concentrate on making music.

3. **Click on the Stop button when you are finished recording.**

   Now you can preview your recording to see whether you are satisfied enough to put it on the Web.

4. **Click on the Play button to play your sound back.**

5. **Click on the Save button (Mac) or select File⇨Save from the Sound Recorder menu bar (PC) in order to save your file.**

   If you want to try another take, repeat Steps 2–4 and then save your file.

One kid's opinion

I made a Web page for my brother Ethan, who belongs to a rock band called the Premonimum Jesters. Ethan helped me include the sound file on his page. I think the Web is a great way for a band that's just starting out to get lots of attention. Ethan's band lists the titles of its songs, and advertises its CD, too. You wouldn't believe the response they've gotten from having their own Web page. They're really excited about it.

Chapter 13

Painting Your Pages with Color and Graphics

● ●

In This Chapter

▶ Understanding Web color palettes

▶ Creating your own horizontal rule

▶ Converting an image to a format that can be displayed on the Web

▶ Coloring fonts, links, and backgrounds

● ●

*E*ven though the human eye can distinguish millions of different colors and many computer drawing programs let you create TrueColor graphics that contain as many as 16.7 million colors, Web browsers can display only a mere 256 colors. A set of colors such as this is called a *palette*. The quality of the graphic images you see on Web pages is also limited by the quality of the computer monitors on which those pages appear, and many monitors can display only 256 colors. This chapter begins by explaining a bit about how browsers and monitors display colors. Understanding these basic subjects will help you create better graphics for your Web pages. In this chapter, you find out how graphics are displayed on Web pages and how to create some simple graphics yourself.

Using the Web Color Rainbow

When you create drawings for a Web page with a program such as Super Paint or LView Pro, it's a good idea to use the same palette of colors used by Web browsers. You might see this palette referred to as the browser-safe palette or the Netscape palette. Some graphics programs have this palette built in, but in order to use this special set of colors, you have to select it as an option before you start drawing or editing a graphic. If the browser-safe palette isn't built in, you can download it from the Web and then use it if your graphics program has an option for opening external palettes.

Open your browser, select File⇨Open or Open Location, and enter one of the following URLs in order to download the Netscape palette to your hard disk. Windows users should enter this URL; ftp://ftp.mvassist.pair.com/pub/win/NS2COLOR.ZIP. Macintosh users should enter this URL: ftp://ftp.mvassist.pair.com/pub/mac/NS2colors.sea.hqx.

Trying out the browser palette

If you use exactly the same colors that are built into a browser, the browser has to do less work to display the graphics you create. And when you use the browser-safe palette, you're using the palette that is built into the most popular browsers: Netscape Navigator and Microsoft Internet Explorer. By using these colors, you'll ensure that your colors will appear the way you want, no matter what browser or computer operating system your visitors are using. Colors that aren't in the Netscape or Internet Explorer palette will have to be simulated by your visitor's browser, and they might look different.

The graphics program you use to make a drawing or edit a photo (see Chapter 10) often gives you the option of using a palette of 256 colors. Use the 256-color option if it's available. Chances are this set of colors is the same as the browser-safe palette.

Web Workshop, from Vividus Corporation, is designed for creating Web pages. Because it comes with the 256-color palette, you don't have to copy the browser palette. Windows 95 users can download Web Workshop from the CD that comes with this book. Mac users can download a copy from the Vividus Corp. Web site (http:///www.vividus.com/). You can also read more about Web Workshop in Appendix B.

After you copy or download the browser palette, you need to copy it into your graphics program so that you can use its 256 colors. Not all graphics programs let you copy a separate palette. In your program's menu options, try to find one that says Load Palette. You can follow these steps to download it from the Web (note the file extension, .pal):

1. **Start Paint Shop Pro, and select File⇨New to create a new image or File⇨Open to edit an existing one.**

   A white drawing area appears in the Paint Shop Pro window, and a new set of menus appears in the menu bar.

2. **Select Colors⇨Load Palette.**

   The Open Palette dialog box appears.

3. **Navigate to the palette you want to use (such as NS2COLOR, if you downloaded this earlier), and click on O̲pen.**

   The palette is now loaded into the program. A miniature version of the palette appears in the Color palette area on the right side of the Paint Shop Pro window.

Two graphics programs that let you use the Netscape palette are Paint Shop Pro (for Windows 95 users only) and GraphicConverter (for Mac users only). Paint Shop Pro, by JASC, Inc., is a powerful and highly recommended graphics program for Windows 95. You can download it from the JASC, Inc. Web site (http://www.jasc.com/) and try it out for 30 days. If you decide to keep the program, you are asked to pay a $69 shareware fee.

GraphicConverter, by Thorsten Lemke, is a full-featured program that lets you convert graphics files from one format to another or even make simple drawings. It's available as shareware for $35 and can be downloaded from http://www.hotfiles.com/macuser/software/.

Monitoring Web colors on computer screens

As I mentioned earlier, your computer monitor may also be limited in its capability to *colorize*. While some monitors can display thousands or even millions of colors, many can display only 256 colors — and might be described as *nearsighted*.

Lots of computer users go for months or even years without realizing that their computer monitors can be adjusted to show more colors, make images more detailed, or give their computer desktop a different color or pattern. It's a good idea to test your monitor and see what its capabilities are, so you can better understand the options your Web site visitor may or may not have.

Mac users: If you decide to use Web Workshop to create Web pages (see Chapter 6) and make your own drawings (as described later in this chapter), you may need to change the number of colors your Mac monitor displays. You have to tell your monitor to display "256" colors instead of "Thousands" of colors.

Check your computer monitor to see how many colors it is displaying right now, and what other color palettes it can display. Windows 95 users should click on the Display icon in the Control Panel window and then click on the Appearance tab, which contains the color settings. Mac users can select Control Panels from the Apple menu and then select Monitors. The Monitors dialog box appears. Make sure the Colors radio button is selected. Then choose 256 (rather than Thousands).

Using tables to arrange images and text

Some kids' pages use tables to arrange text and images next to each other (see Chapter 7). To follow the steps in this sidebar, go to the Kaitlyn's Korner page at `http://www.bayne.com/wolfbayne/kaitlyn/korner.html`. This page includes a table that has been divided into two rectangular areas called "cells." In the cell on the left, Kaitlyn has inserted a photo of her own smiling face. In the cell on the right, she's inserted another image, this time a textual image that gives the name of her Web site.

How do you add a table to your Web page? You can use a Web page tool that lets you create tables, such as Netscape Editor or HotDog (both of which are described in Appendix B). You can also add the HTML table commands to the source HTML for your Web page. Here is the HTML for the page that creates the table seen in Kaitlyn's Korner:

```
<center>
<table border=5 cellpadding=3
   cellspacing=3>
<td><IMG align=center
   SRC="graphics/kaitlyn.gif"
   ALT="Kaitlyn's Photo"></td>
<td><IMG align=center
   SRC="graphics/banner.gif"
   ALT="Site Banner"></td>
</table>
</center>
```

The first line beginning with `<td>` contains the contents for the left cell (the one that contains the photo of Kaitlyn). The second line beginning with `<td>` contains the contents of the right cell (the one with the text).

To add your two images to your table, replace the text contained between the quotation marks in the two lines in the preceding HTML. Say that you have a photo of yourself named `me.jpg` and a banner for your Web page saved as a GIF image named `banner.gif`. To change the preceding HTML, you follow these steps:

1. **Open the HTML file for your Web page in a text editor such as Notepad (if you have a PC) or SimpleText (if you use a Mac).**

2. **In the first line beginning with `<td>`, delete the text** `graphics/kaitlyn.gif`. **Be careful not to delete the quotation marks.**

3. **Enter the name for your file:** `me.jpg`.

4. **Delete the text after** `ALT`.

   In other words, delete "Kaitlyn's Photo," but don't delete the quotation marks.

   This step provides a couple of words that will appear in place of the image if the visitor to this Web page has turned off image display.

5. **Enter a couple of words that describe your photo ("My Smiling Face," or something similar).**

   This line of HTML should read as follows:

   ```
   <td><IMG align=center
   SRC="me.jpg" ALT="My Smiling
   Face"></td>
   ```

6. **Follow Steps 1 through 4 for the second line beginning with** `<td>`.

   In this case, enter the name of your banner image (`banner.gif`) and a couple of words that describe this image ("Welcome to My Web Page," or something similar).

   This line of HTML should read as follows:

   ```
   <td><IMG align=center
   SRC="banner.gif" ALT="Welcome
   to My Web Page"></td>
   ```

7. **Select File⇨Save to save your changes in your text editing program.**

   Be sure to put the image files `me.jpg` and `banner.gif` in the same folder or directory as your Web page so a Web browser can find them without having to look through other directories on your Web site.

Saving Your Web Color Rainbow

After you create a drawing, no matter how many colors it contains, you must save the image as a small computerized "snapshot." That is, you must save it in a GIF (Graphics Interchange Format) or JPEG (Joint Photographic Experts Group) format, both of which enable a browser to compress the file so that a Web browser can quickly and easily copy and show it.

See Chapters 7 and 10 for more about GIF and JPEG formats. The important facts to remember are these:

___ Web browsers can't display images in bitmap (BMP), Macintosh (PICT), Tagged Image File Format (TIFF), ZSoft PCX, or other graphics formats. You need to convert these formats to GIF or JPEG. You can do this with any number of graphics programs.

See "Step 5: Save your image in GIF format" later in this chapter to see how to convert a file format by using LView Pro.

___ GIF works best with drawings such as cartoons or line art.

___ JPEG squishes a file more than GIF, but some of the information in an image might be lost.

Usually your graphics program gives you a choice of several levels of JPEG compression. The higher the compression, the more the image suffers. The image may become bumpy, and tiny dots may form around the edges.

You'll probably start seeing a new graphics format called PNG (Portable Network Graphics) on the Web before long. PNG files have the filename extensions (surprise, surprise) .png.

Making Your Own Horizontal Rule

A *horizontal rule* is a line or other graphic image that runs from the left margin of a Web page to the right margin and that helps to separate one part of a Web page from another part. Creating a horizontal rule demonstrates what you've just learned about drawing and saving files. In this section, you will create a horizontal rule by using the Paint program that comes with Windows 95 to draw a bitmap image. You will have to convert the image from bitmap to GIF format (a format that a browser can display). You will do this by using the shareware graphics program, LView Pro. LView Pro works only on a PC. Mac users can use Paint, Super Paint, or even GraphicConverter, which has a simple set of painting tools.

A version of LView Pro is on the CD that comes with this book (see Appendix D).

Step 1: Draw your image with Paint

Here's how to draw your own rule using Paint:

1. **Open Paint by selecting Start➪Programs➪Accessories➪Paint.**

   The Paint window opens.

2. **Click on the paintbrush icon, and draw a star.**

   You may have better luck with the diagonal line, too. Go ahead; just try and draw it. The quality doesn't have to be the greatest. In fact, a hand-drawn effect is what you're trying to achieve. If you make a mistake, click on the eraser tool and erase the part of the star that doesn't seem right. Then click on the paintbrush and keep working.

3. **Click on the paint can tool, click on a color in the color palette at the bottom of the Paint window, and then click inside the star with the edge of the paint can.**

   Check out Figure 13-1 to see the Windows 95 Paint window and the star I drew.

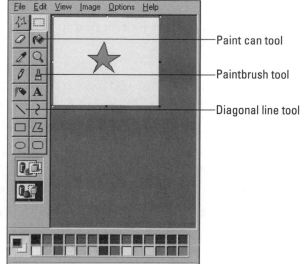

Paint can tool

Paintbrush tool

Diagonal line tool

Figure 13-1:
Paint
comes with
Windows
95 and is a
good
program for
beginners
who want
to create
simple
images for
their Web
pages.

4. **Select File⇨Save to save your star as a bitmap image.**

   The Save dialog box appears.

5. **Give your star a filename (how about `starline.gif`).**

6. **Click on the arrow to the right of the Save as type text box.**

   The Save as type menu drops down containing options for saving the file with various levels of color *(color depths)*.

7. **Select 256 Color Bitmap from the drop-down menu.**

   Remember the browser-safe 256-color palette you read about earlier? This is it!

8. **Click on Save to save the file.**

Step 2: Copy your image

After you draw a single star image, you can just copy and paste it to create a long horizontal line of stars, as follows:

1. **Click on the Select tool (the dotted rectangle shown in Figure 13-1) in the upper-right corner of the Paint tool palette.**

2. **Draw a box around your star to select it. Click just above and to the left of the star, and pressing your mouse button, drag your mouse down and to the right.**

   The selection rectangle appears around the star, which means you have selected the star. (The rectangle can be any size.)

3. **Select Edit⇨Copy.**

   The star is copied, and you can now paste it next to the first star you drew.

4. **Select Edit⇨Paste.**

   A second star appears with a selection rectangle around it. Click on the rectangle, and pressing your mouse, drag this new star to the right so it's next to the original one. (The two need not line up exactly; in fact, it's better if they're slightly off-line.)

5. **To resize the Paint window (so you can keep pasting stars and elongating your line), select Image⇨Attributes.**

   The Attributes dialog box appears.

6. **In the box next to Width, type the number 2000. In the box next to Height, enter 125, and then click on OK.**

   The Attributes dialog box closes, and the Paint window becomes long and narrow.

7. **Repeat Step 4 as many times as you want.**

   Your line of stars should be about 4–5 inches long. You may want to paste as many as 10–15 stars.

8. **When your line of stars is long enough, select File⇨Save.**

   You can also choose Save As to preserve your original single star and save the line of stars with a new filename. In this case, be sure to select 256 Color Bitmap by clicking on the arrow next to the Save as type text box, as mentioned in the sixth step in the preceding section, "Step 1: Draw your image with Paint."

9. **Select File⇨Exit to close the Paint program and return to your Windows desktop.**

If you're not attached to stars as a graphic image, feel free to choose your own image and turn it into a horizontal rule that you can use on your Web pages. A simple circle filled with an interesting pattern or a snakelike squiggly line repeated over and over might be good. It's up to you; the possibilities are endless. Here's another tip: After you paste a star or other image and before you place that image, select Image⇨Flip/Rotate. The Flip and Rotate dialog box appears. Click on the circle next to Rotate by angle. Then click on one of the angle options (90, 180, or 270 degrees). The selected star will be rotated, thus adding a new effect to your line full of stars.

Step 3: Open your image in LView Pro

After you have your basic image, you need to save it in GIF or JPEG format so a Web browser can display it. You do this by using a program such as LView Pro. In this case, you're going to save your star image in GIF format because the image is a *line art* drawing (a drawing made up lines and simple colors) as opposed to a photo. Here's how you open the image in LView Pro:

1. **Copy LView Pro to your hard disk from the CD that comes with this book (see Appendix D).**

   In the process of installing the program, a folder called LView Pro is created on your hard disk. This folder contains the program itself.

2. **Open the LView Pro folder, and then double-click on the green LView 32 icon to open the program.**

   An empty, white LView Pro window appears with a toolbar to the right.

3. **From the program's menu bar, select File⇨Open to work on the star you just drew and saved.**

   The Open Image File dialog box appears.

4. **Locate the star image you just saved by clicking on the arrow to the right of the box at the top of the dialog box that is labeled Look In.**

5. **Select the folder on your hard disk where you saved your image, click on the name of the image file to select it, and then click on Open.**

   The line of stars opens in a new LView Pro window (see Figure 13-2).

   Take a moment to scroll through the LView Pro menu options (particularly the Retouch menu) to get an idea of the cool ways you can use this program to change the appearance or the file format of an image. Some LView Pro options for retouching scanned photos are explained in detail in Chapter 10.

Step 4: Crop your image

One good way you can prepare an image you've drawn for the Web is to crop it. *Cropping* an image means you select only the part you want to appear in your final presentation; you eliminate the areas that aren't essential. That way, the image takes up less room on a Web page, and the file size is reduced, too. LView Pro makes it a snap to crop an image. Just follow these steps:

LView Pro toolbar ⌐

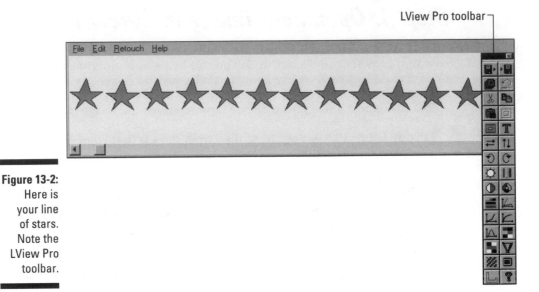

Figure 13-2:
Here is
your line
of stars.
Note the
LView Pro
toolbar.

1. **Click on the Crop tool in the LView Pro toolbar, which is just above the text tool, the letter T (refer to Figure 13-2).**

   When you move your mouse over the LView Pro working area, it appears as a set of crosshairs.

2. **Using the crosshair tool, click just above and to the left of the line of stars, and dragging your mouse down and to the right, draw a long rectangle around all of the stars.**

   A bright red rectangle is drawn around your stars. If you don't get all the stars the first time, don't worry. You can click-and-drag on one of the little handles in the corners of the rectangle to make it a different size (see Figure 13-3).

3. **Select Edit⇨Crop!**

   The image "snaps down" to the area you selected (in other words, it's cropped).

Step 5: Save your image in GIF format

Prior to adding your image to your Web page, you must save the image in GIF or JPEG format, as follows:

1. **With your cropped image still visible in the LView Pro window, select File⇨Save as.**

   The Save Image as dialog box appears.

┌Click here

Figure 13-3:
Click on one
of these
handles to
resize the
selection
rectangle.

2. **Enter** `starline.gif` **in the File name box.**

3. **Click on the arrow next to the Save as type box, and select GIF 89a (.gif) from the drop-down menu.**

    This format allows you to save your image with a transparent background later on, if you want.

That's it. Now you can add your rule to your own Web page or even offer it to your cybervisitors by including a line on your Web page and telling those visitors that they can copy your star-rule because you are designating it as copyright-free clip art.

You clever young Web designers probably already realize that there's a way to make a nontransparent image transparent: Simply make sure that the background of the image is the same color as the background of your Web page. If both your image and the Web page have a white background, the image will seem transparent, even though it's not.

Making image backgrounds transparent

After you create a GIF image, you can use a graphics program such as LView Pro to make the background of the image *transparent*. A transparent image doesn't have a visible background; it seems to be floating on the Web page. You don't have to make an image background transparent, but doing so *can* make your Web page look more elegant and professional.

However, you can do this with only a GIF image; JPEGs can't have background colors. The Help file that comes with LView Pro contains a pretty good tutorial on how to make a transparent background. Open the image you want to make transparent, select Help⇨Contents, and click on the Search button at the top of the Help window. The Help Topics: LView Pro dialog box appears. Scroll down the list of topics, and double-click on Frequently Asked Questions. The very first question explains how to make an image background transparent.

Setting Web Page Colors

OPEN

Graphic images add color to a Web page, but they're not the only Web page elements that can turn your page from a gray-and-black rectangle to an easy-on-the-eyes peacock. You can paint several other parts of a Web page in different colors:

- **Selected text:** This can be the "body text" on a Web page as well as any headings you have created.

- **Link text:** This is text that is highlighted as a clickable hypertext link (normally underlined and in a color).

- **Active links:** These are links that have a special color that appears only when they are *active*: They change color while someone is actually clicking on them.

- **Followed links:** These are links that have been followed. They were clicked on recently. (This helps visitors "retrace their steps" through a Web site if they're trying to find a page they visited earlier and can't remember the address.)

- **Backgrounds:** Web pages can have a solid color, or they can use a graphic image as "wallpaper."

When you're selecting colors for your Web page, remember to provide enough contrast between the background of the page and the text and images that will appear "on top of" that background. Use dark type with a light background and light type with a dark background, and you'll be fine.

CLARE DECLARES

One kid's opinion

The best way to plan a background is to be aware of the colors you want to use, not only in the background itself but in the text and the links that are going to appear on top of the background. Keep the colors simple. I've found that using shades of gray works well in the background. For the page that I made about my school jazz band, I used black and a dark gray, and the text and the photos on the page showed up fine.

Part V
Behind the Curtain: How Web Pages Work

The 5th Wave — By Rich Tennant

"OH SURE, $1.8 MILLION DOLLARS SEEMS LIKE A LOT RIGHT NOW, BUT WHAT ABOUT RANDY? WHAT ABOUT HIS FUTURE? THINK WHAT A COMPUTER LIKE THIS WILL DO FOR HIS SAT SCORE SOMEDAY."

In this part . . .

When I was a kid, I loved to take things apart to see how they worked. I would take the back off a clock to figure out what made the hands move. If you're like me, you'll love this part. The techie world of HTML, HTTP, and servers is spread out before you.

When you make the move from being a Web surfer to being a Web publisher, a little background is essential. In Part V, you learn those background essentials: what HyperText Markup Language is and how it works, how to create links on your pages, and what actually happens when you move your Web page files from your computer to a mysterious and important machine, called a Web server, located somewhere else on the Web.

Don't worry if you're not a natural-born techie, the concepts in Part V are explained in simple language. So go ahead and impress your friends by casually dropping nuggets of background information about absolute versus relative paths and the client/server system.

Chapter 14

Adventures in the Land of HTML

· ·

· ·

*W*elcome to HTML: The Game! You are about to embark on an exciting adventure — an adventure that will take you from the *Land of Boring Old Pencil and Paper* to the *Kingdom of Exciting Cyberspace.* On the way, you'll discover things like the following:

✓ **HTML code:** A powerful language you have to decode

✓ **Hidden messages:** HTML instructions that transform words and pictures

✓ **Learning levels:** Degrees of HTML sophistication that take you from your status as a person only a few people know to your goal of being a star in Cyberspace

The object of the game is to take your family photos, your family stories — about parents, brothers, and sisters — and your family adventures, and turn them into Web pages that you can present to your countless new friends in the Kingdom of Cyberspace.

Lots of kids and lots of families all over the world are forming this new Kingdom of Cyberspace. By sharing information such as descriptions of their homes and their family histories, they are joining together to create a virtual community. You, too, can be part of this community where even people who live in different places and speak different languages can communicate.

Cracking the HTML Code

No matter what language you speak with your friends, to communicate with your new friends in the Kingdom of Cyberspace, you have to speak the language of HTML. In the kingdoms of olden days, you knew where knights lived and what they stood for by the banners they carried. They were like a code. Like those distinctive banners, HTML encodes your images and words so that they can go on Web pages.

Maybe you're the kind of kid who is bored by pageantry. You would just as soon skip the jousting matches, majestic ceremonies, and lavish banquets and go straight to your place on the throne in the castle. That's okay. You don't have to know about banners if you don't want to. These days, lots of programs can help you make your own Web pages without having to be an HTML pro. (Some of these are mentioned in Appendix B, and some are on this book's CD; see Appendix D.) On the other hand, understanding a little HTML is a good thing: You'll know what all the menus and dialog boxes in those Web tools are referring to. And a little basic HTML also comes in handy when you want to correct a problem in one of your pages or if you want to copy someone else's HTML formatting instructions and adapt them to your own family page contents.

Welcome to the tag quest

Imagine that you have sallied forth on your trusty steed, ready for HTML adventure. You approach the gates of Cyberspace, only to be stopped by a knight in shining armor who blocks your path and demands:

"Passwords, please!"

Passwords, you ask? In order to get access to Cyberland and begin to learn HTML, you have to understand some basic words in the language of HTML. You don't have to be fluent in HTML — you just need to know the right access code to gain entry.

HTML Passwords

These few words are all you need to gain entrance to Cyberland. Go ahead. Wave them in the face of the guard: "Browser," "Start Tag," "End Tag."

- **Attribute:** An attribute is an addition to an HTML tag that provides more specific information about what function the tag is supposed to perform. In the tag `<BODY BGCOLOR="red">`, `BGCOLOR` is an attribute to the `BODY` tag.

✔ **Bookmark:** Helps you find a page on the Web so that you can return to it right away, just as you'd mark a page in a book. Your browser keeps a record of the URL for a Web page in its bookmark list. When you want to return to the page, you just click on its name.

✔ **Browser:** A program like Netscape Navigator or Microsoft Internet Explorer that translates and displays HTML code so that you are able to read it on your computer screen.

✔ **Pixel:** A very tiny square that is one part of a computer image. Lots of pixels combined together produce a graphic that you see on a computer screen. Each pixel can be assigned a different color.

✔ **Tag:** Most HTML instructions consist of two tags. The first one is called a *start tag* (for example, <B>). The second one is an *end tag*. The end tag has a forward slash (for example, </B>). Any text contained between these two tags gets formatted in *boldface font* (which is what the B signifies). Here's an example:

```
<B> This text will be bold </B>
```

Level 1: HTML "control" room

Here in Cyberland, people wave banners. The object is to match up the correct *start* and *end* banners. When you have assembled enough banners, you can move on to the next room of the castle. In order to find the right banner to display your message, you have to crack the HTML code and figure out what each formatting instruction does. Right now, you're in the first room in the castle — the "control" room. This is where you create the banner that formats your Web page document as a whole (as opposed to formatting individual words or phrases, which happen in the next room).

To get started, reach up on the wall and pull down your first banner.

The <HTML> tags

Your first banner is <HTML>. It's a tag with two halves. For now, you receive only the first half of this tag (the start tag). You'll receive the second half when you complete your first HTML Web page and are a real citizen in the Kingdom of Cyberspace.

Stash the <HTML> tag in your packet, and move on to the next banner. Reach up and take down the next one.

The <HEAD> tags

The <HEAD> banner has two parts: a start tag (<HEAD>) and an end tag (</HEAD>). You only need the start tag right now.

This banner comes right after <HTML>. Text does not go between these two tags; instead, general instructions about the document as a whole go between the <HEAD> and </HEAD> tags. Just cut it out. There are a few instructions, but the only one you really need to be concerned with at this point is the one that lets you give your document a title.

The <TITLE> tag

This HTML tag was discussed in Chapter 2, so you may be familiar with it already. The two tags <TITLE> and </TITLE> go on either side of the title of your Web page, like this:

```
<TITLE>Colleen's Stupendous Web World</TITLE>
```

Your title appears in the title bar, which is the bar at the top of your visitors' browser windows. Take your <TITLE> and </TITLE> tags and move down the trail.

Secret messages: the Comments tag

The Comments tag <!- -> lets you do something really magical: You can enter messages that don't show up on your page when it appears on the Web. Who do you want to read your *secret* messages? Why, people like yourself — Web page authors who are looking around and trying to learn from someone else's HTML instructions!

You're probably wondering, what kinds of messages to leave for these HTML enchanters? Do you have to enter your messages as some kind of code? You can say anything you want in plain English, as long as you put your messages between the hyphens. Often Web page authors use these tags to identify themselves; they might include a copyright notice, or give an e-mail address. Here's an example:

```
<!-This page created by Andre Magee, age 14->
```

As long as you enter your message after the <!- and before the ->, it won't show up on your page, only in the HTML, which, of course, is in the background.

Reviewing your tags

It's time for a quick review of the banners you've learned about so far. You examined the tags that are contained in the HEAD section of an HTML page. This section contains general information that pertains to the document as a whole. Every document begins with `<HTML>`, followed by `<HEAD>`, `<TITLE>`, and `</TITLE>`. You can also add comments if you want. Then the `</HEAD>` tag ends this part of your HTML page. It looks like this:

```
<HTML>
<HEAD>
<TITLE> </TITLE>
</HEAD>
```

Level 2: HTML "main content" room

Now it's on to the next part of your Web page HTML adventure — the part that contains your words and images. Just take your `</HEAD>` tag and go through this castle door . . . down this passageway . . . into the next room. Now take another tag called `<BODY>`. Now you have acquired what you need to gain entrance to the BODY section of your HTML page.

The `<BODY>` tag

The `<BODY>` and `</BODY>` tags (note the forward slash in the end BODY tag) enclose the BODY of an HTML document. Now that you have the start tag, `<BODY>`, you can explore the big new room you're in. It looks pretty bare, doesn't it? Don't worry. You'll soon fill it up with information about you, your family, or your friends.

Start by putting something on the walls of your bare Web space. You do that by setting your page's background with the `<BODY BGCOLOR>` tag. By adding a special word and a series of characters after the `<BODY>` tag, you can easily assign a color to the background of your Web page. This special addition to BODY is called an *attribute,* and it looks like this:

```
<BODY BGCOLOR="red">
```

Here's all you need to do:

1. **Type one blank space after** BODY.

2. **Type** BGCOLOR=" **(no blank spaces here).**

3. **Type one of 16 standard color names in HTML, like this:**
   BGCOLOR="green."

   The color names are black, gray, maroon, purple, green, olive, navy, teal, silver, white, red, fuchsia, lime, yellow, blue, and aqua. They are supported by most, though not all, Web browsers, but have the advantage of being easier to remember than the numeric hexadecimal code that can also be used.

4. Be sure to add the second quote (") mark and the (>) symbol.

Note: You don't need to use the </BODY> tag (the end tag) when setting the color; this tag comes at the end of the HTML document itself.

Know where you're heading: the <Hn> *tags*

Headings are like the furnishings in your Web page room: They are the organizers, the dividers for main sections of your document. Take a banner off the wall of this room: You'll see that there's a start tag, <Hn>, and an end tag, </Hn>. Any words between these two tags are presented as a *heading* by a Web browser. The *n* in the tag is just a placeholder, an arbitrary letter that is used for this example; you're really supposed to enter a number between 1 and 6. The top-level headings on a page are coded H1; the H2 headings are slightly smaller; H3 headings are smaller still, and so on. H6 is as small as you can go. Here's a very simple example:

```
<H1>This is an H1 Heading</H1>
<H2>This is an H2 Heading</H2>
<H3>This is an H3 Heading</H3>
<H4>This is an H4 Heading</H4>
<H5>This is an H5 Heading</H5>
<H6>This is an H6 Heading</H6>
```

Figure 14-1 shows how the preceding HTML shows up in a Web browser.

Figure 14-1:
Headings in HTML; notice that each <Hn> tag inserts a blank space both above and below it.

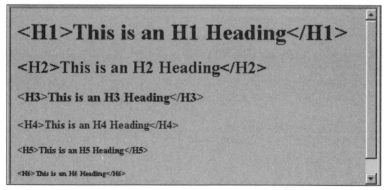

The <P> *paragraph tag*

Now you can actually start to type some text in your HTML document. Simply pick the <P> banner off the wall and insert it at the end of every paragraph you type. The <P> tag inserts one blank space — and only one — after one paragraph and before the next one, like this:

```
Here is one paragraph…<P>
…And here is another!<P>
```

Whatever you do, don't enter carriage returns at the end of a document; Web browsers don't recognize them at all, and they just won't show up when your document appears in the browser window. By the way, <P> is one of those tags that doesn't have an end tag.

The
 line break tag

If you just want to break a line at a particular spot but don't want to add a blank space, use the <BR> tag. Like <P>, <BR> doesn't have an end tag.
 is particularly well suited to things like poems, as shown here:

```
There's no vocabulary<BR>
For love within a family, love that's lived in<BR>
But not looked at, love within the light of which<BR>
All else is seen, the love within which<BR>
All other love finds speech<BR>
This love is silent.<BR>
—T.S. Eliot<P>
```

The <BR> line break tag is one of those tags that comes with only a start tag, <BR>, and does not require an end tag. There is no </BR>. However, some Web authoring tools add </BR> for some reason, so don't be surprised if you see it when you view the source HTML for some documents.

The <BLOCKQUOTE> *tag*

Any text enclosed between <BLOCKQUOTE> and </BLOCKQUOTE> is indented on both the right and the left, and blank spaces are inserted above and below the text.

Figure 14-2 shows examples of the <P>, <BR>, and <BLOCKQUOTE> tags.

Some of the best kid-friendly HTML tutorials on the Web are published by schools. For example, check out the Forty-Five Minute HTML Primer (http://www.grossmont.k12.ca.us/HTMLClass/Primer.html) or the even speedier Eight-Minute HTML Primer (http://web66.coled.umn.edu/Cookbook/HTML/MinutePrimer). If your school is connected to the Internet, ask your teacher whether the school has bookmarks to some of these sites. If your school doesn't have its own HTML primer, you can probably accumulate tons of extra credit by creating one after you become HTML literate and make your own family Web site.

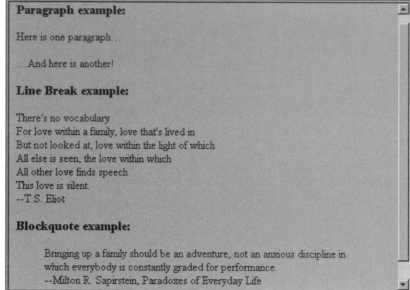

Figure 14-2:
You can use
the `<P>`,
`<BR>`, and
`<BLOCK-
QUOTE>`
tags to
make your
text look
just the way
you want.

Level 3: The "text formatting" room

Now you're moving — it's on to Level 3 of HTML development. After you learn to break paragraphs into different segments, you can grab some tags that let you add magical charms to individual words and phrases. You can also divide major sections of text by inserting horizontal rules.

Making text `<B>old` and `<I>talic`

Knights who were designing their banners liked to use distinctive colors and symbols, but if they put too many on, the banner would be confusing. It's the same with words. As everyone knows, sometimes it's good to give your words a little emphasis so people can pay attention to the most important things you have to say. But it doesn't look good if you SHOUT by using ALL CAPS or too many exclamation marks!!!

Two HTML tags let you make text bold or italic:

```
<B>This text will be bold</B>
<I>This text will be italic<I>
```

There is also an underline tag (`<U> </U>`), but it's not a good idea to use an underline tag on a Web page. Can you imagine why? Because words or phrases that are supposed to serve as clickable hyperlinks are almost always underlined. People are accustomed to clicking on the underlined text to go to another location. If you underline text simply to give it emphasis, people may get frustrated or confused when they click on it and nothing happens.

It's easy to overuse bold and italic on a Web page, and large blocks of bold or italic type can be really hard on the eyes (and even harder to read on a computer screen). So use them only when you really want to add some ***ooomph*** to what you're saying.

Following the horizontal ⟨HR⟩ rule

Now it's time to grab the first tag that produces a visual effect on your Web page: the simple and reliable horizontal rule tag, ⟨HR⟩. The ⟨HR⟩ tag is simple and effective: Just type ⟨HR⟩ anywhere in your document (usually it's better to insert one after a paragraph, list, or a section), and a rule is drawn across the width of the browser window in which your page appears. By the way, ⟨HR⟩ only has a start tag.

One neat thing about ⟨HR⟩ is that although anyone who reads your Web page can make the browser window narrower or wider, depending on the size of the viewer's computer monitor, the ⟨HR⟩ rule adjusts to fit the window. The horizontal line always fills the screen, no matter what size it is.

Usually, the horizontal rule is not a solid black line, rather it appears to have a *shadowed* effect. Most Web page tools will let you change the rule, so you can make it solid black, wider, or narrower than the basic ⟨HR⟩ rule. If you are typing the HTML yourself or looking at someone else's Web page, you may want to know the HTML attributes for these variations. They look like this:

- ⟨HR SIZE=*N*⟩ makes the rule wider in pixels. Pixels are the tiny dots that make up the graphics you see on a computer screen; about 72 pixels equal one inch, so pixels are pretty small. ⟨HR SIZE=5⟩ makes the rule 5 pixels wide.

- ⟨HR WIDTH=*N*⟩ makes the rule something less than the entire width of the browser window. *N* can be a value in pixels or a percentage of the browser window. ⟨HR WIDTH=50%⟩ makes the rule half the width of the window.

- ⟨HR ALIGN=CENTER⟩ centers a rule that you have already made less than the width of the window by adding the attribute WIDTH. You can also use ⟨HR ALIGN=LEFT⟩ or ⟨HR ALIGN=RIGHT⟩.

- ⟨HR NOSHADE⟩ makes the rule solid black.

You can combine these ⟨HR⟩ or any other HTML attributes by typing a blank space between each one. For example, if you want to make a solid black rule that is centered and also one-third the width of the browser window, you type:

```
<HR WIDTH=33% ALIGN=CENTER NOSHADE>
```

The same caution that applies to using bold and italic text applies to rules, too: Don't overuse rules or your page will be divided into too many sections and have a caterpillar-like look (see Figure 14-3).

Arranging Web page elements with lists

As mentioned in Chapter 2, lists are a great way to break up the text in a Web page and direct your reader's eye to special elements in a series of elements. You can use three kinds of lists in your HTML pages:

- ✔ **Bulleted lists:** Present a series of items that are preceded by a bullet and indented from the main body of the text. The list you're reading now is an unnumbered list, but it uses check marks in place of the bullets.

- ✔ **Numbered lists (also called ordered lists):** These are often used to present a sequence of events or actions. Each item in the list is preceded by — surprise! — a numeral: 1, 2, 3, and so on.

- ✔ **Definition lists:** These are sometimes called *glossary lists*. Each item in the list has two parts: the definition term, which is flush-left with the main text, and its definition, which is usually indented on a separate line below the item being defined.

Lists in HTML are pretty straightforward. Bulleted and numbered lists have a similar structure: The entire list is enclosed by a start tag and an end tag. <UL> and </UL> are used for Bulleted lists, and <OL> and </OL> enclose numbered lists. Each list item is preceded by the tag <LI>. Here are some examples:

Bulleted list:

```
<UL>
<LI>Quest
<LI>Dubbing
<LI>Missive
<LI>Joust
<LI>Banquet
</UL>
```

In a bulleted list, each one of the <LI> tags is replaced by a *bullet*.

Numbered list:

```
<OL>
<LI>Meet in mortal combat
<LI>Crown ceremoniously
<LI>Send missive
<LI>Hold vigil
```

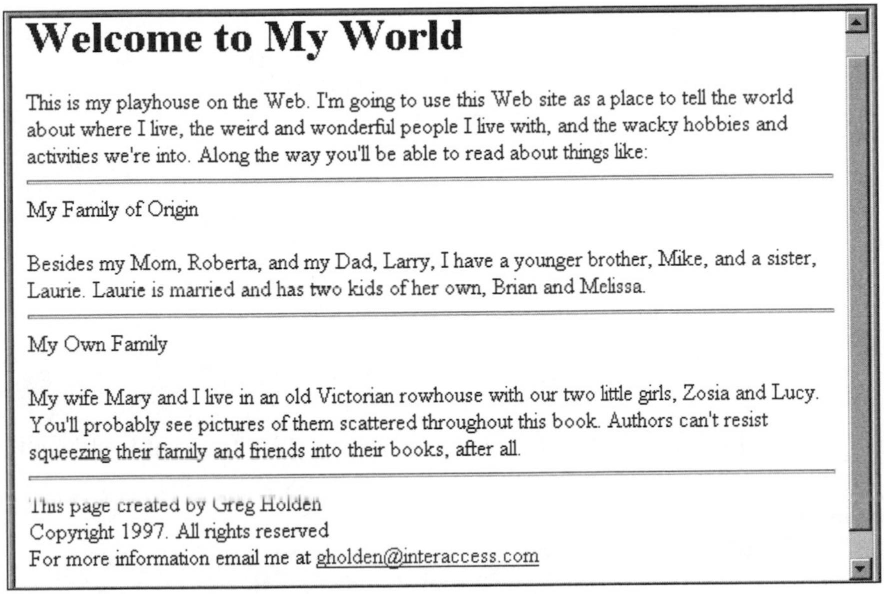

Welcome to My World

This is my playhouse on the Web. I'm going to use this Web site as a place to tell the world about where I live, the weird and wonderful people I live with, and the wacky hobbies and activities we're into. Along the way you'll be able to read about things like:

My Family of Origin

Besides my Mom, Roberta, and my Dad, Larry, I have a younger brother, Mike, and a sister, Laurie. Laurie is married and has two kids of her own, Brian and Melissa.

My Own Family

My wife Mary and I live in an old Victorian rowhouse with our two little girls, Zosia and Lucy. You'll probably see pictures of them scattered throughout this book. Authors can't resist squeezing their family and friends into their books, after all.

This page created by Greg Holden
Copyright 1997. All rights reserved
For more information email me at gholden@interaccess.com

Figure 14-3: Don't turn your Web page into a Very Hungry Caterpillar by adding too many horizontal rules.

```
<LI>Ascend to the throne
</OL>
```

In an ordered list, each one of the <LI> tags is replaced by a *numeral*. Don't type 1, 2, and 3 yourself, or you'll end up with two sets of numbers before each item.

Definition list:

In a definition list, the tags <DL> and </DL> enclose the entire list. Each term to be defined is preceded by <DT>, and each definition is preceded by <DD>.

```
<DL>
<DT>Good triumphs
<DD>The enchanter is defeated.
<DT>Justice prevails
<DD>The wicked are vanquished.
<DT>Tranquility rules
<DD>Might serves right.
</DL>
```

Another thing you can do with lists wasn't mentioned earlier: If you're really ambitious about presenting items in order, you can even nest a list within a list. In the following example, an unordered list is *nested* within an unordered list. The nested list is indented so you can see it more clearly; it will be indented when displayed by a browser, too:

```
<OL>
<LI>Find coat of arms
<LI>Cut banner from colored cloth
<LI>Put flag atop castle
<LI>Take to events, such as:
    <UL>
    <LI>Matches
    <LI>Banquets
    <LI>Ceremonies
    </UL>
<LI>Flaunt it!
</OL>
```

The output of this list as it appears in a Web browser is shown in Figure 14-4.

Figure 14-4:
You can help make your Web page memorable by presenting a series of items in an HTML list.

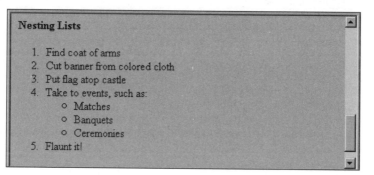

If you can't get enough HTML and want to explore the subject to your heart's content, check out *HTML For Dummies,* 2nd Edition, by Ed Tittel and Steve James, or *HTML For Dummies Quick Reference,* 2nd Edition, by Deborah S. Ray and Eric J. Ray, both published by IDG Books Worldwide.

Plenty of sites on the Web are designed to help you learn HTML in a user-friendly way. The classic HTML guide for beginners is the "HTML Quick Reference" (http://www.cc.ukans.edu/info/HTML_quick.html). Another good place to start is the Tao Html site (http://www.taoh.html), which collects links to lots of HTML resources. One of the best HTML tutorials is "Writing HTML: A Tutorial for Creating WWW Pages" by the Maricopa Center for Learning and Instruction (http://www.mcli.dist.maricopa.edu/tut/).

Level 4: Decorate your rooms!

So far you've learned various ways to present text in the BODY section of an HTML document. You've learned how to use HTML to make paragraphs and line breaks, to make selected text bold and italic, and to turn selected text into hyperlinks that lead your visitors around the Web or around other files on your own site.

Now it's time to get visual with your Web site, to show people your family life. It's time to grab that last tag, the one that inserts images into an HTML document, the <IMG> tag.

The <IMG> tag is used to specify an image file such as a photo you've scanned, a drawing you've made in a paint program, or a piece of clip art you've copied from an art archive on the Web. In order to be displayed by a Web browser, these files must be saved in a graphics format such as GIF or JPEG. These formats do a couple of things to a computer image:

- ✔ They compress the data in the image to make the file size smaller so it can get from one place to another on the Web more easily.
- ✔ They make the image cross-platform — that is, visible to people on the Internet who are using different types of computers or browsers.

After you create a graphics file, here's the tag you need to get the file into your Web page (see Chapters 10, 11, and 13 for information about creating graphics files):

```
<IMG SRC="image.gif">
```

<IMG> uses only a start tag. The other components of this tag should be pretty understandable:

- ✔ SRC stands for Source and is an attribute to the IMG (image) tag.
- ✔ The equal sign (=) connects a file to the attribute.
- ✔ "image.gif" is the file that will be displayed.

In plain English, this line of HTML is saying something like: "I want you to display an image here, and the source for the image is a file called image.gif."

Unless all of your Web site files are in the same directory on your server, you have to specify one of the pesky relative addresses mentioned in Chapter 15 so that your visitors' browsers can find the image file on which you want them to feast their eyes:

```
<IMG SRC="../photos/house.jpeg>
```

Now you can pat yourself on the back: You've learned how to use all the components that go into making a great HTML Web page. Just go through this door and pick up your final tags to put all the pieces together:

```
</BODY>
```

This tag closes out the BODY section of your Web page.

```
</HTML>
```

This is the last tag in any Web page.

There are plenty more HTML tags where these come from, to be sure. However, the tags covered in this chapter are the basic tags that you need whether you're creating a Web page from scratch, editing, or just trying to interpret someone else's HTML.

Table 14-1 reviews all the tags you've used so far.

Table 14-1	Basic HTML Tags
HTML Tag and Tag Pair	*Purpose*
`<HTML> </HTML>`	Tells a browser that this is an HTML document. These two tags enclose the entire document.
`<HEAD> </HEAD>`	Contains information that pertains to the HTML document as a whole, such as the title.
`<TITLE> </TITLE>`	Encloses the title of your Web document.
`<!-comments->`	Lets you insert comments into the HTML that won't be displayed by a Web browser.
`<BODY> </BODY>`	Encloses the BODY of an HTML document. The BODY contains the text and images that appear in a Web browser's window.
`<BODY BGCOLOR="color">`	Sets the background color for the Web page.
`<Hn> </Hn>`	Contains text for a heading; *n* is a number from 1 to 6.
`<P>`	Ends a paragraph; inserts a blank space between the current paragraph and the next one.

(continued)

HTML Tag and Tag Pair	Purpose
` `	Breaks a line without adding a blank space.
`<BLOCKQUOTE> </BLOCKQUOTE>`	Indents a block of text on both the right and left margins.
`<B> </B>`	Contains text to be displayed as bold.
`<I> </I>`	Contains text to be displayed as italic.
`<HR>`	Inserts a horizontal rule.
`<UL> </UL>`	Encloses a bulleted list.
`<OL> </OL>`	Encloses a numbered list
`<LI>`	Marks a list item in either a numbered or bulleted list.
`<DL> </DL>`	Encloses a definition list.
`<DT> <DD>`	Marks definition terms or definitions in a definition list.
`<IMG SRC="image.jpeg">`	Inserts an image file to be displayed on the page.

If you're pretty HTML-literate, you can use an HTML tag called META to insert some neat "hidden" information in your son's or daughter's HTML pages. META is used to store information that is scanned and then indexed by the Internet search services like Excite and AltaVista. You can use META to specify a description of your family Web site that the search services will use when returning your site in a search question. You can also insert some keywords that make it more likely that people will find your site when they make a request to a search service. `<META>` goes between the `<HEAD>` and `</HEAD>` tags of an HTML document, like this:

```
<HEAD>
<META NAME="DESCRIPTION" CONTENT="your description here">
<META NAME="KEYWORDS" CONTENT="family, mom, dad (add your
own keywords here)">
</HEAD>
```

Reading about HTML tags and seeing where they fit in the structure of an HTML document is only one way to enter the Kingdom of Cyberspace, but it's by no means the only way. You can also take a peek at how other people's pages are put together. Just choose View⇨Source or View⇨ Document Source from your browser's menu bar. After a few seconds, you'll see the HTML appear in a separate window.

Cyberspace, Here I Come

Now it's time to put together all you have learned and create your own Web page for everyone to enjoy. An HTML document is nothing more than a plain text document that is saved with the file extension .htm or .html. This document is then displayed in a Web browser window. (Web browsers only display plain text documents, not files created in MacWrite, Nisus Writer, or another snazzy word-processing program's native format.)

To prepare your HTML document from scratch, you can enter the text and the HTML tags in any word-processing program. If you use a program like Microsoft Word or WordPerfect, you must save your file in text-only format. If you use a plain text program like SimpleText or WordPad, your file will be in the correct format already, so you only have to select File⇨Save, and a Web browser will be able to recognize the format.

Setting up your workspace

In order to create, test, and revise your HTML document, you need to get the right software up and running on your computer (assuming, of course, that you aren't using one of the Web page authoring tools described in Appendix B). Here is all you need:

- The word-processing program you will use to enter your HTML.

- The Web browser you will use to preview your work. You don't have to dial into your Internet provider when you are working on your Web page; you can open your browser without connecting and work "offline."

Entering your own HTML

Just follow these steps to create your HTML page:

1. **Open your word processor.**

   Use a program that automatically saves text documents in plain-text format such as Notepad (Windows 95) or SimpleText (Mac).

2. **Type** <HTML>.

3. **Press Return or Enter to go to a new line.**

4. **Type** <HEAD>.

5. **Press Return again, and so on.**

Technically, you don't have to enter each line of HTML on its own separate line, but it makes your file much easier for *you* to read and correct later on. Here's what you might type:

```
<HTML>
<HEAD>
<TITLE>My Home Page</TITLE>
</HEAD>
<BODY BGCOLOR="white">
<H1>Welcome to My World</H1>
This is my playhouse on the Web. I'm going to use this
Web site as a place to tell the world about where I
live, the weird and wonderful people I live with, and
the wacky hobbies and activities we're into. Along the
way you'll be able to read about things like:<P>
<UL>
<LI>Some stories I've written
<LI>The trip I took to Washington, D.C. with my class
last fall
<LI>A paper I wrote on the solar system and the Voyager
expedition
</UL>
<HR>
This page created by [YourName]
Copyright 1997. All rights reserved
For more information email me at [Your email address]
</BODY>
</HTML>
```

6. **To save your document, select File⇨Save.**

   The Save dialog box appears.

7. **Give your new HTML document a simple name that ends in** .html **if you are using a Mac or** .htm **if you're using Windows. Call it** welcome.htm.

8. **Click on OK to save your document.**

9. **Open your Web browser if it isn't already open.**

10. **If you are using Microsoft Internet Explorer, select File⇨Open. If you're using Netscape Navigator, select Open⇨Open File. Navigate to your** welcome.htm **document, and then click on Open to open the file.**

    The contents of your browser should look more or less like Figure 14-5. Congratulations! The gates of the Kingdom of Cyberspace are now thrown open to you, because you have created your first HTML Web page.

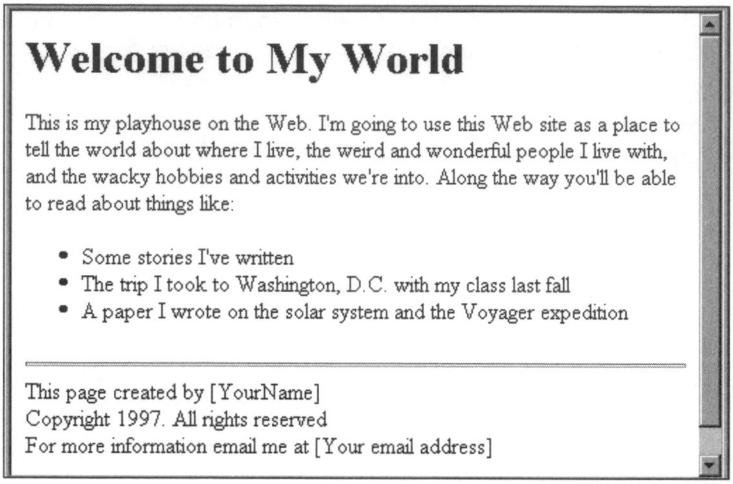

Welcome to My World

This is my playhouse on the Web. I'm going to use this Web site as a place to tell the world about where I live, the weird and wonderful people I live with, and the wacky hobbies and activities we're into. Along the way you'll be able to read about things like:

- Some stories I've written
- The trip I took to Washington, D.C. with my class last fall
- A paper I wrote on the solar system and the Voyager expedition

This page created by [YourName]
Copyright 1997. All rights reserved
For more information email me at [Your email address]

Figure 14-5: It's always exciting to open your own HTML in a Web browser and see your words and images presented in a Web page.

If you are working on a Mac, there's a cool way to open your new HTML document: You can drag and drop the icon for your HTML document atop the icon for Netscape Navigator or Microsoft Internet Explorer. The browser will launch and display your file automatically.

Making revisions

One of the coolest aspects when you are ready to sally forth with your own Web page is making adjustments to the HTML code and instantly seeing the effect in your browser's preview window. Here's how to make changes using the test.htm document you just created:

1. **Open your HTML document.**

2. **Scroll to the first paragraph of text, and change the "p" in the word "playhouse" to a capital "P," and then enter the `<B>` and `</B>` (bold) tags around the phrase "Playhouse on the Web," like this:**

```
<B>Playhouse on the Web</B>
```

Next you create a "dummy" link to a document you haven't created yet. The purpose of this is simply to give you some practice in adding an *anchor* (see Chapter 15 for more about anchors) to an HTML document.

3. **Scroll down to the first item in the bulleted list you created earlier ("Some stories I've written").**

Assume for the purposes of this exercise that you created another Web page that contains some of your own short stories (if you want to *really* do this, you can follow the exercise described in Chapter 3).

A note about browser differences

You say your browser window doesn't look exactly the same as the ones you see in this book? Maybe the type fonts are different? Welcome to the Web! A fundamental feature of Web pages is that their appearance depends on how the individual user has configured the browser software. A given page can be displayed with Helvetica type on a beige background on one user's screen and with Times Roman type on a white background on another user's screen. You can specify background colors and even type fonts (if you use advanced HTML features like style sheets, which are way beyond the scope of this chapter), but there's no guarantee your viewers will be able to see your Web page contents the way they look on *your* screen. For this reason, it's usually best to concentrate on the content of what you are presenting — the words and images, and how well they work together — rather than on the exact layout of the page.

4. Enter the following anchor tags around the word "stories."

The line should look like this:

```
<LI>Some <A HREF="stories.htm">stories</A> I've written.
```

5. Select File⇨Save to save the changes you just made.

6. Now bring your Web browser to the front of your computer screen.

The file welcome.htm should still be displayed. It doesn't display the changes you made, however. In order to see those changes, reload the page. (If you are using Netscape Navigator, select View⇨Reload.)

Presto! The words "Playhouse on the Web" should appear in bold, and the word "stories" should be underlined as a hyperlink.

Testing your work

Long live the ruler of Cyber-Kingdom! But before you ascend in triumph to your throne, gather a few of your subjects. Ask a loyal servant or two to look over your Web page before it goes out into the Cyber-Kingdom. Right after you post your page, call one or maybe a couple of your faithful friends and ask them to find your page and tell you what they think. Not only will their giggling indicate whether they "get" your joke, but they will also be able to tell you if your colors and graphics are showing up the way you thought they would.

HTML validation services

Like showing up at the jousting match without your trusty steed or your tested sword, a little mistake in an HTML page can make the whole page look bad. Proofreading and testing your pages is important, but if you don't have someone to serve as your Web proofreader, what can you do? Believe it or not, you can submit your HTML to one of several places on the Web that will check your code automatically and report back any mistakes. The validation is done by a computer program rather than a real person. Try it! There's nothing to lose, and it doesn't take very long to get your results.

Here are some validation services you can visit:

- ✔ htmlchek: (`http://uts.cc.utexas.edu/~churchh/htmlchek.html`)
- ✔ Weblint: (`http://www.cen.uiuc.edu/cgi-bin/weblint/`)
- ✔ Yahoo!: (`http://www.yahoo.com/Computers_and_Internet/ Information_and_Documentation/Data_Formats/HTML/ Validation_Checkers/`).

If you're wondering why you should bother to have someone else validate your HTML, you can find a pretty good essay on the subject at `http:// www.earth.com/bad-style/why-validate.html`.

But, enough about yucky stuff. Let me be among the first to welcome you to the Kingdom of Cyberspace. It's very exciting that you are a new citizen of a wonderful new community.

One kid's opinion

I never sat down and forced myself to learn HTML, but I know a little bit of it just from being on the Web. A lot of it I learned from other books. I also use the Web page authoring program World Wide Web Weaver, where you just fill in the information, and the program inserts the tag for you. (World Wide Web Weaver is on the CD that comes with this book, by the way.) After a while, I just picked HTML up without really thinking too much about it. Surprisingly, it's not that hard to learn.

Chapter 15

Links in Your Web Chain

• •

In This Chapter

▶ Making a link within a Web page

▶ Creating a link to another Web site

▶ Turning an image into a clickable link

▶ Creating navigation buttons

▶ Using button bars

• •

*G*ood Web pages don't exist in isolation. The Web is all about bringing people together, and one of the ways Web page authors like you can add your own strands to the incredible network of pages connected in the World Wide Web is by adding *hypertext links* to your pages. If you have surfed the Web, you have probably seen these links. They are bits of text or graphic images (usually underlined and highlighted in a color) on a Web page that are connected to another location. When you click on a link, your browser jumps to another location, either on the same Web site or to a page on another Web site.

This chapter explains how links work. You find out how to create basic Web page links and how to make graphic images such as navigation buttons serve as links that take your visitors where you want them to go.

Making Clickable Text Links

This section discusses the various components that make up a link on a Web page. Anchors are discussed, as well as the kinds of links you may want to make on your Web pages to connect them to other parts of your site and to the rest of the Web. To add links to your Web pages, you need to know the kinds of links that are available. You can make three basic types of links:

✔ **External links:** These links connect your visitor to another page on another Web site.

✔ **Same-page links:** Clicking on these links takes your visitor to another location on the same Web page.

   ✔ **Same-site links:** These links take your visitor to another page on your Web site.

Anchors identify the two parts of a link

In order to make a link, you need to have a *starting point* and a *destination*. The *starting point* is the text or image you provide for your visitors to click on. The *destination* is where you want your visitors to go.

In the world of Web publishing and HTML, these two parts of a link are known as *anchors.* You might compare them to an anchor on a boat sitting in the ocean. An anchor is joined to the boat by a rope or a chain. One end (call this the starting point) is fixed to the boat. The other end (call this the destination) rests on the bottom of the ocean. ***Note:*** See Chapter 14 for more information about using HTML.

The basic tool for making hypertext links in HTML is the *anchor tag.* It has a start tag and an end tag (which always has a forward slash), and looks like this:

```
<A> </A>
```

Any text contained between the `<A>` and `</A>` tags is magically transformed into a clickable link on which your Web page visitors can click to travel wherever you want them to go. Here's how these two anchor tags make a link in HTML:

   ✔ **The starting point:** This is the text or image that serves as the clickable link. Text is usually underlined and highlighted in a color so people can recognize it as a link. Images that serve as links are usually outlined with a blue border. The default color for links is blue, but you can change it (see Chapter 13).

   ✔ **The destination:** The first anchor tag, `<A>`, is combined with an important attribute called HREF (Hypertext Reference). This tag sets the destination for the link.

When you put the two parts together in HTML, they look like this:

```
<A HREF="destination">TEXT</A>
```

In the preceding line, `destination` is the place where you want the user to go after clicking on the highlighted text. (You should replace `TEXT` with your own text.) The destination of a link can be a URL to another page or Web site; it can also be an internal reference to a location within the same document.

The following sections show how to set the starting and destination points for each of the three types of links. In the first case (an external link), you see how to make the link by entering the HTML yourself. In the second example (a same-site link), you see how to use my favorite Web page authoring program, which comes with versions of Netscape Navigator called Netscape Gold and Netscape Communicator. The program is called Netscape Editor or Netscape Composer, depending on your version of Netscape. This program makes it especially easy to make links. In the third example (a same-page link), you see how to add the HTML or use Netscape Editor.

I like Netscape Editor because it's convenient, easy to use, and it creates all kinds of Web page goodies, such as links and tables (see Chapter 8). You can download it from Netscape's Web site (`http://home.netscape.com/comprod/mirror/client_download.html`) for free. You can also read more about Netscape Editor in Appendix B.

You should always add one additional bit of HTML to identify some alternative text that will be displayed if a viewer can't see the image (some visually impaired viewers use synthesizers to surf the Web). You do this by adding the ALT attribute to the IMG tag, like this:

```
<A HREF="http://www.internets.com/birds.htm"> <IMG
SRC="falcon.gif" ALT="falcon"> </A>
```

In this example, viewers who have image display turned off and who can't see the image `falcon.gif` will see the word falcon.

Linking your page to other Web sites

In some ways, it's easier to make an external link to a distant place on the Internet than it is to a spot just a few paragraphs down the same page.

Making external links with HTML

To make one of these *external links* to someone else's Web site, you enter the complete URL for that particular site in the HTML line `<A HREF="destination">` `TEXT</A>`, where you see the word `destination`, thereby connecting it to the Hypertext Reference `HREF` attribute. (That's a mouthful, isn't it?) Here's what a link to the IDG Books Online Web site would look like, for example:

```
<A HREF="http://www.idgbooks.com">Visit the IDG Web site</A>
```

To make a link to a specific document on someone else's site, you add the directory name and filename of the remote site's URL. The following URL, for example, takes you to a page that contains links to lots of Web sites kids will love to visit:

```
<A HREF="http://www.dummies.com/bonus/great_sw/
default.htm">Links to great Web sites for kids</A>
```

In this example, you see two directory names. The filename is `default.htm`.

When you specify a destination in an anchor tag, you have to provide a Web address or URL leading to that destination so that your visitors' browsers can find the location you want them to visit. You can specify two kinds of addresses: an *absolute address* and a *relative address*. The method of address differs depending on the location of the document you want your visitor to go to.

Absolute addresses

An absolute address is a way of specifying the location of a file by starting with the name of the computer on which the file resides, listing all intermediate folders or directories, and ending with the name of the file.

Relative addresses

A relative address is a way of making a link to a document on your own computer by specifying its location in relation to the document you currently have open. If you are moving from one Web page to another on your own Web server, you don't need to give the full URL for your own Web server; you only need to list directories that lie between the current document and the document you want people to reach, like this:

```
<A HREF="Hobbies/CoinCollecting.html">Read about my coin
collection</A>
```

In this line of HTML, you make a link from the current document to another document you have created, called `CoinCollecting.html`. To get to that file, your reader has to go into a folder called `Hobbies`, which is also on your Web site.

For example, if you are in the directory `/Family/Dad.html` and you want your reader to be able to jump to `Family/Jobs/DadsWork.html`, a directory that is contained within the current directory, you just enter this relative path in your anchor:

```
/Jobs/DadsWork.html
```

If you want your link to go in another direction — that is, to a different directory than the one you are in currently (`/Family/Dad.html`), say to `/Family/Pets/Figaro.html,` you use these dots, (`..`), to specify the subdirectory above this one and then go back down the directory tree to the destination file, like this:

```
../Pets/Figaro.html
```

Here's the anatomy of this link:

- ✔ The dots (`..`) tell a browser to go to the directory above the current one.
- ✔ `/Pets/` is the new directory the browser needs to go to.
- ✔ `Figaro.html` is the destination file contained in the directory `Pets`.

If you are in a hurry and want to keep all the internal links on your Web site simple, just put all of your text and image files in the same directory. That way, whenever you make a link to another file, you don't have to move from one directory to another and worry about dots and slashes; you only have to type the filename, for example: `<A HREF="document.html">link text</A>`.

Making same-site links in HTML

Another common and useful link you'll need to create if you have more than one Web page on your site is a same-site link. By *same site,* I mean that the two pages being linked are stored on the same computer and they are about the same general subject (you or your family, that is). When you first create the pages, they all reside on your computer. When you publish the pages on a Web server, they reside on *that* computer. Either way, they are part of the same Web site.

You use a relative address to make a link from one file to another on your site. In a relative address, you list the directories that lie between the starting point document and the destination document.

Making a same-page link

The links on a Web page don't have to lead your visitors far across the Internet. Some of the most useful links take them from one place on a page to another. These are called *internal links*. A set of internal links is included on the welcome page of the Penzar Family Cyberspace Home Web site (`http://www.geocities.com/Heartland/1302/`), shown in Figure 15-1.

Starting point

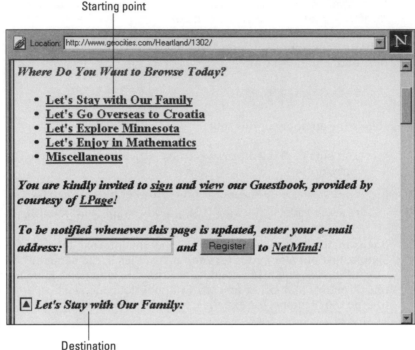

Figure 15-1:
Clicking on
the first item
in this set of
same-page
links takes
you to the
destination —
the heading
shown at
the bottom
of the page.

Destination

Same-page links are *far* easier to create using a Web page authoring program than by entering the HTML tags line by line. For that reason, I'll concentrate on showing how to make a same-page link using Netscape Editor rather than by typing the HTML.

Making a same-page link using Netscape Editor

Netscape Editor adds the HTML for you behind the scenes. You only click on toolbar buttons and enter the text that will serve as your clickable links. It's a two-step process: The first step is to mark the destination for your same-page link. Netscape calls this a *target.* You assign the target a name or a number, and then you mark it with the target toolbar button. Then you identify the text that will serve as the starting point for the link, and tell that link the name of the target it needs to go to.

Here's how to make a same-page link Using the Netscape Editor tools:

1. **Open Netscape Editor (you don't have to be connected to the Web beforehand), and from the Editor menu, select File⇨Open File in Editor.**

    The Open dialog box appears.

2. **Locate the HTML document you want to edit by looking through the folders on your hard disk, and click on OK.**

   The Web page to which you want to add the same-site link should be open in the Netscape Editor window (see Figure 15-2).

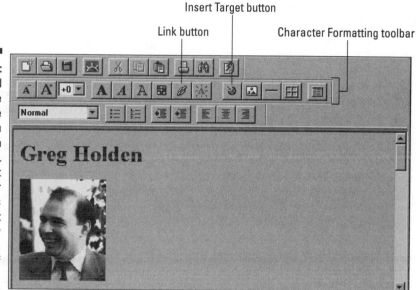

Insert Target button

Link button

Character Formatting toolbar

Figure 15-2:
Using a tool like Netscape Gold, you can open an IITML document and add or revise links without actually seeing a line of HTML.

3. **Position your mouse arrow at the spot in your Web page where you want the new link to appear, and click your mouse button.**

   A text cursor (a blinking vertical bar) appears in the document you are editing. In this example, the cursor should be just before the letter *A* in the heading Announcing My New Club.

4. **Click on the Insert Target button in the Netscape Editor's Character Formatting toolbar, or select Insert Target (Named Anchor).**

   The Target Properties dialog box appears.

5. **Enter the name for this destination, in this case club (see Figure 15-3).**

6. **Click on OK to close the Target Properties dialog box.**

   You return to the Netscape Editor window where you can see your link's destination marked with the target icon with a little red arrow pointing at it.

Figure 15-3:
When using
Netscape
Editor, just
enter the
name for
your link's
target.

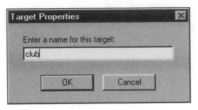

7. **Scroll up to the top of your Web page, and position your text cursor in your Web page document where you want to insert the starting point for your link.**

8. **If you have not yet typed this text, type it now. If you have already typed the text, click just before the text and drag your mouse to select it.**

You'll know when you have selected the text; it will be highlighted in black. For this example, you might type the phrase "Join my new club for guys."

The Properties dialog box appears, with the Link tab in front. The link text you just typed is shown beneath the phrase Linked text, and you should see the word "club" already entered in the "Select a named target in the specified file (optional)" text box (see Figure 15-4).

Figure 15-4:
After you
enter the
text that will
appear as a
highlighted
link, click
on the Link
button and
select the
target that
you want to
link to (in
this case,
"club").

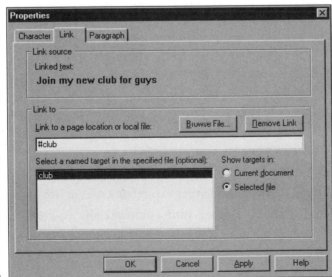

9. **Single-click on the word club to select it.**

   The words #club appear in the text box Link to a page location or local file.

10. **Click on OK to close the Properties dialog box.**

    You return to the Netscape Editor window where the words "Join my new club for guys" are now underlined and highlighted in blue as a clickable link. In order to test this link, you have to view your page in the Navigator browser window. You can't test it in the Editor window.

11. **Select File⇨Save to save your changes, and then select File⇨Browse Document to view your page in the Netscape Navigator browser window.**

    Your Web page opens in the Navigator browser window. Click on the highlighted words, and you should jump down the page to your target. (Actually, the targeted location jumped to the bottom of the Netscape Editor window.)

Using Images as Clickable Links

After you have some experience with making various textual links on your Web pages, you can also try making the same kinds of links using images as the starting points. Giving your visitors images they can click on gives your pages a more professional appearance. If you have an easy way of drawing or scanning images, you should give it a try.

Making a graphic link with HTML

The process is basically the same as it is for making external, same-site, or same-page links; the difference is that when you create the starting point for the link, instead of typing a word or phrase between the <A> and </A> tags, you insert another HTML tag that identifies the image you want people to click on. It seems confusing at first to put an HTML tag inside another set of tags, but once you try it, the process becomes more understandable.

Start with a textual link

For example, on my own home page (http://members.aol.com/gregholden), I have a paragraph about bird-watching. I might want to add a link to a page on the Web that contains links to lots of other bird-watching and bird-related information. If I were adding the HTML myself, I would do the following in order to create a textual version of this link:

1. **Open the HTML instructions for the Web page in a word-processing program, such as SimpleText (Mac) or Notepad (PC).**

2. **Scroll down to the place in the HTML where I want the highlighted starting point text to appear, and enter the following:**

```
<A HREF="http://www.internets.com/birds.htm"> This page has
lots of birding links </A>
```

3. **Save my HTML file by selecting File⇨Save.**

4. **Open my HTML document in a Web browser so I can test the link to make sure it works.**

Change the text to an image

I can also substitute an image of a bird for the highlighted phrase `This page has lots of birding links`. I have an image of a bird called `falcon.gif` that works just fine. To make this image "clickable," I do the following:

1. **Put the `falcon.gif` image file in the same directory as the Web page in which I want to include the link.**

2. **Open my HTML document in my word-processing program again.**

3. **Erase the highlighted phrase and substitute a reference to the image using the IMG tag in HTML, like this:**

```
<A HREF="http://www.internets.com/birds.htm"> <IMG
SRC="falcon.gif"> </A>
```

4. **Select File⇨Save to save my change.**

5. **Open my HTML document in any Web browser.**

   The cool way to do this is to click on the icon for the HTML document and then drag the icon atop the icon for the browser in which I want to view the Web page, and release my mouse button.

   The image appears on my page (see Figure 15-5). I can now test my link by clicking on the image and going to the page I linked to.

Figure 15-5:
An image appears with a blue border around it to signify that the image is a clickable link.

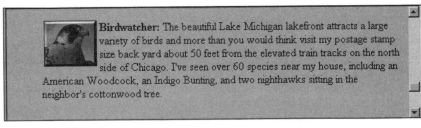

Birdwatcher: The beautiful Lake Michigan lakefront attracts a large variety of birds and more than you would think visit my postage stamp size back yard about 50 feet from the elevated train tracks on the north side of Chicago. I've seen over 60 species near my house, including an American Woodcock, an Indigo Bunting, and two nighthawks sitting in the neighbor's cottonwood tree.

Using navigation buttons

The navigation buttons that you see on many Web pages, and that are labeled Home, Back, or Next, are just clickable images that serve as same-site links. They lead you to different parts of the same Web site. The steps for making navigation buttons are the same as those given in the earlier section, "Making same-site links in HTML," with two differences:

 ✔ You need to obtain a copyright-free navigation button image from an image archive on the Web (see Appendix C) or draw one yourself.

 ✔ Instead of designating a word or phrase to serve as the starting point for the link, you designate a button or other image.

You can make any of the links mentioned in the "Making same-site links in HTML" section by using an image instead of a text link. For example, the first example in the section about relative addresses uses this line of HTML.

```
<A HREF="Hobbies/CoinCollecting.html">Read about my coin
collection</A>
```

If you have an image of a coin that you can use, you change the HTML as follows:

```
<A HREF="
```

```
Hobbies/CoinCollecting.html"> <IMG SRC="coin.gif" ALT="coin
image"> </A>
```

Be careful about using images of U.S. currency on your pages. The U.S. Secret Service doesn't like it. The only way you can legally publish an image of real U.S. money is to make the image either greater than $1^1/_2$ times its original size or less than 75 percent of its original size. It's much safer to use an image of an ancient coin, foreign currency, or to draw the image yourself.

Using button bars

A *button bar* is a series of clickable images that go at either the top or the bottom of a Web page. Each of the images is linked to a different page on the site. Daniel Warsaw includes a series of clickable photos at the top of his Web page (http://www.geocities.com/Heartland/1065/).

Navigation bars can be a series of homemade drawings, too (which is handy if you don't have access to a scanner). Lauren Bush includes some simple clickable images at the bottom of her Web page (http://milo.chem.usouthal.edu/%7Enix/), shown in Figure 15-6.

Figure 15-6:
Draw your own images using some of the techniques described in Chapter 13, and include each of those images a clickable button bar.

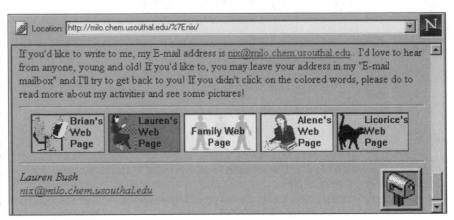

Brief note about imagemaps

Another kind of clickable image that you'll encounter often in your Web surfing is a clickable imagemap. An *imagemap* is an image that has been divided into clickable regions. The designer takes a GIF or JPEG image and, using special map software, divides the image into rectangles, circles, or other shapes. Each one of the shapes is then linked to a Web page. You'll find a nice explanation of imagemaps at the Webheads Web site (`http://www.pitt.edu/~webheads/MAPCLASS/imagemaps.html`). You can also try Felipe's Clickable Gif Map Tutorial-Mac at `http://edb518ea.edb.utexas.edu/html/gifmap.html`. To create a map file, download a copy of WebMap or other Macintosh imagemap programs at `ftp://ftp.uwtc.washington.edu/pub/Mac/Network/WWW/`. Find out about MapEdit and download a trial version from `http://www.boutell.com/mapedit/`.

Things like x,y coordinates, polygons, and maps are all familiar parts of basic geometry. If you can master imagemaps, you can take what you've learned and apply it to your geometry class. An imagemap would make a great extra-credit project!

One kid's opinion

The first time I made a link on one of my Web pages, I used World Wide Web Weaver because it's so much easier. You just click on the Link button, type the address, click on OK, and you're done. When I have to revise the URL for a link, though, I open the HTML file in a word processor and just type the new address. I have to admit that I've never made those internal links that take you from one part of a page to another, though. Those kinds of links only make sense if your page is pretty long, and I keep my pages as short as I can.

Part VI
The Part of Tens

The 5th Wave   By Rich Tennant

"No Stuart, I won't look up 'rampaging elephants' on the Internet. We're studying plant life and right now photosynthesis is a more pertinent topic."

In this part . . .

What do Santa Claus from the North Pole, The Count from Sesame Street, David Letterman from late-night TV, and Part VI all have in common? They all use lists.

Lists are great things when it comes to making Web pages. Lists organize important information in tidy packages that are easy to digest and that make a Web page easy to read.

Part VI, in fact, consists solely of lists that you can look through whether you're brainstorming for ideas or looking to upgrade some Web pages you've already created. You find suggestions for cool add-ons to your pages, great contents you can write about, and some do's and don'ts to observe when making Web pages. You even find the proverbial Top Ten list of well-designed Web pages.

So read through the lists, check 'em over at least twice, and learn some Web page rules that are both naughty and nice. Your present to yourself will be a great Web page.

Chapter 16

Do's and Don'ts for Web Page Authors

In This Chapter

▶ Top ten tips for terrific Web pages

▶ Web page gotchas that you should avoid

Does it seem like every time you turn around someone is reminding you of another rule? Rules at home, rules at school . . . seems like you run into rules everywhere. And you will find rules on the Web, too. But these rules are different. They're meant to help you look good online. Follow these rules, and you're sure to create eye-catching, interesting pages that will bring you lots of visitors and lots of responses.

Top Ten Web Page Do's

✔ **Be creative:** One of the first rules of Web pages is to break the rules: Don't be afraid to do something wild, crazy, and creative. Don't have a wannabe/look-alike page. The Web is no place to follow the crowd and blend in with everyone else. For example, don't simply give your visitors a list of other Web sites that you find interesting. They can do their own Web browsing. Make your page a contribution to the Web community by including information that is totally different. The easiest way to do that is to talk about yourself *(see Chapter 3)*. And after you create text that is uniquely your own, take some time to present it in a way that nobody else has thought of yet. Make yours a worthwhile page to visit.

✔ **Be a designer:** Make an effort to plan your Web page before you ever put your finger on the keyboard. Make a pencil drawing of how you want your page to look. Organize it well so that it is easy to access and view *(see Chapter 5)*. Your audience needs to be able to locate the main topics of a site quickly. Don't make them scroll through two or three computer screens worth of material in order to find something. You are wiser to provide five short Web pages, each, say, no more than 1 1/2 screens in length, than to have a single page that is several screens long. If you have great material but your page is a mish-mash that takes a full minute to appear in its entirety, you'll defeat your purpose. Do everything you can to put your best foot forward.

✔ **Be a communicator:** Before you create a page, think about why you want to have one, what you really want to say, and the best way to say it. Use all the tools at your disposal. Talk to your family, get the addresses for your friends' Web pages, scour your homework for material you can put online (see *Chapter 3* for suggestions on topics you can talk about). Then after you complete a draft, double-check to be sure you've expressed your ideas and materials clearly and concisely. No one does a perfect job the first time out. Take some extra time to fine-tune your work. Kids might ask Mom or Dad to look over your page and correct any typos or other mistakes. Don't be bashful about asking for help; everyone makes mistakes, and a little help with proofreading goes a long way.

✔ **Be a teacher:** You don't need a textbook and a chalkboard to spread knowledge. And kids, when you have your own Web page, *you* get to play the role of teacher, for a change. Make sure your audience learns something worthwhile by visiting your page. Even if you don't consider yourself to be an expert, your visitors can all learn from you or about you when you present, in your own special way, a topic you dearly love. Like Ed Methuey in Australia (`http://www.geocities.com/Enchanted Forest/3545`), you might create a whole page about sharks. So do some research, have some experiences, and then share what you've learned or done.

✔ **Be an entertainer:** Bring in the clowns. Yuk it up. Everyone likes to have fun and be entertained by what they see on the Internet. Make your page a fun place to visit. Crack a joke, tell a riddle, make a really "bad" pun. But more important, be a storyteller. Don't just say, "I like junk food." Go into detail about what you like and why you like it. Don't just say, "I went fishing on my vacation." Tell about where you went and what you caught or were trying to catch. Describing your feelings will make your viewers feel something. After all, your goal is to connect with each audience member emotionally.

✔ **Be personal:** If your visitors want to look at a cartoon, they'll turn on the TV. When they open your Web page, they want to get to know you, not Bugs Bunny. Show them who you are and tell them what you think. How? By writing in your own words, arranging photos of yourself or other photos that you've taken, creating your own images, and presenting sounds and videos that you have made. Talk about your family, for example. (Also, fill out the exercises on the CD that accompanies this book.) Don't worry if it looks homemade. That's the point. You're striving to be 100 percent natural.

✔ **Be visual:** A picture is worth a thousand words. Yes, your text is important, and you should do your very best to find good words and arrange them effectively. But don't put a page on the Web that's filled with only words. You can find many, many ways to please the eye as well as the mind on the Web. Use images, photos, video, color, textures, and any other graphic elements you can to communicate visually and delight your audience.

If you don't have access to a scanner, never fear. Lots of kids create fine Web pages that don't include a single photo. You can borrow clip art to use on your pages *(see Chapter 9)* or make your own drawings *(see Chapter 13)*.

✔ **Be an explorer:** Visit lots of other sites on the Web to learn new things. Doing that will make you a better Web publisher. It helps to know what's out there so that you know how you compare. "More leads to more" when you're talking about being on the Web. The more you use the Internet, the more excited you get about it. Then when you bring that excitement home to your own Web page, people get excited about what you've done and do more good stuff themselves. Tell people about other sites that you admire and provide a link to each one *(see Chapter 15)*. But be sure you say a word or two about why you like the site and what people might discover there. That way, they won't waste their time by checking out a site that doesn't interest them.

✔ **Be up-to-date:** On the Web, it's pretty clear what's hot and what's not. One of the worst insults you can get is to be called the keeper of a *cobWeb* page. So make sure your page is always fresh by updating it often. Add new things and remove dated material. Don't put up a page and leave it unattended for long periods of time and don't just keep tacking new stuff onto the old stuff. Your viewers will wonder why they should care about your page if it doesn't mean enough to you to make it current *(see Chapter 5)*.

Another good reason to update your page is that you get the chance to rework and improve it. Web pages aren't written in stone (or, more accurately, on paper). Don't be afraid to consider your site as being under construction and something you can always upgrade.

You can keep involved with your page by responding quickly to e-mail from your visitors. Why not set a certain day of the week or of the month to check and update your page? That's also a good way to remind yourself to make sure the links you have to other pages are still correct.

✔ **Be a friend:** Friends are friends no matter how they meet. Be willing to share yourself on the Web and get to know others, too. If you meet enough people, you might be able to start up your own *cyberclub*. Check out Debbie Hayes's cyberclub site for girls (`http://www.geocities.com/RodeoDrive/3294/index.html`).

When you look around your classroom, you may see only one or two kids who share your interests. On the Web, however, you can always connect with as many soul mates as you have the time to visit. E-mail other kids who have pages that you admire or would like to get to know better. Be ready to listen, and be ready to talk. Together, you and your new friends will come up with ideas that neither of you might have thought of yourself. That's what friends are for.

Top Ten Web Page Don'ts

Don't do this, don't do that — you've probably heard about plenty of things you shouldn't do, either at school or at home. However, the following list of don'ts is different. They're intended to help you avoid possible pitfalls and problems you can run into when creating Web pages and to keep your Web page looking good so you'll get lots of positive feedback from your visitors.

✔ **Don't overdo it:** Plenty of "kitchen sink" Web pages put all of their contents on a single document. Divide your text and images into several pages (see *Chapter 4* for ideas on how to organize your pages). Include a maximum of one or two topics on each page. Don't clutter any one page with more than, say, five or six visuals.

✔ **Don't use big images:** Keep any GIF or JPEG files to 30K or less in size. Large graphics take too long to appear, and your viewers with short attention spans will go elsewhere. Reduce the size by cropping your files as tightly as you can *(see Chapter 10).*

✔ **Don't use copyrighted material:** Use clip art on your page, or else get permission in writing from the author or authors of art that you use *(see Chapter 9).* This rule applies to things like written material, photos, graphics, sounds, and videos, too. When in doubt, ask.

✔ **Keep backgrounds readable:** Avoid bright background colors that are hard on the eyes. Also, avoid busy background textures. Make sure the type is readable on whatever color you choose. Your text, for example, will get lost if there's not enough contrast between the type and background *(see Chapter 13).*

✔ **Don't make "surprise" links:** If you provide links on your pages to large files, such as video or audio files, be sure to warn people of their size and how long it might take to download them.

- ✔ **No caterpillars!:** Don't insert so many horizontal rules or bars across your page that your page begins to resemble one of these crawly creatures.

- ✔ **Keep URLs simple:** Use short filenames that are easy to remember. Don't use too many numbers or unusual characters such as the percent sign (%).

- ✔ **No "Under Construction:"** Web pages are always under construction, and you really don't have to point it out by adding this label or graphic to your page.

- ✔ **Don't get obscure:** Avoid slang or obscure terms that might leave your visitors, particularly members of your foreign audience, scratching their heads and wondering what you're talking about.

- ✔ **No broken links:** Don't put a link on your page without checking to see whether the URL you are using to create the link is spelled correctly and will actually take your visitors to the site when they click on the highlighted text or image.

Chapter 17

Cool Contents for Great Web Pages

• •

• •

Ten Cool Things to Put on Your Web Pages

The highest compliment that Web page authors can receive is to have someone *bookmark* their pages in order to revisit them at a later date (a bookmark, also called a favorite, records and stores the URL of a Web page). Often, the pages that become bookmarks or favorites are the ones that provide visitors with plenty to see and do. This chapter suggests ten words, images, and utilities that you can include to keep your visitors coming back again and again.

Provide games and puzzles

Be a player. Include a game on your page or make up a puzzle or riddle to solve. Use your imagination so that visiting your Web page is an adventure.

You don't have to be a computer programmer to create a game, coloring book, or interactive story. One example is a story called Patty's Adventure, which is included on one of Heather Shade's Web pages (http://www.shadeslanding.com/hms/march/page1.html).

Scan photos so people can see you

If you have a scanner (or can borrow someone else's), your Web page should definitely feature a picture of yourself *(see Chapter 10)*. After that, how about throwing in some photos of your family, pets, friends, house, school, teachers, or city? That said, there's not much point in putting photos on the Web unless their quality is good (just one or two good ones, though, don't go overboard). The images should be sharp and clear. The faces should be big enough to see on the screen. You never know when a Hollywood agent will discover you on your Web site!

Get your creativity online

If you've done it, flaunt it. Show visitors your drawings, paintings, and photos. Let them read your poems and short stories. What's that you say? Your latest accomplishment is a weaving that covers an entire wall or a sculpture that's taller than you are? Maybe what you're most proud of is a costume you made for a play or the science project that won first prize. Take a photo and put it on your page. Or just tell people a joke that you like, or suggest a book or movie you've enjoyed recently. If it's yours, your visitors want to see it.

Make a GIF animation

Creepy and crawly isn't just for Halloween anymore. Your Web page doesn't need to sit frozen in time. Like many other young Web page authors, you can include one of several types of animations on your page. An *animation* is an image that seems to move in some way or another. Animations add a feeling of liveliness and extra excitement to a page. An animation can also call attention to something, such as an invitation to send you e-mail. If you have some artistic ability, you can try to create your own animated GIF, as described in *Chapter 11*. Otherwise, you'll find plenty of locations around the Web where generous artists have made animated images available for you to copy and use on your own pages, either for free or for a small fee. The following sections suggest a number ways to include animations on your Web pages.

Animated GIFS

Yikes, it's alive! Animated GIFs are made up of several different images saved in a GIF format that allows them to be played one after another like a miniature movie. These animations require relatively small amounts of memory. Besides that, they're fun and make your page a more interesting and lively page to visit. If you don't want to make your own animated GIFs *(see Chapter 11)*, you can find and use clip art *(see Chapter 9)*.

Make your own headings

Make your headings as unique as you are. Open a painting program and draw your own snappy headlines *(see Chapter 13* for information about using painting programs). Don't worry if your headings look clumsy or childish; the point is that they truly convey your personality. Hand-drawn headlines add a friendly, cheerful, personal look to your page, like the one on Debbie's Home Page (`http://www.li.net/~edhayes/debbie.html`).

Make your page really "count"

Statistics are popular on Web pages. Here are some ways to help your visitors keep track of where they are and what time it is.

Day and date

Make a date. Sure, everyone has a calendar hanging on the wall. But when a visitor sees the day and date on your page, they get the message that it's a *happening* place. Ask your Internet Service Provider if day and date utilities (often called server-side includes) are available that you can put on your Web page *(see Chapter 7)*.

Counters

How do I visit thee? Let me count the ways. A counter is a utility that records the number of visits that have been made to a Web page. A counter resides on the Web server, which is the computer that holds your Web pages. Counters add more graphic interest to your page and help you keep track of how many times your page has been visited. Your Internet Service Provider might let you make a link on your Web page to one of its counters so that the number of visits can be displayed *(see Chapter 7)*.

Give your visitors a place to say hello

Sign in, please! Guestbooks (as described in *Chapter 7*) are pages that contain text boxes where visitors can type something about themselves and send you a comment on how they liked your page. A guestbook gives you important feedback so that you can improve your page. Plus, you can make new friends.

Fill your page with nice furnishings

"It's not much, but I just call it my home page," you may say, modestly. But underneath, you're glowing with pride when you create beautiful graphics. Some people call them Web page *furniture,* while others call them *eye candy*. Whatever you want to call them, add nice buttons and bars to your page, start paragraphs with large decorated letters of the alphabet, or break up blocks of text by inserting some icons.

Color your page with wallpaper

As long as you are making Martha Stewart proud with furniture, don't overlook your background patterns. If used effectively, they give your page depth and visual interest. You may want to check out Rachel's Page (`http://www.mcs.net/~kathyw/rachel.html`), which contains a nice background. Or make your own background pattern from a picture you like *(see Chapter 13)*. Anything to keep the walls from closing in on your viewer is the effect you're trying to create.

Add some sound to your page

Turn up the volume: Add a musical background that people can listen to while visiting your page. Or find sound bites that give that extra bite to your page. People have five senses, so don't leave out the hearing one. *Chapter 12* has some suggestions for how to add sound to your pages. (Remember, though, to include alternative text to your sound file for visitors who don't have sound cards or who have impaired hearing.)

Ten Ways to Get Personal on Your Web Page

The next "set of ten" concerns aspects of your life that you can talk about online. Some of these are discussed in *Chapter 3,* although others are topics that aren't covered in that chapter.

Make a special presentation

Do you like a particular musical group, a special TV show, unicorns, dinosaurs, horses, or elephants? You may want to devote an entire Web page (or series of pages) to your one special interest. David Cain has a whole page devoted to snakes at `http://www.charm.net/~jcain/david.html`.

Link your page to the Web

The only thing better than finding a page that interests you is having it provide a link to another page that shares that interest. Don't just put in a link for no good reason. Add links that really relate to something that is already on your page (as explained in *Chapter 15*). It's more fun than playing leapfrog.

Be a tour guide

You don't have to wait until you get a chauffeur's license to offer the cook's tour. For example, what if your Web page were to have the title, "My Room and My Things"? You might give visitors a tour of your room and the things you really like having around you. Do you have posters or pictures on the wall? Do you have stuffed animals? What are your favorite toys or souvenirs? What are your favorite things and why? Do you share your room with a brother or sister? Do you keep it messy or clean? Well, enough of my ideas. Put on your official hat and wow visitors with a great description of your room or the location of your choice.

Describe your heroes and she-roes

Whom do you admire and why? Put your heroes' pictures on your page. Tell visitors what it is that you admire about them or want to develop in yourself. Then they may want to find out more about a person who is special enough for you to highlight. Or they may just be glad they got to know you a little bit better.

Describe your summer (or other) vacation

Tell visitors in pictures and words about your last vacation. What did you learn from traveling? Don't just give them a list of dates and places. By sharing anecdotes and describing scenes in great detail, you can help your visitors feel like they were actually with you. Everybody likes to add to their frequent flier miles by using their imaginations.

Celebrate your family heritage

Roots aren't just for trees. Tell visitors about your family heritage or your family history. Did your family recently arrive from another country? Which one? Your Web visitors will want to know about customs and clothes — and especially about food.

Celebrate holidays and birthdays

The problem with holidays is that most of them last only 24 hours. But on the Web, the celebration of holidays can go on all year long. Show visitors your Halloween costume, your family's Christmas tree, or your Chanukah candles. If you're Irish, make a page about St. Patrick's Day. What do you know about the history of these holidays?

Celebrate your birthdays

Show visitors pictures of your birthday party and the gifts you received. What astrological sign (Pisces, Aquarius, and so on) are you? Who else was born on your birthday? Nothing brightens up an un-birthday more than sharing the fun that happened on a real birthday.

Start a cyberclub

Start a club on the Web dedicated to a specific purpose. Maybe a club for girls or boys or babysitters. You name it, the Web is the place to join up.

Take a survey

Maybe you're more interested in collecting information than giving it out. Maybe you search for opportunities to do research. Do you want to ask people about something? Develop a questionnaire about anything, and see what people think. Check out Katie's Kewl Page (http://www.blinn.com/katie/). It lets people tell Katie about their favorite music, or give feedback on other topics.

Chapter 18

Ten (Actually, Eleven) Winning Web Pages

· ·

In This Chapter

▶ Pages that make a great Web presentation

▶ Pages that supplement content with nonintrusive graphics and color

▶ Pages that are simple yet friendly

· ·

*D*o you get a lump in your throat when athletes climb up to the winner's platform wearing gold medals and holding bouquets of flowers, and then their national anthem starts to play? Those are thrilling moments to be sure, but another very important part is when the commentator mentions that a sports figure has achieved his or her personal best. The Web pages featured in this chapter have lots of stuff going for them, but they are here solely because they captured my imagination.

These Web pages show that a lot of time, effort, and love went into making them. They are personal expressions: They tell you something about their young authors' personalities, things they are passionate about, people they admire.

The purpose of this chapter isn't to start a Web page competition of Olympic proportions. Instead, you are being encouraged to look at some of the home pages spotlighted, along with others that you find along the way, and think about what you can learn from them. What works for you is cool. What doesn't fit your very own special self may be interesting, but should be left alone.

Funniest? Cleverest? Strangest? Nerdiest? Touchingest? Prettiest? Come up with unique categories, and have your own award ceremony with friends or family members. Defend your favorite at a debate to choose the top pick. There can be more than one winner, don't forget.

Pages with Flashy Multimedia and Animation

This first group of pages includes a number of interactive multimedia-type goodies: lots of color, sounds, animations, and interactive features such as frames and forms. Yet the bells and whistles don't overwhelm the contents, and the authors' personalities still come through.

Ayal's Home Page

```
http://agdec1.technion.ac.il/ayal.html
```

Game of chess, anyone? Ayal takes on all comers on his page. You can actually play a game of chess with him by clicking on a link. But the best reason to visit is to take a look at his use of frames. The left frame on his page contains a clickable imagemap (see *Chapter 15*): Click on the white region labeled Miffy, for example, and you are taken to a page about a cartoon rabbit named Miffy. This new page appears in the right frame of the page. Only the contents of this right frame change; the left and top frames don't change. Frames are subdivisions of an individual Web page; each frame, in fact, is a miniature Web page within a Web page. You can set up frames so that a click on a link in one frame makes the contents of another frame change.

Nicole's Home Page

```
http://www.geocities.com/EnchantedForest/2926/
```

Nicole's home page, like lots of other kids' pages, uses music in the background (see *Chapters 7 and 12* for more on how to do this). Sometimes putting tunes in the background can be risky because what's cool to you can be intrusive or irritating to some visitors. Nicole's page, like many others, uses a song that we didn't find overly complex or distracting: the theme from *Forrest Gump*. She also uses nice background colors and lots of animated GIFs.

Sarah's 'Très Cool' Homepage

```
http://www.angelfire.com/wv/sarpage/index.html
```

Sarah Gravelines has been mentioned elsewhere in this book and has won several Web awards (such as number 1 in PowWow's Top Ten list) for her hand-drawn headline, nice photo of herself, and lots of interesting contents on her Web page. She also has a guestbook, a Web page counter, and the current time (all mentioned in *Chapter 7*). Her page truly lives up to its name!

Pages that Combine Nice Layout and Organization

These pages use innovative layout techniques, called tables, to present lots of page contents in a compact space. The pages have much to say, but it's easy to find the most important information.

Kaitlyn's Korner

```
http://www.bayne.com/wolfbayne/kaitlyn/korner.html
```

Kaitlyn Ruth and her mom collect jokes from other kids and publish them on Kaitlyn's page. (My 4-year-old daughter and I had fun going through the list of "knock-knock" jokes.) But the page doesn't limit itself to chuckles. The table at the top of the page lets Kaitlyn present her photo next to her page's heading. A lot of personal information about Kaitlyn is also well presented. Good organization makes this page easy to navigate.

Heather's Happy Holidaze Page

`http://www.shadeslanding.com/hms/`

You'll find lots of graphics on 7-year-old Heather Shade's sophisticated page, but they all work because she planned one focus: holidays. Each holiday page is either interactive or includes animation, or both. Although the ideas were Heather's, the Web page is by her mom. The links to each holiday page are presented in a big table (see Figure 18-1).

Pages with Great Contents

Colors and flashy animations are great, but they're wasted if you don't actually have anything to say on your Web page. The kids who created the Web pages in this section have lots of good information to contribute to their fellow cybersurfers.

Amy's Home Page

`http://www.bayside.net/users/kidsetc/amy.htm`

If you need a button to wear to the St. Patrick's Day parade, you can print out one from 10-year-old Amy's page. Amy's personality shines through just by the use of a few simple graphics, including smiling flowers and one of Amy's own drawings. Click on the drawing shown in Figure 18-2, and you see a photo of Amy herself. While you're visiting Amy's world, take note of the variety of backgrounds used and how readable the text is on all of them. Amy also uses a table to organize the links to some of her favorite sites. Plus, she includes background music, and she loves Elvis, too!

Derya Davenport's Home Page

`http://www.cs.bilkent.edu.tr/~david/derya/derya.html`

Would you like to meet an 11-year-old British girl named Derya Davenport who has lived in Turkey all her life? Reading this page will give you some very good ideas on how to publish your own magazine on your home page (not to mention instructions on how to build a robot!). Plus, you'll learn a lot about diverse cultures. Remember the name of the author, who's shown in Figure 18-3. She's well on her way to becoming a well-known writer. Derya's page also uses a nice, simple background (see *Chapter 13* for more on backgrounds).

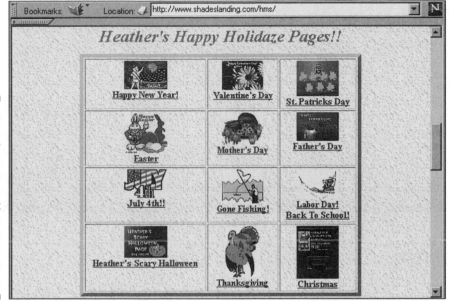

Figure 18-1:
A table is a great way to present a lot of links in a compact format, as shown on 7-year-old Heather's Web page.

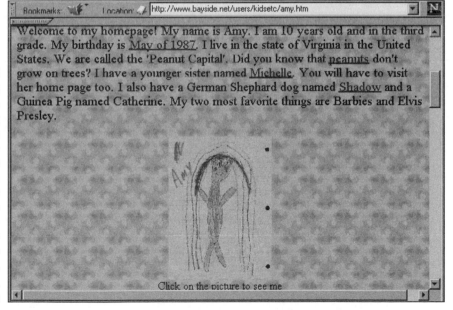

Figure 18-2:
This excerpt from Amy's Home Page shows how well written it is and how Amy isn't afraid to let her personality shine through.

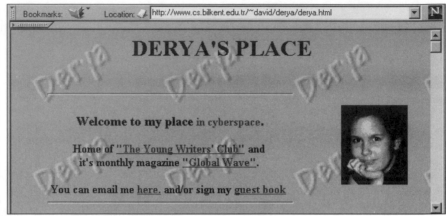

Figure 18-3:
Derya
Davenport
uses her
Web page
to publish
her poems
and stories,
as well as
her online
writers'
magazine.

Graphics that Spice Up Text

I'm a writer, so I tend to like Web pages in which the author's golden prose doesn't get obscured by backgrounds that are too bright, background music that won't stop, or animations that take too long to appear. These two pages have flashy graphics, but they don't overwhelm the contents; the two complement one another, just as they should on a good Web page.

Cosanna's Page

`http://midxpress.com/midxpress/cos/cos.htm`

This page gets high marks for effective use of graphics and color. Right away, you are introduced to the personality behind the page with 13-year-old Cosanna's photo prominently displayed (see Figure 18-4). Cosanna uses an interesting technique in presenting the images as shapes with the background removed rather than as ordinary photos in a rectangular form. Although the background texture is strong, the text has good contrast and is quite readable. The ratio of text to images is good. The page flows nicely because a lot of thought went into the placement of the elements.

Sophie's Page

`http://homepages.enterprise.net/ted.hall/sophie.html`

Icons are a happening thing on Sophie Winsley's page. It's a very attractive page graphically, with a sky-blue background, a Java applet, animations, and lots more. Content-wise, the page is full of interesting information about where Sophie lives — on the Isle of Man, near Great Britain. The balance between text and graphics is good, and the design is clean and functional.

Figure 18-4:
Cosanna's Page uses transparent images and homemade lettering, but the graphics are balanced by lots of interesting contents, too.

Simple and Friendly Pages We Love to Visit

Simpler is often better when it comes to Web pages. You don't have to overwhelm your visitors with lots of multimedia that creep along as your browser struggles to download them. These pages do a great job with relatively simple graphics.

Peggy's Page

http://cres1.lancs.ac.uk/~esarie/peggy.htm

Easy on the eyes is one way to describe this Web page by Peggy Rosina Edmondson-Noble, who lives in England. The page uses a simple gray background with an interesting paperlike texture, as well as a plain black line drawing at the top of the page. The graphics let you concentrate on the contents. Readers feel that they have really gotten to know the author and that they like her a lot. You'll probably like Peggy's pony, William, too; You can even send e-mail to him! This page is proof that a lack of bells and whistles doesn't mean a lack of impact.

Matt G-J's Home Page and Hotlist

`http://bvsd.k12.co.us/~ginsberm/`

If your favorite language is HTML, you'll find someone to communicate with on this page. It was completely created by Matthew Ginsberg-Jaeckle, a student at Boulder High School in Boulder, Colorado. You find lots of links to pages that help you learn HTML, along with pages with research material to help with homework assignments.

The Best of the Rest: Other Notable Kids' Pages

When you get right down to it, just about every Web page contains some technique you can apply to your own site. Here are three kids' Web pages that have ideas you may want to borrow:

Rachel's page (`http://www.mcs.net/~kathyw/rachel.html`): True, this site hasn't been updated in a long time, but it was good when it was created, and it's still good. Have you ever wondered how to describe your feelings about something that's hard to put into words? Lots of emotions are conveyed on this site — love, sadness, and appreciation — as Rachel pays tribute to her mother, who died after helping get the Web site started. It's really an effective way to keep memories alive. Thanks so much for sharing, Rachel.

The Teel Family Web Site (`http://www.teelfamily.com/`): Okay, so this isn't a kids' page as such, but kids are in it. Obviously, Matthew and Susan Teel and their family have lots of time to work on their Web pages during the long winters in Chugiak, Alaska. Their site shows it. They've got their own family logo, their own domain name, cool photos, and they use simple white page backgrounds.

Kel's Place (`http://www.toptown.com/centralpark/Kel/index.htm`): Here you find terrific graphics combined with good content to create a great site. Kelly R. makes use of a high-tech feature called *server push,* which she uses to update information about a missing person every few minutes. She's also got a page about adoption, a subject she knows well.

Part VII
Appendixes

"I SAID I WANTED A NEW MONITOR FOR MY BIRTHDAY!
MONITOR! MONITOR!"

In this part . . .

Where's the beef? In the last part of this book, you find lots of useful information to put some flesh on the bones of your Web page projects. You can take your pick of hardware and software programs that you can use to be a Web publisher. You learn about Web page authoring programs so you can decide which ones you want to try out yourself. You get to check out the numerous lists of Web sites that provide free art, sounds, and other useful goodies you can put on your pages.

And you find out how to open the *Creating Web Pages For Kids & Parents* CD-ROM and install the Web browsers and other programs that are on the CD.

Appendix A

Assembling Your Web Page Toolbox

● ●

*W*hen you make the progression from simply surfing the Web to adding your own trickle to the flood of information being published online, you become very aware that your computer crawls along, software programs take forever to download, and that you doze off while waiting for a cool clip art animation to appear on a Web site.

So before your computer runs out of memory and goes on strike right in the middle of a Web page project, check out the equipment you already have and assess your needs:

___ Take stock of how much computer memory and processing speed you have available. Fill out the checklist at the end of this appendix and take it to a computer store if you need to make some purchases.

___ Evaluate your level of satisfaction with your present Internet Service Provider (if you have one). Find out what kind of Web page publishing options your provider gives you. You may want to shop around for a faster connection and more space on a Web server (some more pros and cons are described in Chapter 6).

___ Make a list of software you have and the software you need programs for creating Web pages (see Chapters 1 and 6) and drawings (see Chapter 13), for adjusting photos (see Chapter 10), or for whatever you want to do.

___ Shop around. Either online or in computer stores, get prices on a faster modem or a new disk drive. Get the fastest equipment and the largest chunk of memory you can afford — your investment is sure to pay off in the long run.

Getting Your Computer Up to Speed

Your computer must be powerful enough to handle your graphics files. The following sections offer some suggestions on what you need to create Web pages.

Check out your CPU

Your Central Processing Unit (CPU) determines how fast you work on your computer. For creating Web pages on a Mac, it's best to have a PowerMac computer, a Performa, or a Quadra. You should be running System 7.1 or later. Older Macs like the SE and LCII, will creak along. PC users will be in great shape with a Pentium processor, but a 486 processor is okay, too.

The type of processor is often shown on the front of the computer: 6100/66 or 7200/90 on a PowerMac, for example. The first number is the chip your computer uses; the part after the slash is the "clock speed" at which the computer does its stuff. If you have a 486/66 PC, your computer has a 486 processor and runs at a clock speed of 66 MHz, which is a minimum for processing on the Web. Anything that's 66 MHz and up is okay.

Upgrading your computer so that it browses the Web and lets you create Web pages quickly doesn't have to cost a fortune. You don't necessarily have to purchase a whole new computer, either. A new Pentium processor may cost about $200. You may also be able to get a great bargain by making a bid on computer equipment at the ONSALE online auction house (`http://www.onsale.com/`).

Boost your memory banks

If you want to be really nice to your computer, go out and buy it some memory. You should certainly have a minimum of 8MB RAM and 16MB is better. If you can install even more than that, your computer will happily turn out as many Web pages as you desire.

RAM stands for Random Access Memory, which is the built-in memory your computer uses to run software programs. (*ROM,* by the way, is Read Only Memory that is built into a computer or CD and can't be altered.) The other kind of memory on your computer is *hard disk* (or hard drive) storage, which you can copy over and reuse as long as you don't use it up. *Virtual memory* is memory you can take from a hard disk (on a Macintosh) and designate as RAM. You can use virtual memory to bring your RAM up to 16, 24, or 32MB, but you'll be robbing yourself of disk storage space. Your computer will run better (that is, have plenty of space or crash less frequently) if you buy real RAM and install it yourself. On a PC, installing RAM is as easy as installing a memory card; on a Mac, you may want a technician to do the work for you.

Table A-1 lists the programs you need to operate most Web page browsers, Web page authoring tools, and graphics programs and the memory and processing speeds they require.

Table A-1	Program Memory Requirements	
Program	*Memory (Minimum)*	*Processor (Minimum)*
Netscape Communicator	8MB (Windows 95) 16MB (Mac OS)	486 or later 68020 or PowerPC
Internet Explorer 3.01 for Windows 95	8MB RAM and 5–10MB hard disk space	386 or later
Internet Explorer 3.0 for Windows 3.1	4MB RAM and 1.7–3.8MB hard disk space	386 or later
Internet Explorer 3.0 for Mac	8MB and 2.2–7.7MB hard disk space	68030 or PowerPC
Adobe PageMill 2.0	8MB (Mac OS) and 10MB hard disk space	68020 or PowerPC
FrontPage 97 for Windows	8MB and 30MB hard disk space	486 or later
FrontPage 1.0 for Mac	16MB and 30MB hard disk space	PowerPC
HotDog Professional 3	16MB (Windows 95)	486 or later

RAM is getting cheaper all the time. Prices vary widely, though, depending on the type of computer you have. One way to do some comparison shopping is to calculate the price per megabyte of RAM. A price of $49.99 for 8MB RAM is $6.25 per megabyte, for example.

Hard disk storage

It's alarmingly easy to use up disk space when you're surfing the Web, creating graphics, and downloading software. Every time you visit a page on the Web, the graphics on that page (and often, the text) are copied to your hard disk. If you start running out of space on your hard disk, you have some options:

__ Do some housecleaning! Get rid of files you don't need.

__ Clean out your e-mail inbox; throw old messages you don't need in the Trash or Recycle Bin, and empty the trash.

__ Reduce the space on your hard drive (otherwise known as disk cache) that your Web browser uses to store graphics files whenever you visit a Web page. You do this in the Cache dialog box in Netscape Navigator's Network Preferences. In Microsoft Internet Explorer, you click on the Settings button in the Advanced dialog box in Internet Explorer's Options settings.

__ Break down and get a new hard disk: You can purchase a 1GB (gigabyte) internal disk drive for less than $200.

Get Connected!

If you don't yet have a way of connecting to the Internet from home and you want to create family Web pages, you need to get an Internet connection soon. Sure, you can connect to the Internet from school or work, but where's the family fun in that? If you do have a connection, whether you are online already or are looking for a faster connection, here are a couple of other alternatives that you can use to get a faster connection.

Let your modem do the talking

Slow is cool when you're with your special friend and want the minutes to last forever, but when you're sitting in front of a computer, fast is a blast. If you are poking along with a modem that transfers 14,400 bytes or even only 9,600 bytes of data per second, consider upgrading to something faster, such as a 28,800 or 33,600 baud modem. (These are all analog modems, as opposed to a digital ISDN modem mentioned later.) The move from 14,400 to 28,800 is a noticeable improvement; it will put some wind in your sails and make your surfing a breeze.

Businesses that connect to the Internet have all kinds of exotic high-speed options with techie-sounding acronyms, such as ATM, ADSL, and so on. For most home users, though, calling a computer that is connected to the Internet, and thus getting a temporary connection to the Internet yourself, is the most practical solution. Here are a couple of other alternatives for families wanting to get online:

  ✔ **ISDN Service (Integrated Services Digital Network):** ISDN, which is offered by some telephone companies, involves running a new digital phone line to your house. Digital lines can carry both voice and data. ISDN has a couple of advantages. It gives you either 56K or 128K access to the Internet, which is faster than most modems (though in my experience, not *dramatically* faster). Besides getting the ISDN line for your computer, you get two new POTS (Plain Old Telephone Service) lines for your regular phone calls. If you're using the only phone line in the house to connect to the Internet, ISDN will help free up the phone for everyone else.

  The big disadvantage is that ISDN is a bit of an investment. You have to buy an ISDN modem, you have to pay to get it installed, and you have to pay a monthly ISDN fee on top of your regular bill. Besides that, your Internet provider will probably charge you a higher monthly fee to connect via ISDN. (Makes the 56 Kbps analog modem mentioned earlier look pretty attractive, doesn't it?)

✔ **Web TV:** If you already have a computer, why get Web TV?

- It frees up the family phone — you know that thing that is glued to your ear more often than not.

- It frees up your regular computer so someone can do homework or actual work while someone else in the house surfs the Web.

- The screen tends to be bigger than most computer screens (although the resolution depends on the quality of the TV).

- Instead of filling your head with passive commercial entertainment, you can actively get information on the Internet.

On the downside, you have to buy a set-top box, a hand-held controller, and a keyboard. You also have to pay a monthly fee to the WebTV network, and you may need to install another phone line because WebTV uses a regular telephone jack. Most Web sites aren't yet designed for TV and just won't look very good on a TV screen.

Find yourself a Web space provider

After you get your computer and your modem ready, you need to get onto the Internet. Here are brief overviews of the most common options. For more information, see Chapter 6.

✔ **Commercial online providers:** Commercial online providers (you might call them COPs) are the well-known companies America Online, CompuServe, Prodigy, and Microsoft Network. Like everything else, they have their good and bad points. One very good point is that they give you access to the Internet from virtually anywhere in the world.

Points against COPs: Millions of people are using these services at any one time, so access can be slow. Parts of the site you want to visit are occasionally busy (particularly on lunch hours and just before 5 p.m. on weekdays), and the system may occasionally get overloaded and crash.

✔ **Major Internet providers:** Several big Internet providers give Internet access to users over a very wide area — the whole country or even around the world. If you want to connect to the Internet while you are traveling, these providers can be a good option because they typically offer toll-free numbers that you can dial from practically anywhere.

In case you are looking for a provider, look no farther than the CD accompanying this book. It includes the software you need to connect to the Internet using AT&T's WorldNet Service.

> ✔ **Local service providers:** Many smaller Internet companies serve customers primarily in their local area. They may not offer as much as the commercial or national providers in the way of ready-made Web content or chat groups, but they have one big advantage: They often provide better service than bigger companies. Sometimes, having someone to patiently answer all of your questions over the phone can make a big difference, particularly if you're a newcomer to the Internet.

What kind of Internet provider should you choose? Talk it over with your parents. If you plan to be on the Internet a lot (either several days a week or perhaps every day), choose a provider that charges you a flat monthly rate for unlimited access to the Web: typically, about $19.95 a month. The essential factors, though, are how much Web space a provider will give you and what you can do with it.

Web Server Space

Along with giving you access to the Internet, your provider should give you storage space on one of its *Web servers.* Web servers are helpful computers that remain connected to the Web all the time and serve up Web pages. Be sure to find out what a provider will give you before making a choice. Here's what to look for:

> ✔ **Memory:** You'll probably find that 2MB of space for your personal pages on a Web server is more than enough to begin. If you plan on making your site really extensive, ask your provider if you can pay a little extra for 5MB or 10MB of space. Also make sure your provider doesn't charge you for every kilobyte, or even every byte, of data you transfer to the server. This kind of "hidden" cost can add up quickly.
>
> ✔ **Content restrictions:** Most providers get very grouchy when it comes to content that they consider offensive, obscene, or otherwise not nice. Some providers will give you 2MB or so to put up your own personal pages but charge extra if you are running a for-profit business. Be sure you talk to a customer service representative and find out exactly what you can do and how much it will cost.
>
> ✔ **Domain name:** Choosing your own domain name for your Web site can be even more fun than getting one of those vanity license plates for your car. A domain name is an easy-to-remember word or phrase that you can use in the Internet address (also called the URL) for your Web site. Not only does it look cool to have a simple domain name, but also it's easy to remember. Instead of an URL like

```
http://www.geocities.com/users/1915/
```

you can have an address like

```
http://www.johnsons.com/
```

An organization called InterNIC keeps track of domain names in order to avoid disputes. To get a domain name, you have to pay a $100 application fee to keep your name registered for two years and a yearly $50 maintenance fee thereafter. Some providers will help you apply for a domain name; others won't allow one at all. Ask your provider for its current policy.

If you're interested in applying for a domain name, visit InterNIC at `http://rs.internic.net/`. You can search for a name you want to use and see whether anyone is already using it on another Web site.

✔ **FTP Space:** When you are shopping for Web server space, be sure to ask whether you can upload and download files easily using FTP (File Transfer Protocol).

Also, find out whether your friends can get access to files you want them to download. On AOL, the process is hardly straightforward; with other providers, it's a no-brainer.

Table A-2 compares Web space offerings for three providers.

Table A-2	Web Server Space for Your Home Page		
Provider	*Space*	*Restrictions?*	*Cost?*
America Online	2 to 10MB	Yes	No
EarthLink	2MB	No	No
InterAccess (a local Chicago provider)	10MB	No	$1/month

It's shop 'til you drop time, so call a family forum to put together your wish list. Make sure you keep control of the credit card and resist the temptation to order from mail-order software sites on the Web. Although security on the Internet is getting better, no one claims that it's perfect. To be safe, pick out what you want on the Internet, and then call a toll-free catalog mail-order number to order directly.

Before you order, go over the following list, take stock of your computer equipment, and jot down what you need to purchase.

General information

___ Computer maker

___ Model

Detailed information

___ CD-ROM drive speed

___ Clock speed (MHz)

___ Hard drive space (MB)

___ Modem

___ Monitor

___ Operating system (version)

___ Other hardware

___ Paint/drawing program

___ Processor

___ RAM (MB)

___ Scanner

___ Web browser

___ Web page software

Appendix B
Cool Tools for Wonderful Web Pages

• •

*L*ong, long ago, when the World Wide Web was in its "spider-nursery" stage (I'm kidding, of course; actually it was only a few years ago), the only way you could create a Web page was to type all those funny-looking HTML instructions in a file using a word-processing program.

Happily, you can now choose from a veritable cornucopia of software programs that help you create, format, and edit Web pages faster than you can say, "Start your browsers!"

This appendix describes a few of the Web page authoring tools that are especially good for young people or beginning Web publishers. They are easy to use and understand.

Some of the programs described here are included on the CD that accompanies this book (see Appendix D for details about the CD). Though other programs listed here may not be on the CD, you can download them from the Web. If you have an account with the commercial online service CompuServe, you can use a program that CompuServe provides its members, called Home Page Wizard, to easily create your own Web pages.

Each program's description tells you the following:

- ✔ Where you can download or find the program
- ✔ How much memory you need on your hard drive to run the program and the minimum processor requirements
- ✔ Whether the program is available for Windows 95, Windows 3.1, or for the Mac
- ✔ Pros and cons of the program, as well as some of its notable features

The intent of this list is to save you time (and, in some cases, money) by pointing you to the program that's right for you, based on your level of experience. For that reason, the programs are organized into beginning-level, intermediate-level, and advanced-level categories. I provide detailed information only about programs that I've tried and that I think are suitable for the age range in question. Many more programs are out there, but I'm highlighting my favorite ones for Windows or Mac users.

Beginning-Level Web Page Tools

These tools are especially great for younger kids or for beginning Web page authors in general. They guide you through the process of putting together a Web page as painlessly as possible.

Web Workshop (Windows/Mac)

Web Workshop, by Vividus Corporation, is a great Web page tool for kids. The first thing you notice when you start up Web Workshop is that it's fun to look at. The colors are pleasing, and the tools for drawing, adding text, and making clickable links are easy to find. Besides that, Web Workshop has a number of other advantages:

- **Built-in sound:** The program comes with a built-in sound recorder. If you have a microphone attached to your computer, you can add a music excerpt or voice message to your pages without having to enter the HTML tags (see Chapter 12).

- **Clip art:** Web Workshop comes with lots of ready-made drawings, backgrounds, and dividers. You add them to your pages by simply clicking on a small "thumbnail" version of the graphic itself.

- **Drawing tools:** You can draw your own headings or other works of art right in Web Workshop. Otherwise, you'd have to create the image in a Paint-type program and then convert the image to GIF or JPEG format (a process described in Chapter 13).

The big drawback to Web Workshop is that it may be too simple for older kids. There's no way to add a photo to a page, and the pages you create don't have lots of room for text. It's a great tool for starting out, but when you want to make your programs more sophisticated, you should switch to one of the other programs listed in this appendix.

A trial version of Web Workshop is on the CD that comes with this book.

Web Workshop Facts and Figures

Be sure to set your monitor to 256 colors before you start using Web Workshop (actually, the program will tell you to do this if you try to start up with your monitor set to thousands or millions of colors). You can copy the version for Windows 95 users on the CD that comes with this book. Mac or Windows 3.1 users can download a trial version from Vividus' Web site (`http://www.vividus.com/`). You can try out the software for 30 days; after that you have to purchase it. Here are the system requirements and purchasing information:

- ✔ **RAM:** 8MB

- ✔ **Disk space:** 20MB

- ✔ **Price:** $29.95

- ✔ **System:** Windows 3.1, Windows 95, Macintosh 68030 or Power PC, System 7.1 or later

- ✔ **Monitor:** VGA or better color monitor is required

Intermediate-Level Tools

These programs aren't targeted directly at young people, like Web Workshop, but they are well-suited to kids ages 9 to 15, as well as other Web page beginners. These programs also let you create Web pages while hiding the HTML instructions from you. You select menu options and click on toolbar buttons, and the program adds the HTML for you "in the background."

Adobe PageMill (Windows/Mac)

Adobe PageMill is one of the best commercial Macintosh Web page creation tools around. What's more, a prerelease or "beta" version of the program was just released for Windows users as this book went to press. By the time you read this, you may be able to download or purchase a final Windows release.

PageMill is a great tool for both beginners and experienced Web page authors. Here are some reasons why:

- ✔ **HTML-free:** The program lets you create and format Web pages without ever having to see a line of HTML instructions. Tables, frames, and other complicated layouts appear in PageMill exactly as they will appear when your visitors see your page in their browser windows.

- ✔ **Support for animations:** PageMill lets you preview animations before you post your pages on the Web.

Adobe PageMill 1.0 Tryout is on the CD that comes with this book.

Adobe PageMill Facts and Figures

You can find out more about PageMill at the Adobe Systems Incorporated Web site (http://www.adobe.com/prodindex/pagemill/main.html). Adobe has another piece of software called SiteMill that includes some of the PageMill features and adds some tools that help you organize and maintain a set of Web pages (see Chapter 3). SiteMill is only available for the Macintosh, however; you can find out more about SiteMill at (http://www.adobe.com/prodindex/sitemill sm2main.html). Here are the system requirements and purchasing information for PageMill:

- ✔ **RAM:** Windows 95: 8MB minimum, 16MB recommended; Windows NT: 16MB minimum, 24MB recommended; Macintosh: 8MB

- ✔ **Disk space:** 20MB for Windows 95 or NT; 10MB for Macintosh

- ✔ **Price:** $99

- ✔ **System:** Windows 95 and NT: 486 processor minimum, Pentium-based processor preferred; Macintosh: 68020 or faster or Power PC processor, System 7.1 or later

- ✔ **Monitor:** VGA or better color monitor is required

Netscape Editor (Windows/Mac)

Netscape Editor is a program that lets you edit, create, and preview Web pages. This program is included in the version of the Netscape Navigator program called Netscape Navigator Gold.

The version of Navigator included on the CD is only for browsing the Web; if you want to create Web pages, consider downloading Navigator Gold from Netscape's Web site.

Netscape Editor is the program I use most often when I'm working on Web pages — not because I have stock in Netscape Communications or want to promote them for a particular reason, but because the program has these good points:

- ✔ **Convenient:** Call me impatient, but I like being able to switch from the Navigator browser to the Editor by simply selecting File➪Edit Document, File➪Open File in Editor, or another menu option. I don't have to launch a separate program in order to work on Web pages.

- ✔ **Easy previewing:** When I want to preview a page I'm working on, I simply select File➪Browse Document while I'm working in Netscape Editor. Then I can see my new page in the Navigator browser window.

- ✔ **Cross-platform:** Netscape Editor is available for Windows 3.1, Windows 95, and Mac users.

- ✔ **Tables:** Netscape Editor lets you create tables easily. Tables are not supported by all Web page tools.

On the downside, Navigator Gold requires a lot more memory than the regular version of Navigator, and it tends to operate slowly if you don't have enough memory (see the memory requirements below).

Note: Navigator Gold may have been replaced by a newer program called Netscape Communicator by the time you read this book. For those of you who like to keep track of such things, Navigator Gold is one of the version 3 releases of the program, and Communicator is version 4. The Web page tool in Communicator is called Netscape Composer rather than Netscape Editor. Both Netscape Composer and Netscape Gold work virtually the same way, however.

Netscape Navigator Gold Facts and Figures

Like the other popular versions of the Web browsers manufactured by Netscape Communications Corp., Navigator Gold can be downloaded for free from Netscape's Web site (`http://home.netscape.com/comprod/mirror/client_download.html`). However, in order to get technical support for the program or to receive discounts on newer versions when they come out, the company asks you to become a registered user and purchase the program. You can find out more about purchasing Navigator Gold at `http://home.netscape.com/misc/quick_purchase/index.html`.

- **RAM:** Windows 3.1: 4MB minimum, 8MB recommended; Windows 95 and NT: 6MB minimum, 8MB recommended; Macintosh: 7MB minimum, 9MB recommended

- **Disk space:** Windows 3.1: 3MB; Windows 95 and NT: 9MB; Macintosh: 6MB

- **Price:** $79

- **System:** Windows 3.1, Windows 95, and Windows NT: 386SX processor minimum; Macintosh: 68020 or faster processor; System 7.1 or later

- **Monitor:** Black-and-white or color monitor

Advanced-Level Tools

Don't get the wrong idea here. "Advanced-level" doesn't mean these programs are difficult to use. On the contrary: Allaire HomeSite and World Wide Web Weaver in particular are highly recommended for their user-friendly interface.

These programs are different from the other two categories in that they add HTML instructions to the contents of your Web pages as you are working on them. Usually, the HTML is formatted in a different color or typeface in order to distinguish it from the text and the images you want to appear on-screen. But looking at the HTML along with the contents gives this program a more techie-feeling than the other two programs, which has both an upside and a downside. On the upside, it's a great way to learn HTML; on the downside, it may seem intimidating to some users.

Allaire HomeSite (Windows)

Allaire HomeSite, a program that was developed by Nick Bradbury and is now owned by Allaire Corporation, is an easy to use yet powerful Web page editor. It doesn't make the HTML for your Web page invisible; when you click on one of the HomeSite toolbar buttons, the program enters the HTML tags in your document. But HotDog and World Wide Web Weaver do that, too. One big advantage of HomeSite is that it comes with wizards for more advanced page layouts (such as the ones described in Chapter 8).

HomeSite's advantages include:

- ✔ **Wizards:** Wizards are helpful utilities that guide you through a particular task on the PC. HomeSite comes with Wizards that help you create pages that contain frames and tables.

- ✔ **Page previews:** HomeSite is configured so you can quickly preview the pages you are working on in Microsoft Internet Explorer. (You can use Netscape Navigator if you want, but Internet Explorer will work more quickly because it is HomeSite's internal browser program.)

- ✔ **Link verification:** HomeSite can automatically verify that any links you have added to your documents are accurate; it can even check how long it will take to access a site once you or your visitors click on a link.

A trial version of HomeSite 2.0 is on the CD.

Allaire HomeSite Facts and Figures

You can download a more recent trial version of HomeSite or find out more about the program at Allaire's Web site (http://www.allaire.com/products/homesite/overview.cfm).

- ✔ **RAM:** 8MB, 16MB recommended
- ✔ **Disk space:** 2MB
- ✔ **Price:** $39.95
- ✔ **System:** Windows 95 and NT (not Windows 3.1)
- ✔ **Monitor:** Black-and-white or color monitor

HotDog (Windows)

HotDog from Sausage Software is a good Web page tool for kids who have experience making Web pages and who like working with HTML. Actually, HotDog is also a good tool if you want to learn HTML. That's because HotDog combines user-friendly tools like buttons and menus with actual tags. When you click on a toolbar button labeled "H1," for example, you see the HTML tags added in the document you are creating. HotDog has some other good features, too:

- ✔ **Tables support:** You can create tables with HotDog.

- ✔ **Browser support:** HotDog can be configured to work with many different browsers.

- ✔ **Interface:** HotDog is especially easy for Windows 95 users to work with because it uses the Windows 95 interface.

Since HotDog is only available for PC users, it's a good alternative to World Wide Web Weaver (which is only available for Mac users).

Trial versions of HotDog are on the CD that comes with this book.

HotDog Facts and Figures

HotDog comes in two versions: HotDog and HotDog Express. HotDog is a full-featured Web page editor for people who don't mind working with HTML. HotDog Express lets you make pages without having to see HTML instructions. You can copy and install a trial version of HotDog from this book's CD. If you want to purchase a copy of HotDog, find out more from Sausage Software's Web site (`http://www.sausage.com/`).

- ✔ **RAM:** 8MB minimum, 16MB recommended

- ✔ **Disk space:** 2MB

- ✔ **Price:** $99.95

- ✔ **System:** 486 or better, Windows 95, NT

- ✔ **Monitor:** Black-and-white or color monitor

World Wide Web Weaver (Mac)

World Wide Web Weaver, from Miracle Software, Inc., has been around for a few years, which is a pretty long time in terms of the Web. The program's creators have refined and strengthened the software so that it does some very cool things that you can't do with other programs. World Wide Web Weaver is great for kids who have created a few pages already and who want to start adding cool features like forms, tables, or frames. Here are some of the things that this "kewl tool" provides:

- ✔ **Frames support:** World Wide Web Weaver lets you divide a Web page into separate frames without having to enter the HTML instructions yourself.

- ✔ **Tables support:** The program also lets you create Web page tables easily.

- ✔ **Browser support:** You can configure World Wide Web Weaver to work with any Web browser you want.

- ✔ **Forms support:** You can create forms that let your Web page visitors enter information about themselves and type messages. World Wide Web Weaver provides the complicated computer scripts called CGIs that process the information so you can read it.

World Wide Web Weaver is great, but it has one big limitation: It's only available for the Macintosh. Another thing you should know is that the program does not completely "shield" you from having to see HTML instructions. As you format headings, paragraphs, lists, or other page elements, you see the tags in your document.

You will find a version of World Wide Web Weaver on the CD that comes with this book.

World Wide Web Weaver Facts and Figures

World Wide Web Weaver comes in two versions: a commercial version that you can purchase for $59 and a lite version that doesn't have as many features but costs only $25. At the time of this writing, Miracle Software, Inc. (`http://www.miracleinc.com/`) is also offering a package of decorative elements and GIF and JPEG images for Web pages for a discount price of $49 if you purchase World Wide Web Weaver for $89.

✔ **RAM:** 68000 Macintosh 3.5MB, Power Macintosh 5.5MB

✔ **Disk space:** 7.5MB

✔ **Price:** Commercial version $89 (includes two free upgrades); $59 (without upgrades); lite version $25

✔ **System:** Any Macintosh with 7.0 or above (upcoming version 2.1 requires Quicktime 2.5)

✔ **Monitor:** Black-and-white or color monitor

BBEdit (Mac)

BBEdit differs from the other programs listed here in that it is primarily intended for editing text and formatting it in HTML. This program is great if you have a lot of text documents you have to turn around. It's not really intended to lay out pages, although it does enable you to add images and specify colors. BBEdit is ideally suited for marking up text. Then, when you are ready to create a Web page, you can use another tool such as PageMill or World Wide Web Weaver to combine the text with images, colors, and other design elements. Advantages include:

✔ **Spell-checking:** BBEdit comes with a built-in spell checker so you can catch those nasty typos and "gotchas" that will make you look bad online.

✔ **Forms and tables tools:** BBEdit lets you format forms and tables.

✔ **HTML checking:** BBEdit checks your HTML and all links you have made and tells you about mistakes you need to correct.

The CD with this book includes a demo version and a lite version of BBLite.

BBEdit Facts and Figures

Although BBEdit contains lots of features, its memory requirements are remarkably small. The program can even be "stripped"
of its documentation and other nonessential features in order to
fit on a single floppy disk. You can find out more at the Bare
Bones Software Web site (`http://www.barebones.com/
bbedit.html`).

- **RAM:** 700K to 1.8MB
- **Disk space:** 4MB
- **Price:** $119
- **System:** Any Macintosh with System 7.0 or later
- **Monitor:** Black-and-white or color monitor

Microsoft FrontPage (Mac/Windows 95)

Last but by no means least, *Microsoft FrontPage* is one of the most powerful
programs around for creating pages and maintaining an entire a Web site.
FrontPage is actually made up of several separate programs. One *(FrontPage
Editor)* lets you edit Web pages without having to type HTML. Another
(FrontPage Web Server) lets you explore your Web site and test your pages
before you put them online. Another one *(Image Composer)* lets you edit
images. Yet another *(FrontPage Web Publisher)* helps you move your files to
a Web server.

FrontPage is like a luxury car with lots of automatic controls. It includes cool
Wizard-type utilities called WebBots that help you create interactive forms
and even "discussion areas" where visitors to your site can place messages.
As described in Chapter 4, FrontPage lets you visualize the layout of your
Web site and quickly change the way your pages are linked together.

OPEN

Microsoft FrontPage Facts and Figures

Microsoft FrontPage is expensive, both in terms of its memory requirements and its purchase price, but if you are serious about making Web pages and weaving a group of related pages into a Web site, this program is definitely worth the money. You can only purchase FrontPage; you can't download a demo or shareware version to try out. You can read more about FrontPage at the Microsoft Web site (http://www.microsoft.com/frontpage/).

- **RAM:** Windows 95: 8MB; Macintosh: 16MB minimum, 24MB recommended

- **Disk space:** Windows 95: 15MB; Macintosh: 30MB

- **Price:** $99.95

- **System:** Windows 95: 486 or higher processor; Macintosh: PowerPC-based Macintosh computer running at 100 MHz or higher, System 7.5.3 operating system or later, and Open Transport 1.1 or later

- **Monitor:** Windows 95: VGA or higher-resolution video monitor (SVGA 256-color is recommended); Macintosh: Macintosh-compatible monitor with Thousands of Colors mode or better

Appendix C
Online Resources for Kids and Parents

● ●

*T*he good news is that you can find a lot of resources on the Web. The bad news is that the good stuff can be really hard to find. This appendix is organized in categories and provides directions to sites you may find useful. But, remember, the Web changes constantly. Although the sites listed here were current when the book was being written, some sites have no doubt changed or disappeared altogether. So don't be surprised if your browser cannot find a Web address you type or if a Web site listed in this appendix is no longer at the given address. You may have to search for something similar. You might also try looking for a "missing" site by shortening the address — deleting everything after the .com (or .org or .edu).

Graphics for Your Web Pages

Creating Web pages is fun, but it takes time. To save time, you can go to the sites in this section and find graphics and other goodies to put on your Web pages.

Animated GIFs

Animated GIFs, described in Chapter 11, are yours for the taking from lots of places on the Web. Here are a few sites where you can begin.

AGL Free Animated GIFs and Postcards

http://www.arosnet.se/agl/

This site offers a searchable database of animated GIFs.

Club Unlimited Animated GIFs

`http://www.wu-wien.ac.at/usr/h95a/h9552688/local.html`

You can choose from 2,500 animated GIFs for free!

Victorian Animated GIFs

`http://www.victoriana.com/animate/animated.html`

This site has some unusual and beautiful Victorian animated GIFs based on old drawings, and they are free to download.

Animations and Graphics for your Web site

`http://www.cyberspace.com/~tup/`

This site contains a wide assortment of Web page decorations such as icons and horizontal rules, as well as animated GIFs that you can put on your Web site.

Kristy's Desktop Creations

`http://kwebdesign.com/kdesk/`

This site has great animated art for kids, including animated cursors, kids icons, and designs that you can use in the background of a Web page (the area of the page on which the type and other contents appear, that is; see Chapter 13).

Rose's Animated GIFs

`http://www.wanderers.com/rose/animate2.html`

Rose's page offers a great collection arranged alphabetically and instructions on how to make your own animated GIFs.

Clip Art

At one time, if you wanted to use an image from a clip art book, you'd get a pair of scissors and cut out the image. Now, you can download plenty of graphics from sources such as those in this section. If you want to find out more about how to download graphics and other files from the Web, you can find some suggestions in Chapter 9.

Barry's Clip Art Server

`http://www.barrysclipart.com/`

This site has a huge collection of clip art, backgrounds, animated GIFs, and nearly anything else you can imagine. The term "clip art" doesn't always mean the artwork is absolutely free, of course; it means that the authors (who still hold the copyright to their creations) have made their artwork freely available for you to copy. Be sure to read about all use restrictions or fees before you start copying.

Free Art @ Solarflare

`http://www.solarflare.com/freeart/`

This site provides sets of graphics that share the same theme (Halloween or weddings, for example), as well as other images for personal and not-for-profit Web sites.

The Clip Art Universe

`http://www.nzwwa.com/mirror/clipart/`

This site includes a galaxy of pictures, backgrounds, dividers, buttons, and animated GIFs. You'll also find links to some graphics programs you can download from the Web.

Icon Mania

`http://www.gamesdomain.co.uk/tigger/icon/index.html`

This site is a great resource for kids. It has icons, clip art, and links to other art resources especially for young people.

Backgrounds You Can Copy

Background images are patterns and designs that you can add in the background of a Web page (as described in Chapter 13). As long as the pattern you choose contrasts well with the type and other images on the page, background images can be a lot of fun, especially if they're free. Look around for one to grab for yourself or for ideas that you can make from scratch.

The Netscape Background Sampler

`http://home.netscape.com/assist/net_sites/b backgrounds.html`

This site has some very nice simple backgrounds with instructions on downloading with Netscape.

MacDaddy's Background Sampler

```
http://neuromancer.hacks.arizona.edu/~macdaddy
backgrounds.html
```

MacDaddy's Background Sampler offers 110 backgrounds.

Julianne's Background Textures

```
http://www.sfsu.edu/~jtolson/textures/textures.htm
```

Here you find a nice collection of background textures that are organized according to color.

Computing Services Centre Backgrounds

```
http://www.cityu.edu.hk/webimage/backgrnd/index.htm
```

These backgrounds, many of which are based on items from nature (wood, rocks, sky, water, and so on) are provided by the Computing Services Centre of the City University of Hong Kong.

Buttons, Bars, and Icons

If you're thinking about using buttons, bars, or icons, you can find lots of them here, along with some good ideas for other graphics to spice up your golden prose and lovely photos on your Web pages.

Free Art for HTML

```
http://www.mcs.net/~wallach/freeart/buttons.html
```

This site includes 3-D bars and buttons, 3-D initial capital letters, initial Victorian capital letters, and animated cartoon people.

Pam Bytes Free Backgrounds

```
http://www.tgn.net/~pambytes/free.html
```

This site includes coordinated sets of backgrounds. You find matching buttons, icons, and bars, as well as other individual icons and graphics. Plus, it's a good place to find holiday graphics.

Comprehensive Web Page Resources

This book and the other books in the *Kids & Parents* series published by IDG Books Worldwide will help you create great Web pages and use your computer in new and exciting ways, but you can find even more information on the Web itself. The following sites are learning centers that will teach you about Web page design, working with HTML, and other aspects of Web publishing.

Web Designers' Paradise

```
http://www.desktoppublishing.com/webparadise.html
```

This page lives up to its name because it's a virtual paradise for people who are interested in designing Web pages. You'll find information on many of the cool Web page features described in Chapter 7, such as counters and guestbooks, as well as some more advanced topics not discussed in this book, for example, imagemaps.

Online Web Page Tutorials

Your style of learning is not the same as anyone else's, so it pays to look around for different kinds of teachers. Many Web sites will start at the very beginning, give you step-by-step how-to's on creating an HTML document from scratch and adding content and images. They'll even provide you with elements to put on your Web page.

HTML Goodies
```
http://www.htmlgoodies.com/
```

This page includes an HTML primer, an HTML tutorial, a complete list of HTML commands, graphic resources, and more.

Create It ~ 101
```
http://www.geocities.com/SiliconValley/6658/
```

This page includes tutorials, online classes, backgrounds, buttons, icons, lines, a color chart for fonts and backgrounds, and information on how to publicize your page on the Web.

Beginner's Guide to HTML

```
http://www.ncsa.uiuc.edu/General/Internet/WWW
HTMLPrimer.html
```

The University of Illinois National Center for Supercomputing Applications (NCSA) offers the classic HTML beginners guide at this site.

Free Web Page Services

Here's a list of sites that (like GeoCities, described in Chapter 1) will host your Web page for free.

FREE Homepages at FREE-Way

```
http://www.vivanet.com/~woodj/money-mart/freeway
homepages.html
```

If you want to put a page on the Web for free, check out this site's list of free Web page services.

GeoCities

```
http://www.geocities.com/BHI/freehp.html
```

This site provides users with 2MB of free space and a free e-mail account. GeoCities offers a program that helps you create a Web page that is tailor-made for those with little or no experience in HTML code.

Tripod

```
http:www.tripodomplanet/homepager/
```

This site is okay if you need only 200K for your home page. However, if you plan to publish more than a few simple pages, you're likely to run out of space.

Angelfire Communications

```
http://www.angelfire.com/freepages/index.html
```

Angelfire Communications operates a popular, free Web page site that offers Web page utilities similar to those provided by GeoCities.

Scanning Services

Didn't find a scanner in your stack of birthday presents? Photos are a great addition to any Web page, and if you don't have a scanner, you can turn to these services, which prepare your photos for the Web (a subject discussed in more detail in Chapter 10).

Phydeaux Production/HTML Goodies Scanning Service

```
http://www.htmlgoodies.com/scan.html
```

All scans (up to ten) are $1.00 each. If you order 10–20, they are 85 cents each. More than 20 are 75 cents each. Minimum order is $5.00.

Information Partners Photo Scanning

```
http://www.tccom.com/photoscan/
```

Photos are $2 each and slides are $10 for the first slide and $3 for each additional one. Delivery by e-mail only.

Appendix D
About the CD

• •

*T*he folks at IDG have put together a terrific assortment of software programs that you can use to start creating Web pages and make your Web surfing a more rewarding experience. You can use some of the programs to create graphics and chat with others on the Web. These programs will truly help you to take charge of your computing and become a Webmaster.

System Requirements

Your computer should meet the following system requirements for using this CD:

- ✔ A PC with an Intel processor or equivalent running Windows 3.1 or Windows 95, or any Macintosh with a 68020 processor or better running System 7.1 or higher (System 7.5 recommended)

- ✔ At least 8MB total RAM installed in your computer (16MB or more highly recommended for better performance with Windows 95 and Power Macintosh computers)

- ✔ At least 40MB hard disk space available on a PC and 55MB hard disk space on a Mac for installing all the software on the CD (less space needed if you don't install every program)

- ✔ A CD-ROM drive — double speed (2x) or faster

- ✔ A sound card with speakers (for PCs)

- ✔ A monitor capable of displaying at least 256 colors or grayscale

- ✔ An Internet connection with a 14,400 Kbps or faster modem (needed to use some of the software on this CD)

What Do I Do First with the CD?

Using the CD is pretty simple, whether you're using a PC with Windows 3.1 or Windows 95 or a Macintosh. Windows users have a program on the CD that's called an *interface* in geek-speak. You can use it to easily install or run software on the CD.

Getting started in Windows 95

If you're running Windows 95, try these steps to start using the CD.

1. **Insert the CD in your computer's CD-ROM drive.**

2. **Wait a moment to see if the interface starts up automatically.**

   If you see a message that tells you that icons for the CD will be installed, congratulations! If you quit from the interface, restart it later by ejecting and reinserting the CD, or with the CD still in the CD-ROM drive, just double-click on the My Computer icon and double-click on the CD-ROM icon. Move on to the section, "What You'll Find."

   If nothing happens after a minute, see the following section.

Getting started in Windows 3.1

All Windows 3.1 users (and some Windows 95 users) need to install icons to your Start menu or Program Manager to get started. To install the icons, follow these steps:

1. **Insert the CD in your computer's CD-ROM drive.**

2. **Windows 3.1: In Program Manager, choose File⇨Run.**

   Windows 95: Click the Start button, and choose Run.

3. **In the Run dialog box, type** `D:\INSTALL.EXE`**.**

   Substitute your actual CD-ROM drive letter if it is something other than D.

4. **Click on OK.**

   The *Creating Web Pages For Kids & Parents* icon is installed in a program group named IDG Books Worldwide.

Note: To start the CD interface, open the IDG Books Worldwide program group (Windows 95 users will find an item named IDG Books Worldwide in their Start⇨Programs menu), and double-click on the icon in Windows 3.1 (select the icon in Windows 95) to run the CD.

For Macintosh

You take advantage of the Mac's easy-to-use desktop to use this CD. Just pop the CD into your CD-ROM drive. When the CD-ROM icon appears on your desktop, double-click on it. A window appears showing folders named after each category of software on the CD. For more information about the categories of software, see the following section.

What You'll Find

Here's a summary of the software you'll find on this CD. Windows users should start the CD interface and then click on the software category listed on the interface window that you'd like to explore. A list of programs in that category appears. For more information about a program or demonstration software, click on the name of the program. To install or run the software, just click on the Install or Run button.

Mac users can find the software on the CD by double-clicking on the folders named after the categories listed in this section. Depending on the software, you can drag the software's folder from the CD to your hard drive to install it on your computer, or you can double-click on the item on the CD to run or launch the software. Explore and enjoy!

Note: In the following list, items followed by an asterisk (*) are shareware or trial products. If you like the shareware product, you should pay the program's author for the software. Trial software limits the program's features or the length of time you can use the program.

AT&T WorldNet Service (for Mac OS/Windows)
In the Internet category

If you don't have an Internet sevice already, AT&T WorldNet Service can get you started. You have to pay for this service, so have your credit card handy during registration.

When asked for a registration number, use **L5SQIM631** if you use AT&T as your home's long-distance service, or use **L5SQIM632** if you use another long-distance service.

Note: If you already have an Internet service, please note that AT&T WorldNet Service software makes changes to your computer's current Internet configuration and may replace your current Internet service's settings.

Windows 95 users have a choice of installing AT&T WorldNet software that uses Netscape Navigator 3.0 or Microsoft Internet Explorer 3.0 Web browsers. Everyone else gets a version of Netscape Navigator only.

NetPresenz, (Mac OS) and WS_FTP LE (Windows)*
In the Internet category

After you create your pages and check the links to make sure they work, you'll need a program like WS_FTP or NetPresenz to move your pages to a Web server. Both programs transfer files via File Transfer Protocol (FTP).

WS_FTP LE is freeware to students, educators, and others noted in the program's doocumentation.

BBEdit 4.0 Demo, BBEdit Lite 4.0, World Wide Web Weaver Demo* (Mac OS), Alliaire HomeSite*, HotDog Professional*, HotDog Standard*, and Web Workshop* (Windows/Mac)*
In the HTML Editors category

These programs allow you to try your hand at creating Web pages more or less through HTML, the programming language for making Web pages.

Web Workshop is Web page creation software designed specifically for kids. It has a friendly interface and lots of free backgrounds and images you can add to your Web pages by pointing and clicking. This trial version of Web Workshop, which is for either the Mac or Windows 95, is fully functional for only 30 days. If you have a working Internet connection and an e-mail address, you can create a sample Web page and publish it at the Vividus Web site for free for 30 days. To purchase a copy or download a more recent version, go to the Vividus Corporation Web site at `http://www.vividus.com/`. BBEdit 4.0 Demo is a trial version of the commercially-available BBEdit 4.0. It's like the full product but will not allow you to save or print. BBEdit Lite, a less powerful version of BBEdit 4.0, is freeware.

Claris Home Page 2.0 Trial (Mac OS/Windows 95) and PageMill 2.0 Tryout* (Mac OS)*
In the Web Page Programs category

These trial versions of Claris Home Page 2.0 and PageMill 2.0 let you create Web pages without an understanding of HTML. Claris Home Page Trial is fully functional for only 30 days after you install it, and PageMill 2.0 Tryout is like the full version, except that it does not allow you save or print your work.

GraphicConverter, Icon Mania!* (Mac OS), and LView Pro* (Windows 95)*
In the Graphic Tools category

With GraphicConverter and LView Pro, you can open many graphic files and modify them for use on Web pages. Icon Mania! is an application for the Macintosh that lets you create, edit, swap, and manage icons quickly in one easy-to-use program. As a bonus, you get a huge collection of clip art icons. You can use these icons to spice up the files on your own computer or to create thumbnail previews to the images on your Web pages. After trying out the demo version included on this CD, you can purchase the full version from Dubl-Click for $39.95 when you download it from the Dubl-Click Software Web site at `http://www.dublclick.com/IconMania.html`.

LView Pro software is © 1993–1996 by Leonardo Haddad Loureiro. For more information on this software, visit the LView home page at `http://www.lview.com` on the World Wide Web.

Art For Kids Demo, Kids PowWow (Windows), Templates/Exercises/ClipArt (Mac OS/Windows)*
In the Potpourri category

The Internet contains lots of free images whose authors make them available as copyright-free "clip art" that you can copy and use on your Web pages. Art For Kids for Windows 95 users, by Moving Pixels, includes a selection of predrawn images you can color yourself, as well as puzzles and images you can paint over. You can purchase a more extensive version on CD-ROM or floppy disk by visiting the Moving Pixels Web site at `http://www.magna.com.au/~tonyb/afk.htm`.

After you create your Web pages, you'll be burning to tell others what you've accomplished. The free kids PowWow for Kids will help you do it. The free kids PowWow is an exciting and popular program that lets kids chat safely on the Web. It's included on the CD just for fun. The program, which is for Windows 3.1, Windows 95, and Windows NT users, includes safety precautions to minimize the likelihood of kids chatting with dangerous adults. In order to use PowWow, you must have an e-mail address. You send an e-mail message to Tribal Voice Software (the makers of PowWow) requesting a password. Then Tribal Voice provides you with more instructions on how to connect to its chat site and find other kids. To find out more and get the e-mail address, go to the Tribal Voice Web site at `http://www.tribal.com/kids.htm`.

Sample Web pages and clip art as described in Chapters 3 and 8 are also included in the CH3IDEAS and CH8TMPLS folders on the CD. PC users can find the items in the POTPOURI folder. Mac users can find the items in the Potpourri category folder.

Bookmarks/Favorites

The CD contains a set of Web page addresses called *bookmarks* (by Netscape Navigator) — or *favorites* (by Microsoft Internet Explorer). A bookmark/favorite is a record of the address of a Web page (otherwise called a URL) that is stored by your browser so that you can easily return to that page later on.

We have assembled a collection of useful URLs for you to check out. The same set of addresses is presented in four different versions located in CD. You need to import or open the version that's right for your browser and operating system.

Many of the addresses in this list take you to the kids' Web pages mentioned in this book. Other links take you to clip art sites or places where you can download software that's useful for creating Web pages.

Here is how to access or import either the Bookmarks or Favorites file.

Netscape Navigator users (Mac and Windows):

1. **Connect to the Internet, start up Netscape Navigator, and select W̲indow⇨B̲ookmarks.**

   The Bookmarks window opens.

2. **Select F̲ile⇨I̲mport from the Bookmarks window's menu bar.**

   The Select Bookmarks File dialog box opens.

   Mac users: The standard Finder dialog box opens.

3. **Click on the arrow to the right of the Look i̲n text box, and select drive D, or substitute your CD-ROM drive letter if it is something other than D.**

   Mac users: Click on Desktop to the display the disk drives you have available, including the CD for this book.

   The bookmark file is `kidpages.htm` and is located in the POTPOURI\Links directory (Mac users: the Bookmarks/Favorites folder, inside the Potpourri folder) on the *Creating Web Pages For Kids & Parents* CD.

4. **Select the file, and click on Open.**

   A folder named Creating Web Pages appears in your bookmarks window. This directory contains the list of bookmarks.

5. **Close the Bookmarks window.**

   You return to Netscape Navigator's main window.

6. **Click on Bookmarks, select Kidpages, and choose a site from the collection.**

   Navigator browses to the Web page, which will open in the browser window.

Microsoft Internet Explorer for Macintosh users

1. **Connect to the Internet, start Internet Explorer, and choose Favorites⇨Open Favorites.**

   The Favorites window appears.

2. **Choose File⇨Import.**

3. **Use the dialog box to open the** `Kidpages.html` **file, located in the Potpourri folder, inside the Bookmarks/Favorites folder.**

   A folder named `Kidpages.html` appears at the bottom of your Favorites window.

4. **Close the Favorites window.**

   You return to Internet Explorer's main window.

5. **Click on Favorites, select Kidpages, and choose a site from the collection.**

   Internet Explorer browses to the Web page, which will open in the browser window.

Microsoft Internet Explorer for Windows 95 users

We've provided a program on the CD that makes importing of the Favorites easy. Just start the interface, and choose the POTPOURI category. Click the item named Web Page Templates, and follow the instructions on-screen. A folder containing the Kid Pages favorites will be copied to your Windows\ Favorites folder. After the program is done, just connect to the Internet, open Internet Explorer, choose Favorites⇨Kid Pages, and select the page you want to browse.

Microsoft Internet Explorer for Windows 3.1 users

Unfortunately, Internet Explorer for Windows 3.1 doesn't provide an Import command for Favorites. However, you can still open the `kidpages.htm` file and click on the items that appear.

1. **Connect to the Internet, start Internet Explorer for Windows 3.1, and choose File⇨Open.**

2. **Click the Open File button.**

3. **In the dialog box, select your CD-ROM drive (most of you may know it as drive D), open the POTPOURI folder, then open the BOOKMARK folder, and finally open the Links folder.**

4. **Open the** `kidpages.htm` **file.**

You can click on any link you see in the page to go to that site. If you want to add a link to your Favorites menu, just click on the link with your right mouse button to bring up a tiny menu that appears on your mouse pointer. Choose "Add to Favorites" to add the link.

If You've Got Problems (Of the CD Kind)

We tried our best to compile programs that work on most computers with the minimum system requirements. Alas, your computer may differ, and some programs may not work properly for some reason.

The two likeliest problems are that you don't have enough memory (RAM) for the programs you want to use or you have other programs running that are affecting the installation or running of the program. If you get error messages like "Not enough memory" or "Setup cannot continue," try one or more of these methods and then try using the software again:

✔ **Turn off any antivirus software that you have on your computer.** Installers sometimes mimic virus activity and may make your computer incorrectly believe that it is being infected by a virus.

✔ **Close all running programs.** The more programs running, the less memory available to other programs. Installers also typically update files and programs. So if you keep other programs running, installation may not work properly.

✔ **Some of the software on this CD may require special utility programs, such as QuickTime.** Try reading any files named README.TXT included in the software's folder on the CD for more information on installing the utility software you need.

✔ **Have your local computer store add more RAM to your computer.** Adding extra memory can really help the speed of your computer and allow more programs to run at the same time.

If you still have trouble installing the items from the CD, please call the IDG Books Worldwide Customer Service phone number: 800-762-2974 (outside the U.S.: 317-596-5261).

Index

AT&T WorldNet℠ Service

A World of Possibilities…

Thank you for selecting AT&T WorldNet Service — it's the Internet as only AT&T can bring it to you. With AT&T WorldNet Service, a world of infinite possibilities is now within your reach. Research virtually any subject. Stay abreast of current events. Participate in online newsgroups. Purchase merchandise from leading retailers. Send and receive electronic mail.

AT&T WorldNet Service is rapidly becoming the preferred way of accessing the Internet. It was recently awarded one of the most highly coveted awards in the computer industry, *PC Computing's* 1996 MVP Award for Best Internet Service Provider. Now, more than ever, it's the best way to stay in touch with the people, ideas, and information that are important to you.

You need a computer with a mouse, a modem, a phone line, and the enclosed software. That's all. We've taken care of the rest.

If You Can Point and Click, You're There

With AT&T WorldNet Service, finding the information you want on the Internet is easier than you ever imagined it could be. You can surf the Net within minutes. And find almost anything you want to know — from the weather in Paris, Texas — to the cost of a ticket to Paris, France. You're just a point and click away. It's that easy.

AT&T WorldNet Service features specially customized industry-leading browsers integrated with advanced Internet directories and search engines. The result is an Internet service that sets a new standard for ease of use — virtually everywhere you want to go is a point and click away, making it a snap to navigate the Internet.

When you go online with AT&T WorldNet Service, you'll benefit from being connected to the Internet by the world leader in networking. We offer you fast access of up to 28.8 Kbps in more than 215 cities throughout the U.S. that will make going online as easy as picking up your phone.

Online Help and Advice
24 Hours a Day, 7 Days a Week

Before you begin exploring the Internet, you may want to take a moment to check two useful sources of information.

If you're new to the Internet, from the AT&T WorldNet Service home page at www.worldnet.att.net, click on the Net Tutorial hyperlink for a quick explanation of unfamiliar terms and useful advice about exploring the Internet.

Another useful source of information is the HELP icon. The area contains pertinent, time saving, information-intensive reference tips, and topics such as Accounts & Billing, Trouble Reporting, Downloads & Upgrades, Security Tips, Network Hot Spots, Newsgroups, Special Announcements, etc.

Whether online or off-line, 24 hours a day, seven days a week, we will provide World Class technical expertise and fast, reliable responses to your questions. To reach AT&T WorldNet Customer Care, call **1-800-400-1447.**

Nothing is more important to us than making sure that your Internet experience is a truly enriching and satisfying one.

Safeguard Your Online Purchases

AT&T WorldNet Service is committed to making the Internet a safe and convenient way to transact business. By registering and continuing to charge your AT&T WorldNet Service to your AT&T Universal Card, you'll enjoy peace of mind whenever you shop the Internet. Should your account number be compromised on the Net, you won't be liable for any online transactions charged to your AT&T Universal Card by a person who is not an authorized user.*

*Today, cardmembers may be liable for the first $50 of charges made by a person who is not an authorized user, which will not be imposed under this program as long as the cardmember notifies AT&T Universal Card of the loss within 24 hours and otherwise complies with the Cardmember Agreement. Refer to Cardmember Agreement for definition of authorized user.

Minimum System Requirements

IBM-compatible Personal Computer Users:
- IBM-compatible personal computer with 486SX or higher processor
- 8MB of RAM (or more for better performance)
- 15–36MB of available hard disk space to install software, depending on platform (14–21MB to use service after installation, depending on platform)
- Graphics system capable of displaying 256 colors
- 14,400 bps modem connected to an outside phone line and not a LAN or ISDN line
- Microsoft Windows 3.1x or Windows 95

Macintosh Users:
- Macintosh 68030 or higher (including 68LC0X0 models and all Power Macintosh models)
- System 7.5.3 Revision 2 or higher for PCI Power Macintosh models: System 7.1 or higher for all 680X0 and non-PCI Power Macintosh models
- Mac TCP 2.0.6 or Open Transport 1.1 or higher
- 8MB of RAM (minimum) with Virtual Memory turned on or RAM Doubler; 16MB recommended for Power Macintosh users

- 12MB of available hard disk space (15MB recommended)
- 14,400 bps modem connected to an outside phone line and not a LAN or ISDN line
- Color or 256 grayscale monitor
- Apple Guide 1.2 or higher (if you want to view online help)
  If you are uncertain of the configuration of your Macintosh computer, consult your Macintosh User's guide or call Apple at 1-800-767-2775.

Installation Tips and Instructions

- If you have other Web browsers or online software, please consider uninstalling them according to the vendor's instructions.
- If you are installing AT&T WorldNet Service on a computer with Local Area Networking, please contact your LAN administrator for setup instructions.
- At the end of installation, you may be asked to restart your computer. Don't attempt the registration process until you have done so.

IBM-compatible PC users:
- Insert the CD-ROM into the CD-ROM drive on your computer.
- Select *File/Run* (for Windows 3.1x) or *Start/Run* (for Windows 95 if setup did not start automatically).
- Type *D:\setup.exe* (or change the "D" if your CD-ROM is another drive).
- Click *OK*.
- Follow the onscreen instructions to install and register.

Macintosh users:
- Disable all extensions except Apple CD-ROM and Foreign Files Access extensions.
- Restart your computer.
- Insert the CD-ROM into the CD-ROM drive on your computer.
- Double-click the *Install AT&T WorldNet Service* icon.
- Follow the onscreen instructions to install. (Upon restarting your Macintosh, AT&T WorldNet Service Account Setup automatically starts.)
- Follow the onscreen instructions to register.

Registering with AT&T WorldNet Service

After you have connected with AT&T WorldNet online registration service, you will be presented with a series of screens that confirm billing information and prompt you for additional account set-up data.

The following is a list of registration tips and comments that will help you during the registration process.

I. Use one of the following registration codes, which can also be found in Appendix D of *Creating Web Pages For Kids & Parents*. Use L5SQIM631 if you are an AT&T long-distance residential customer or L5SQIM632 if you use another long-distance phone company.
II. During registration, you will need to supply your name, address, and valid credit card number, and choose an account information security word, e-mail name, and e-mail password. You will also be requested to select your preferred price plan at this time. (We advise that you use all lowercase letters when assigning an e-mail ID and security code, since they are easier to remember.)
III. If you make a mistake and exit or get disconnected during the registration process prematurely, simply click on "Create New Account." Do not click on "Edit Existing Account."
IV. When choosing your local access telephone number, you will be given several options. Please choose the one nearest to you. Please note that calling a number within your area does not guarantee that the call is free.

Connecting to AT&T WorldNet Service

When you have finished installing and registering with AT&T WorldNet Service, you are ready to access the Internet. Make sure your modem and phone line are available before attempting to connect to the service.

For Windows 95 users:
- Double-click on the **Connect to AT&T WorldNet Service** icon on your desktop.
  Or
- Select **Start, Programs, AT&T WorldNet Software, Connect to AT&T WorldNet Service.**

For Windows 3.x users:
- Double-click on the **Connect to AT&T WorldNet Service** icon located in the AT&T WorldNet Service group.

For Macintosh users:
- Double-click on the **AT&T WorldNet Service** icon in the AT&T WorldNet Service folder.

Choose the Plan That's Right for You

The Internet is for everyone, whether at home or at work. In addition to making the time you spend online productive and fun, we're also committed to making it affordable. Choose one of two price plans: unlimited usage access or hourly usage access. The latest pricing information can be obtained during online registration. No matter which plan you use, we're confident that after you take advantage of everything AT&T WorldNet Service has to offer, you'll wonder how you got along without it.

Explore our AT&T WorldNet Service site at http://www.att.com/worldnet.

The Internet For Macs® For Dummies® 2nd Edition	by Charles Seiter	ISBN: 1-56884-371-2	$19.99 USA/$26.99 Canada
The Internet For Macs® For Dummies® Starter Kit	by Charles Seiter	ISBN: 1-56884-244-9	$29.99 USA/$39.99 Canada
The Internet For Macs® For Dummies® Starter Kit Bestseller Edition	by Charles Seiter	ISBN: 1-56884-245-7	$39.99 USA/$54.99 Canada
The Internet For Windows® For Dummies® Starter Kit	by John R. Levine & Margaret Levine Young	ISBN: 1-56884-237-6	$34.99 USA/$44.99 Canada
The Internet For Windows® For Dummies® Starter Kit, Bestseller Edition	by John R. Levine & Margaret Levine Young	ISBN: 1-56884-246-5	$39.99 USA/$54.99 Canada

MACINTOSH

Mac® Programming For Dummies®	by Dan Parks Sydow	ISBN: 1-56884-173-6	$19.95 USA/$26.95 Canada
Macintosh® System 7.5 For Dummies®	by Bob LeVitus	ISBN: 1-56884-197-3	$19.95 USA/$26.95 Canada
MORE Macs® For Dummies®	by David Pogue	ISBN: 1-56884-087-X	$19.95 USA/$26.95 Canada
PageMaker 5 For Macs® For Dummies®	by Galen Gruman & Deke McClelland	ISBN: 1-56884-178-7	$19.95 USA/$26.95 Canada
QuarkXPress 3.3 For Dummies®	by Galen Gruman & Barbara Assadi	ISBN: 1-56884-217-1	$19.99 USA/$26.99 Canada
Upgrading and Fixing Macs® For Dummies®	by Kearney Rietmann & Frank Higgins	ISBN: 1-56884-189-2	$19.95 USA/$26.95 Canada

MULTIMEDIA

Multimedia & CD-ROMs For Dummies® 2nd Edition	by Andy Rathbone	ISBN: 1-56884-907-9	$19.99 USA/$26.99 Canada
Multimedia & CD-ROMs For Dummies® Interactive Multimedia Value Pack, 2nd Edition	by Andy Rathbone	ISBN: 1-56884-909-5	$29.99 USA/$39.99 Canada

OPERATING SYSTEMS:

DOS

MORE DOS For Dummies®	by Dan Gookin	ISBN: 1-56884-046-2	$19.95 USA/$26.95 Canada
OS/2® Warp For Dummies® 2nd Edition	by Andy Rathbone	ISBN: 1-56884-205-8	$19.99 USA/$26.99 Canada

UNIX

MORE UNIX® For Dummies®	by John R. Levine & Margaret Levine Young	ISBN: 1-56884-361-5	$19.99 USA/$26.99 Canada
UNIX® For Dummies®	by John R. Levine & Margaret Levine Young	ISBN: 1-878058-58-4	$19.95 USA/$26.95 Canada

WINDOWS

MORE Windows® For Dummies® 2nd Edition	by Andy Rathbone	ISBN: 1-56884-048-9	$19.95 USA/$26.95 Canada
Windows® 95 For Dummies®	by Andy Rathbone	ISBN: 1-56884-240-6	$19.99 USA/$26.99 Canada

PCS/HARDWARE

Illustrated Computer Dictionary For Dummies® 2nd Edition	by Dan Gookin & Wallace Wang	ISBN: 1-56884-218-X	$12.95 USA/$16.95 Canada
Upgrading and Fixing PCs For Dummies® 2nd Edition	by Andy Rathbone	ISBN: 1-56884-903-6	$19.99 USA/$26.99 Canada

PRESENTATION/AUTOCAD

AutoCAD For Dummies®	by Bud Smith	ISBN: 1-56884-191-4	$19.95 USA/$26.95 Canada
PowerPoint 4 For Windows® For Dummies®	by Doug Lowe	ISBN: 1-56884-161-2	$16.99 USA/$22.99 Canada

PROGRAMMING

Borland C++ For Dummies®	by Michael Hyman	ISBN: 1-56884-162-0	$19.95 USA/$26.95 Canada
C For Dummies® Volume 1	by Dan Gookin	ISBN: 1-878058-78-9	$19.95 USA/$26.95 Canada
C++ For Dummies®	by Stephen R. Davis	ISBN: 1-56884-163-9	$19.95 USA/$26.95 Canada
Delphi Programming For Dummies®	by Neil Rubenking	ISBN: 1-56884-200-7	$19.99 USA/$26.99 Canada
Mac® Programming For Dummies®	by Dan Parks Sydow	ISBN: 1-56884-173-6	$19.95 USA/$26.95 Canada
PowerBuilder 4 Programming For Dummies®	by Ted Coombs & Jason Coombs	ISBN: 1-56884-325-9	$19.99 USA/$26.99 Canada
QBasic Programming For Dummies®	by Douglas Hergert	ISBN: 1-56884-093-4	$19.95 USA/$26.95 Canada
Visual Basic 3 For Dummies®	by Wallace Wang	ISBN: 1-56884-076-4	$19.95 USA/$26.95 Canada
Visual Basic "X" For Dummies®	by Wallace Wang	ISBN: 1-56884-230-9	$19.99 USA/$26.99 Canada
Visual C++ 2 For Dummies®	by Michael Hyman & Bob Arnson	ISBN: 1-56884-328-3	$19.99 USA/$26.99 Canada
Windows® 95 Programming For Dummies®	by S. Randy Davis	ISBN: 1-56884-327-5	$19.99 USA/$26.99 Canada

SPREADSHEET

1-2-3 For Dummies®	by Greg Harvey	ISBN: 1-878058-60-6	$16.95 USA/$22.95 Canada
1-2-3 For Windows® 5 For Dummies® 2nd Edition	by John Walkenbach	ISBN: 1-56884-216-3	$16.95 USA/$22.95 Canada
Excel 5 For Macs® For Dummies®	by Greg Harvey	ISBN: 1-56884-186-8	$19.95 USA/$26.95 Canada
Excel For Dummies® 2nd Edition	by Greg Harvey	ISBN: 1-56884-050-0	$16.95 USA/$22.95 Canada
MORE 1-2-3 For DOS For Dummies®	by John Weingarten	ISBN: 1-56884-224-4	$19.99 USA/$26.99 Canada
MORE Excel 5 For Windows® For Dummies®	by Greg Harvey	ISBN: 1-56884-207-4	$19.95 USA/$26.95 Canada
Quattro Pro 6 For Windows® For Dummies®	by John Walkenbach	ISBN: 1-56884-174-4	$19.95 USA/$26.95 Canada
Quattro Pro For DOS For Dummies®	by John Walkenbach	ISBN: 1-56884-023-3	$16.95 USA/$22.95 Canada

UTILITIES

Norton Utilities 8 For Dummies®	by Beth Slick	ISBN: 1-56884-166-3	$19.95 USA/$26.95 Canada

VCRS/CAMCORDERS

VCRs & Camcorders For Dummies™	by Gordon McComb & Andy Rathbone	ISBN: 1-56884-229-5	$14.99 USA/$20.99 Canada

WORD PROCESSING

Ami Pro For Dummies®	by Jim Meade	ISBN: 1-56884-049-7	$19.95 USA/$26.95 Canada
MORE Word For Windows® 6 For Dummies®	by Doug Lowe	ISBN: 1-56884-165-5	$19.95 USA/$26.95 Canada
MORE WordPerfect® 6 For Windows® For Dummies®	by Margaret Levine Young & David C. Kay	ISBN: 1-56884-206-6	$19.95 USA/$26.95 Canada
MORE WordPerfect® 6 For DOS For Dummies®	by Wallace Wang, edited by Dan Gookin	ISBN: 1-56884-047-0	$19.95 USA/$26.95 Canada
Word 6 For Macs® For Dummies®	by Dan Gookin	ISBN: 1-56884-190-6	$19.95 USA/$26.95 Canada
Word For Windows® 6 For Dummies®	by Dan Gookin	ISBN: 1-56884-075-6	$16.95 USA/$22.95 Canada
Word For Windows® For Dummies®	by Dan Gookin & Ray Werner	ISBN: 1-878058-86-X	$16.95 USA/$22.95 Canada
WordPerfect® 6 For DOS For Dummies®	by Dan Gookin	ISBN: 1-878058-77-0	$16.95 USA/$22.95 Canada
WordPerfect® 6.1 For Windows® For Dummies® 2nd Edition	by Margaret Levine Young & David Kay	ISBN: 1-56884-243-0	$16.95 USA/$22.95 Canada
WordPerfect® For Dummies®	by Dan Gookin	ISBN: 1-878058-52-5	$16.95 USA/$22.95 Canada

Order Center: **(800) 762-2974** *(8 a.m.–6 p.m., EST, weekdays)*

Quantity	ISBN	Title	Price	Total

Shipping & Handling Charges

	Description	First book	Each additional book	Total
Domestic	Normal	$4.50	$1.50	$
	Two Day Air	$8.50	$2.50	$
	Overnight	$18.00	$3.00	$
International	Surface	$8.00	$8.00	$
	Airmail	$16.00	$16.00	$
	DHL Air	$17.00	$17.00	$

*For large quantities call for shipping & handling charges.
**Prices are subject to change without notice.

Ship to:

Name _____

Company _____

Address _____

City/State/Zip _____

Daytime Phone _____

Payment: ☐ Check to IDG Books Worldwide (US Funds Only)

      ☐ VISA   ☐ MasterCard   ☐ American Express

Card # _____ Expires _____

Signature _____

Subtotal _____

CA residents add
applicable sales tax _____

IN, MA, and MD
residents add
5% sales tax _____

IL residents add
6.25% sales tax _____

RI residents add
7% sales tax _____

TX residents add
8.25% sales tax

Shipping _____

Total _____

Please send this order form to:

IDG Books Worldwide, Inc.
Attn: Order Entry Dept.
7260 Shadeland Station, Suite 100
Indianapolis, IN 46256

Allow up to 3 weeks for delivery.
Thank you!

IDG BOOKS WORLDWIDE, INC.

END-USER LICENSE AGREEMENT

Read This. **You should carefully read these terms and conditions before opening the software packet(s) included with this book ("Book"). This is a license agreement ("Agreement") between you and IDG Books Worldwide, Inc. ("IDGB"). By opening the accompanying software packet(s), you acknowledge that you have read and accept the following terms and conditions. If you do not agree and do not want to be bound by such terms and conditions, promptly return the Book and the unopened software packet(s) to the place you obtained them for a full refund.**

1. **License Grant.** IDGB grants to you (either an individual or entity) a nonexclusive license to use one copy of the enclosed software program(s) (collectively, the "Software") solely for your own personal or business purposes on a single computer (whether a standard computer or a workstation component of a multiuser network). The Software is in use on a computer when it is loaded into temporary memory (i.e., RAM) or installed into permanent memory (e.g., hard disk, CD-ROM, or other storage device). IDGB reserves all rights not expressly granted herein.

2. **Ownership.** IDGB is the owner of all right, title, and interest, including copyright, in and to the compilation of the Software recorded on the disk(s)/CD-ROM. Copyright to the individual programs on the disk,™)/CD-ROM is owned by the author or other authorized copyright owner of each program. Ownership of the Software and all proprietary rights relating thereto remain with IDGB and its licensors.

3. **Restrictions on Use and Transfer.**

   (a) You may only (1) make one copy of the Software for backup or archival purposes, or (ii) transfer the Software to a single hard disk, provided that you keep the original for backup or archival purposes. You may not (i) rent or lease the Software, (ii) copy or reproduce the Software through a LAN or other network system or through any computer subscriber system or bulletin-board system, or (iii) modify, adapt, or create derivative works based on the Software.

   (b) You may not reverse engineer, decompile, or disassemble the Software. You may transfer the Software and user documentation on a permanent basis, provided that the transferee agrees to accept the terms and conditions of this Agreement and you retain no copies. If the Software is an update or has been updated, any transfer must include the most recent update and all prior versions.

4. **Restrictions on Use of Individual Programs.** You must follow the individual requirements and restrictions detailed for each individual program in Appendix D, "About the CD." These limitations are contained in the individual license agreements recorded on the disk(s)/CD-ROM. These restrictions may include a requirement that after using the program for the period of time specified in its text, the user must pay a registration fee or discontinue use. By opening the Software packet(s), you will be agreeing to abide by the licenses and restrictions for these individual programs. None of the material on this disk(s)/CD-ROM or listed in this Book may ever be distributed, in original or modified form, for commercial purposes.

5. **Limited Warranty.**

   (a) IDGB warrants that the Software and disk(s)/CD-ROM are free from defects in materials and workmanship under normal use for a period of sixty (60) days from the date of purchase of this Book. If IDGB receives notification within the warranty period of defects in materials or workmanship, IDGB will replace the defective disk(s)/CD-ROM.

   (b) IDGB AND THE AUTHORS OF THE BOOK DISCLAIM ALL OTHER WARRANTIES, EXPRESS OR IMPLIED, INCLUDING WITHOUT LIMITATION IMPLIED WARRANTIES OF MERCHANTABILITY AND FITNESS FOR A PARTICULAR PURPOSE, WITH RESPECT TO THE SOFTWARE, THE PROGRAMS, THE SOURCE CODE CONTAINED THEREIN, AND/OR THE TECHNIQUES DESCRIBED IN THIS BOOK. IDGB DOES NOT WARRANT THAT THE FUNCTIONS CONTAINED IN THE SOFTWARE WILL MEET YOUR REQUIREMENTS OR THAT THE OPERATION OF THE SOFTWARE WILL BE ERROR FREE.

   (c) This limited warranty gives you specific legal rights, and you may have other rights which vary from jurisdiction to jurisdiction.

6. **Remedies.**

   (a) IDGB's entire liability and your exclusive remedy for defects in materials and workmanship shall be limited to replacement of the Software, which may be returned to IDGB with a copy of your receipt at the following address: Disk Fulfillment Department, Attn: Creating Web Pages For Kids & Parents, IDG Books Worldwide, Inc., 7260 Shadeland Station, Ste. 100, Indianapolis, IN 46256, or call 1-800-762-2974. Please allow 3–4 weeks for delivery. This Limited Warranty is void if failure of the Software has resulted from accident, abuse, or misapplication. Any replacement Software will be warranted for the remainder of the original warranty period or thirty (30) days, whichever is longer.

   (b) In no event shall IDGB or the author be liable for any damages whatsoever (including without limitation damages for loss of business profits, business interruption, loss of business information, or any other pecuniary loss) arising from the use of or inability to use the Book or the Software, even if IDGB has been advised of the possibility of such damages.

   (c) Because some jurisdictions do not allow the exclusion or limitation of liability for consequential or incidental damages, the above limitation or exclusion may not apply to you.

7. **U.S. Government Restricted Rights.** Use, duplication, or disclosure of the Software by the U.S. Government is subject to restrictions stated in paragraph (c) (1) (ii) of the Rights in Technical Data and Computer Software clause of DFARS 252.227-7013, and in subparagraphs (a) through (d) of the Commercial Computer—Restricted Rights clause at FAR 52.227-19, and in similar clauses in the NASA FAR supplement, when applicable.

8. **General.** This Agreement constitutes the entire understanding of the parties and revokes and supersedes all prior agreements, oral or written, between them and may not be modified or amended except in a writing signed by both parties hereto which specifically refers to this Agreement. This Agreement shall take precedence over any other documents that may be in conflict herewith. If any one or more provisions contained in this Agreement are held by any court or tribunal to be invalid, illegal, or otherwise unenforceable, each and every other provision shall remain in full force and effect.

CD-ROM Installation Instructions

Important: Before you use the CD, refer to Appendix D for additional system requirements and essential instructions. After you start the CD, the first thing you see is the IDG License Agreement. To use the CD, you need to click on Accept to accept the terms of this agreement.

For Windows 95 users

1. **Insert the CD in your computer's CD-ROM drive.**

2. **Wait a minute to see whether the interface starts up automatically.**

   If you see the picture of a happy Dummies family (that is, after you've clicked Accept to accept the terms of the license agreement), the interface is up and running, and you can follow the on-screen instructions to begin using the software on the CD.

   If nothing appears on-screen after a minute or two, you need to move on to the next step.

3. **Click on the Start button, and choose <u>R</u>un.**

4. **In the Run dialog box, type** D:\ICONS.EXE.

   Substitute your actual CD-ROM drive letter if it is a letter other than D.

5. **Click on OK.**

   The *Creating Web Pages For Kids & Parents* icon is installed in a program group named IDG Books Worldwide.

If you don't have the IDG Books Worldwide group in your Start⇨<u>P</u>rograms menu, to restart the CD interface, double-click on the My Computer icon, and then double-click on the CD-ROM icon. If you do have the IDG Books Worldwide program group, choose the *Creating Web Pages For Kids & Parents* icon.

For Windows 3.1 users

1. **Insert the CD in your computer's CD-ROM drive.**

2. **In Program Manager, choose <u>F</u>ile⇨<u>R</u>un.**

3. **In the Run dialog box, type** D:\ICONS.EXE.

   Substitute your actual CD-ROM drive letter if it is something other than D.

4. **Click on OK.**

   The *Creating Web Pages For Kids & Parents* icon is installed in a Program Manager group named IDG Books Worldwide.

To restart the CD interface, open the IDG Books Worldwide program group, and choose the *Creating Web Pages For Kids & Parents* icon.

For Macintosh users

1. **Insert the CD in your computer's CD-ROM drive.**

2. **Double-click on the *Creating Web Pages For Kids & Parents* icon on-screen to run the CD interface.**

IDG BOOKS WORLDWIDE REGISTRATION CARD

Title of this book: **Creating Web Pages For Kids & Parents™**

My overall rating of this book: ❑ Very good [1]   ❑ Good [2]   ❑ Satisfactory [3]   ❑ Fair [4]   ❑ Poor [5]

How I first heard about this book:

❑ Found in bookstore; name: [6]   ❑ Book review: [7]

❑ Advertisement: [8]   ❑ Catalog: [9]

❑ Word of mouth; heard about book from friend, co-worker, etc.: [10]   ❑ Other: [11]

What I liked most about this book:

What I would change, add, delete, etc., in future editions of this book:

Other comments:

Number of computer books I purchase in a year: ❑ 1 [12]   ❑ 2-5 [13]   ❑ 6-10 [14]   ❑ More than 10 [15]

I would characterize my computer skills as: ❑ Beginner [16] ❑ Intermediate [17] ❑ Advanced [18] ❑ Professional [19]

I use ❑ DOS [20] ❑ Windows [21] ❑ OS/2 [22] ❑ Unix [23] ❑ Macintosh [24] ❑ Other: [25]_____

(please specify)

I would be interested in new books on the following subjects:

(please check all that apply, and use the spaces provided to identify specific software)

❑ Word processing: [26]   ❑ Spreadsheets: [27]

❑ Data bases: [28]   ❑ Desktop publishing: [29]

❑ File Utilities: [30]   ❑ Money management: [31]

❑ Networking: [32]   ❑ Programming languages: [33]

❑ Other: [34]

I use a PC at (please check all that apply): ❑ home [35] ❑ work [36] ❑ school [37] ❑ other: [38] _____

The disks I prefer to use are ❑ 5.25 [39] ❑ 3.5 [40] ❑ other: [41]_____

I have a CD ROM: ❑ yes [42]   ❑ no [43]

I plan to buy or upgrade computer hardware this year: ❑ yes [44]   ❑ no [45]

I plan to buy or upgrade computer software this year: ❑ yes [46]   ❑ no [47]

Name: _____   Business title: [48] _____   Type of Business: [49] _____
)
Address (❑ home [50] ❑ work [51]/Company name: _____

Street/Suite# _____

City [52]/State [53]/Zipcode [54]: _____   Country [55] _____

❑ **I liked this book!** You may quote me by name in future
    IDG Books Worldwide promotional materials.

My daytime phone number is _____

IDG BOOKS
WORLDWIDE
THE WORLD OF
COMPUTER
KNOWLEDGE®

 **YES!**
Please keep me informed about IDG Books Worldwide's
World of Computer Knowledge. Send me your latest catalog.

 **WORLD**
TECHNICAL BOOKS

 **...FOR DUMMIES** ™
BESTSELLING
BOOK SERIES
FROM IDG

 **3-D Visual** ™

 **...SECRETS** ®

 Macworld ®
Books

NO POSTAGE
NECESSARY
IF MAILED
IN THE
UNITED STATES

BUSINESS REPLY MAIL
FIRST CLASS MAIL   PERMIT NO. 2605   FOSTER CITY, CALIFORNIA

IDG Books Worldwide
919 E Hillsdale Blvd, Ste 400
Foster City, CA 94404-9691